THE OTHER 90%

Advance Comments About Robert Cooper and *The Other 90%*

"Every once in a while a book comes along that forever changes our view of what's possible in our daily lives and in the world of work. *The Other 90%* is that kind of book. Based on a lifetime of experience, Robert Cooper's message is powerful, challenging, inspiring, and highly practical. Robert Cooper brilliantly upends conventional thinking about human capacity and awakens unseen possibilities that are within reach of us all. This is vital reading for everyone who wants to bring out more of the best in themselves and others."

—*Nancy L. Badore, Ph.D.,*
founding director of the Executive
Development Center, Ford Motor Company

"A timeless and unforgettable message! Nothing else in the leadership field compares to the emotional intensity and practical value of this book. In inspiring and immediately useful ways, Robert Cooper invites us to a new frontier of possibilities for life and work. Share this book with everyone you know."

—*Ken Blanchard,*
co-author of *The One Minute Manager*

"It took a very productive lifetime for Robert Cooper to produce such a beautifully inspirational and truly insightful leadership book for the digital age!"

—*Stephen R. Covey, Ph.D.,*
co-chairman of Franklin Covey and
author of *The 7 Habits of Highly Effective People*

"A truly illuminating message! Robert Cooper excels in weaving uncommon yet practical truths with highly inspirational guideposts for creating the future. He provides clearly actionable directions for the art and science of stress-free productivity and enhanced health and spirit. In *The Other 90%*, Robert Cooper leads us to discover and deploy our own untapped greatness."

—*Susan J. Duggan, Ph.D.,*
founder and CEO,
Silicon Valley World Internet Center

"Robert Cooper's message can change the future of leadership. . . . When his work was compared to twenty widely recognized leadership experts, Cooper received the highest ratings, including inherent value, usefulness, applicability, and overall results."

—*John C. Horton,*
founder and president,
The Leadership Center, Atlanta

"This is a life-changing book for leaders at every level and in every field. Filled with uplifting and insightful personal stories, scientific breakthroughs, and practical tools from the author's journeys in leadership and life. I have worked with Robert Cooper for nearly a decade and his unique talents for challenging, inspiring, motivating, and educating come shining through on every page. Share this book with everyone who matters to your life and work."

—*Deborah J. Kiley, Ph.D.,*
director of executive development,
Arthur Andersen LLP

"I love this book! Brilliant insights, a powerful and compelling message, and completely practical. *The Other 90%* absolutely hits the mark!"

—*Jim Loehr, Ph.D.,*
CEO, LGE Performance Systems,
advisor to top athletes and executives, and
author of *Mentally Tough* and *Stress for Success*

"*The Other 90%* goes right to the heart of what matters most in leadership and life. Robert Cooper provides compelling yet little-known insights from neuroscience, inspiring stories, and practical new tools. This is priority reading for us all!"

—*Bob Nelson, Ph.D.,*
author of *1001 Ways to Reward Employees,*
1001 Ways to Energize Employees, and
1001 Ways to Take the Initiative at Work

"Robert Cooper's work is vital for everyone who wants to make a difference in their organization, community, or personal life."

—*Barry Z. Posner, Ph.D.,*
dean, Leavey Graduate School of Business,
Santa Clara University, and co-author of
The Leadership Challenge

"*The Other 90%* is a vital wake-up call to find the untapped potential in yourself and others! Professional life in the Information Age makes it too easy to lose sight of what's possible in life and work. Robert Cooper provides bold new ways to discover and apply this hidden value."

—*Martha Rogers, Ph.D.,*
partner, Peppers and Rogers Group, and
co-author of *The One to One Future*

THE

Most people live in a very restricted circle of
their potential being.
We all have reservoirs of energy and genius to
draw upon of which we do not dream

—WILLIAM JAMES, 1899

ROBERT K. COOPER

OTHER 90%

How to Unlock
Your Vast
Untapped Potential
for Leadership
and Life

CROWN
BUSINESS
NEW YORK

Published by Crown Business, New York, New York.
Member of the Crown Publishing Group.

Random House, Inc. New York, Toronto, London, Sydney, Auckland
www.randomhouse.com

CROWN BUSINESS and colophon are trademarks of Random House, Inc.

The Other 90% is a service mark of Robert K. Cooper.

Website: *www.theother90percent.com*

Printed in the United States of America

Design by Helene Berinsky

Library of Congress Cataloging-in-Publication Data

    Cooper, Robert K.
      The other 90%: how to unlock your vast untapped potential for
  leadership and life / Robert K. Cooper.—1st ed.
      Includes bibliographical references and index.
      1. Self-actualization (Psychology)   2. Success—Psychological
  aspects.   I. Title: Other ninety percent.   II. Title.
    BF637.S4 C658 2001
    158.1—dc21
                        2001017340

ISBN 0-8129-3287-0

10 9 8 7 6 5 4 3 2 1
First Edition

To all those who are ready to
claim more of the vast hidden possibilities
of their own lives.

———

To my family:
My wife, Leslie
My children, Chris, Chelsea, and Shanna
My parents, Hugh and Margaret Cooper
My grandmothers, Nora Roby Cooper and Marion Downing
My grandfathers, Hugh Cooper, Sr., and
Wendell Lanphear Downing, M.D.
Who above all engaged me in the search for
what is Possible and Real.

———

How shall I hold my soul
That it may not be touching yours?

—RAINER MARIA RILKE

CONTENTS

My Grandfather's Challenge

Going from-toward; it is the history of every one of us.
—THOREAU

No matter how long we work, no matter how little we sleep, no matter how hard we try, very few of us are achieving the life we have imagined or hoped for. There is another way.

I am thankful every day for the challenge my grandfather gave me early in my life which forms the basis for the challenge and the promise I extend to you.

My father worked long hours and was often away from home when I was growing up. He was a loving parent, but his work, including humanitarian service to world health organizations and with the hospital ship USS HOPE, engaged his energies for extended periods. On numerous occasions, both of my grandfathers committed themselves to spending extra time with me. They shared insights and lessons from their lives that have had an enduring influence on my own.

Hugh Cooper, Sr., had been a surveyor, a minister, a teacher, and a school superintendent. Amid the clutter of memorabilia atop his desk sat a small pewter frame given to him when he was a boy in the late 1880s. Inside the frame, written in script with a fountain pen on a now-yellowed piece of paper were these words: "Give the world the best you have and the best will come back to you."

I stared at that inscription as I stood in the den of his house waiting for him to return from the hospital following his fourth heart attack. I was fourteen years old.

After each of his three previous attacks—in a time before coronary bypass surgery—his physicians had solemnly advised him that there was nothing they could do; he was living on borrowed time. With each return from the brink of death he would call and ask me to come to his house to talk about life and what mattered the most. This time he had been so unsure of his prospects that he called from the hospital and asked me to meet him directly upon his return home. He loved me, and he had something important to tell me.

I heard the front door open and soon my grandmother, stooped from worry, helped her husband make his way, supported by two canes, to his favorite sofa. Sitting heavily, he asked me to take the small pewter frame from his desk and sit beside him.

"They said I wouldn't make it," he said as I came toward him. "I heard the doctors talking when they were trying to make my heart keep beating. They said no one could survive this." He winked at me, his eyes bloodshot but glowing with intensity. "They were wrong, weren't they, Robert?"

Though it was a cold March day, warm sunlight poured into the room through a bank of windows as we sat together.

"I've been thinking," he said, gently pointing toward the frame and gazing at the expression it contained. "My whole life I thought I knew what these words meant. It was simple. Either you gave your best or you didn't. First you went to school and worked hard to get good grades . . ." He drew in a breath, gathering himself.

He had been the first in his family of seven children to finish high school. He went on to graduate from college at the turn of the century and earned a master's degree. "Then," he continued, "once you got a job, you arrived on time every day and worked hard. That was giving your best. From there, the best would come back to you, as a paycheck and a sense of pride."

He looked at me intently, as he almost always did. "My whole life I have been wrong," he said.

"What do you mean?"

"In the hospital, I was thinking about the most exceptional people I've known. They were the ones who kept going when others quit; the ones who found ways to do what everyone else thought couldn't be done. They didn't just hold down a job or work hard. They were reaching deeper inside and finding something more. They made a greater difference. I don't believe they would have understood these words"—he held the frame so we both could see the inscription—"the way I did."

"I remember my parents and other adults in my hometown saying, 'Study hard and work hard but don't let your dreams get too big. If you do that, you'll only be disappointed.' 'Learn to fit in and go along,' they said, 'that's what successful people do.' I got very good at fitting in and going along." His voice trailed off.

"Robert, you're going to hear the same kinds of things from people around you. They're well-intentioned but they're wrong. What if I hadn't accepted it? What if every day I had questioned yesterday's definition of my best? What if I'd listened to my own heart instead of their words? Then I might have kept looking deeper and giving the world more of the best that was hidden inside me."

"And if I'd done that," he said, "more of the best would have come back to me, and to this family, and to you, Robert. But it won't," he said, "because I didn't do it."

"So this is my challenge to you, to live these words." He handed me the frame. There was no glass in it; I ran my fingertips over the words and felt the brittle paper. "But grandfather," I said, not wanting to disappoint him but unsure of how to accomplish what he was asking of me, "maybe when I'm older . . ."

"Age has nothing to do with it. Every day you can learn something more about who you are and all the potential that's hidden inside you. Every day you can choose to become more than you have been. I'm asking you to start right now."

"But how?"

"By looking inside yourself. By testing new possibilities. By searching for what matters most to you, Robert. Few of us ever do that for ourselves. Instead, we hold our breath. We look away. We get by or go along. We defend what we have been. We say, 'It's good enough.' I pray you don't wake up one day and say, 'I've been living my life wrong and now it's too late to make it right.'"

Young as I was, I could still see the pain his regret was causing him, and even then I recognized that the gift he was giving me was as much in his honesty as in the specific words he was so determined for me to hear.

"Robert, all of us are mostly unused potential. It's up to you to become the most curious person you know and to keep asking yourself, What is *my* best? Keep finding more of it every day to give to the world. If you do that, I promise that more of the best than you can ever imagine—and in many ways beyond money—will come back to you."

And it has. Despite my struggles and mistakes along the way, I have learned that there are opportunities for each of us that exist beneath and beyond conventional thinking and self-imposed limits. What my grandfather realized too late that he had not done, he challenged me to do. In this book, I pass that challenge to you.

The Other 90% and More

Human intelligence and spirit are two of the most amazing creations we know, yet most of us use only a tiny percentage of our brilliance or power. It is as if we are each given our own jet airplane at birth. It can fly—it was made to fly—but we don't see it; we don't know what we have. So all we do is polish the wings or fire up the engines each morning for the sound effect, and then close the storage hangar for the rest of the day. How you get that plane flying is what *The Other 90%* is about.

In accepting my grandfather's challenge, little did I realize how it would shape not only my personal life but also my professional path through the many years since his death. His challenge has moved me to independently study life and leadership from a different perspective, as an ordinary man searching for hidden human possibilities. This has encouraged me to travel far and also to observe the world more closely wherever I am, asking uncommon questions of everyday people doing extraordinary things: inventors, parents, children, teachers, business leaders, thinkers, and doers in all walks of life. Time after time, I have seen them do the impossible against all odds. Their actions, large and small, have changed me, stretched my thinking, and awakened more of my heart and spirit along the way. I am not the same person I would have been.

My grandfather believed in the saying, "We use only about 10 percent of our potential in the course of a lifetime." What about the rest of it, he wondered. That's why he started me on a search for what we called "the other 90 percent." He would have been amused to know that a few years ago the old wisdom got revised: studies indicate that we use not one-tenth but *one ten-thousandth* of our capabilities!

Whenever my grandfather would observe me getting caught up on the surface of things, struggling along by habit or expending lots of time or effort trying to produce some small gain, he would ask, "What about the other 90%, Robert?" It was one of his ways of encouraging me to alter my view, look deeper, and be willing to consider hidden possibilities.

I believe that the most exciting breakthroughs of this century will come not only from advances in technology but from a deeper realization of what it means to be most human and alive. Many of the choices that can dramatically change our lives are small and within easy reach, yet few people recognize them or know how to apply them.

William James, a pioneer in philosophy and psychology, said, "All of life is but a mass of small choices—practical, emotional and intellectual—systematically organized for our greatness or grief." When asked if these choices could be altered, he replied, "Yes, one at a time. But we must never forget that it's not only our big dreams that shape reality. . . . The small choices bear us irresistibly toward our destiny."

For centuries, it has been assumed that there are vast limits to human capacity. Now, a host of scientific discoveries prove this wrong, yet the mind-set of limits persists—blocking us from our greatest possibilities and leaving us feeling bombarded by stress, change, and uncertainty. No matter how hard we work, no matter how much we give, we're still not getting what we hoped for.

There is another way.

The next frontier is not only in front of you, it is inside you. You have a vast hidden potential and a destiny beckoning to be lived. So do we all. No one else can live it in your place.

There is no passion to be found playing small—
in settling for a life that is less
than the one you are capable of living.
                                        —NELSON MANDELA

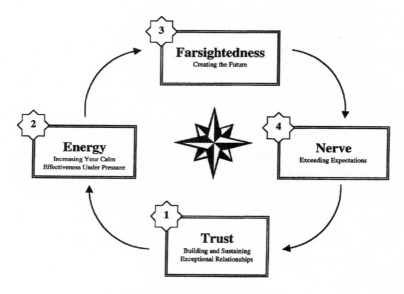

The Four Keystones of
THE OTHER 90%™

FIRST KEYSTONE

TRUST

1

Be an Original

I got off to a bad start in school. When I arrived for my first day, inside was a desk that had an index card on top with my name on it. I walked over and sat down. Lots of kids were milling around. The 8:00 bell rang and the others made their way to their seats. My teacher, Miss Robinson, a rotund woman with grey hair tied up in a bun, gazed sternly as she sized us up.

She clapped her hands and called for attention, which didn't work well. She shouted for quiet. The students near the windows kept jabbering. With a formidable glint in her eyes, she raised something in the air: a thick, metal-edged yardstick, covered with dents, probably from the backsides of the disobedient. She began striking it on the edge of her desk.

It was then that I gauged the distance to the door.

The first thing we did was review the rules. Sit still. On your bottom with your back straight in the molded plastic chair. No speaking unless spoken to by the teacher. No gum chewing. No spit balls. No curse words. No looking cross-eyed. No funny faces. No burping. No laughing. No questions except during Question

Time; no answers except from her. Know your place in line. Don't get dirty or grass-stained during recess. Ask permission to go to the bathroom. Don't get too excited. Don't tell jokes. Never get out of your place in line. Do everything in sequence. The most important thing was the report card, which she called the key to "having a good life."

After about fifteen minutes, I knew this wasn't for me. I imagined my younger friends outside on that sunny September day, playing in the turnaround at the end of our street. I knew they would be getting ready to start a ball game or hike off into one of the nearby wooded parks on some adventure, watching frogs, searching for ghosts, or saving lost dogs. To my young mind, this felt like the key to life, not a report card.

I rose and went for the door.

"Sit down, Robert!" ordered Miss Robinson. All eyes turned to me. I hesitated for only a moment. She was rounding her desk, yardstick in hand. I bolted for the door. The room erupted with shouting children.

"Stop!" she yelled.

By the time I had cleared the edge of the playground and jumped the fence, I encountered a group of safety patrol members, fifth and sixth graders, returning from guarding the street corners, on their way to class.

"Stop him!" shrieked Miss Robinson from the doorway. My shoes were laced tight with double knots. I never looked back.

The exact distance from the schoolyard to the side door of my house was three and a half blocks. My four-year-old friends, who were indeed playing ball in the turnaround, cheered wildly as they saw me running up the final steep hill toward home, chased by someone twice my size with a white belt across his chest and a silver badge. He never got within twenty feet of me.

If Everyone Else Is Doing It, Don't

I began my school life on the wrong foot. But at least it was my own foot. I have always wanted to learn how life could be and how the world really works. Those things are not always emphasized in school curricula.

One of the unwritten codes I came to believe in was, "If everyone else is doing it, don't." Through the years I have learned that when using this approach many individuals in all walks of life have been able to call forth more of their best.

When we suppress our originality, we lose touch with the source of our vitality and initiative. The greatest learning and achievements come not from standardized group work but from the unique efforts of individuals. In this regard, the human spirit has its own set of rules. In many ways, it is rebellious. The imperative to live life differently, on our own terms, keeps building until it breaks through the surface. It is then up to us not to let it fade away.

When Rosa Parks refused to do what everyone else was doing on a December evening in 1955, American history was forever altered. She had been returning home on the bus, at the end of a long day of working. "I was sitting in the front seat of the colored section," as she tells it, "and the white people were sitting in the white section. More white people got on, and they filled up all the seats in the white section. When that happened, we black people were supposed to give up our seats to the whites. But I didn't move. The white driver said, 'Let me have those seats.' I didn't get up." Her courageous refusal to accept an inhumane practice has been hailed as a defining moment of the American civil rights movement.

Thomas Edison is another example. On his first day of school, Edison was brought home by his kindergarten teacher, who told his parents, "He's an imbecile and unteachable." Edison remembers, "I was always at the foot of the class. I felt my teachers saw no potential in me and that my father thought I was stupid."

Virtually deaf, fired from countless early jobs, Edison purposely marched in the opposite direction of conventional thinking—and as a result he played a major role in inventing the twentieth century. He left us with 6,000 inventions that changed the world, three million pages of notes and diagrams, and is credited with founding scientific teamwork.

Another person driven to go against what everyone else was doing was the "Lone Eagle," Charles Lindbergh. Most of us know of him as the pilot of *The Spirit of St. Louis,* the first person to fly solo across the Atlantic. Few of us know that as a researcher at the Rockefeller Institute, he amazed the medical profession by inventing the blood centrifuge and the artificial heart and lung. These life-saving devices grew from his deeply felt desire to do what others weren't doing. When no one else would fly a supply of pneumonia serum from Wisconsin to Quebec to save the life of one of his closest friends, he did it himself.

When the Cooper family council met to discuss my truancy problem, I was firmly reminded that reading, writing, and arithmetic are important skills, and that a five-year-old doesn't get to make the rules. But I could tell from a certain twinkle in my grandfather's eye that no one thought I was entirely at fault, and from a certain sternness in my mother's look that the school officials would be encouraged to create a more hospitable learning environment for newcomers. I returned determined to make the best of my time in school.

As I continued asking questions and showing that I was willing to work hard at the things that mattered, it seemed that many of my teachers—even Miss Robinson—began to go out of their way to treat me as an individual instead of just one of this year's students on a class roster.

In fifth and sixth grade, I served on the safety patrol. I helped protect the other kids from strangers and cars, but I never chased down anyone who was running home. When I could, I talked with them or ran beside them. An independent spirit is never something to take lightly. Without it, no one stands out from the crowd.

Another of the things I learned about originality is that you can't take it for granted. If you want to keep your independence, good intentions or willpower alone won't do it. It takes something rare but very practical: a mechanism that makes it a reality.

One Good Mechanism Beats a Hundred Good Plans

A distinctive, learning-filled life results from a succession of small, specific choices made each day. There's a world of difference between imagining such a fulfilling life and actually living it. It is through taking new actions that we learn to awaken and apply our hidden capacity. If you know by doing, there is no gap between what you know and what you do.

There's something in the way, however. A powerful part of the brain, the amygdala, wants the world to run on routine, not change. Located within the limbic system, an ancient area of the mind that deals with the way you perceive and respond to the world, the amygdala relentlessly urges us to favor the familiar and routine. It craves control and safety, which at times can be vital. Yet the amygdala's instincts, which have evolved over thousands of years, tend to spill over into every aspect of life and promote a perpetual reluctance to embrace anything that involves risk, change, or growth. Your amygdala wants you to be what you have been and stay just the way you are.

Unless you choose to consciously override this brain tendency, you're consigned to repeating the past. One of the most effective ways to get past this limitation is to devise simple mechanisms that help you stand apart from the crowd and reach for what you can yet become. A plan is a fine intention or faraway vision. It may be inspiring, but by itself it usually doesn't amount to much. But once you have a clear sense of what you want, a *mechanism* actually brings it to fruition.

For example, there's a simple mechanism that overcomes our natural resistance to growth or change and helps us be our best. All that is required is to regularly ask these two questions:

1. What's the most exceptional thing you've done this week?
2. What's the most exceptional thing you will do next week?

You can ask each member of a group to answer these questions or you can do it alone—you can schedule a weekly meeting with yourself (every Friday morning in front of the bathroom mirror, for example). The word "exceptional" is defined however you want. It simply means, "What stood out for you?" or "How did you go against the crowd?" or "What real difference did you make to the people around you or the world at large?" Perhaps this week it was something big. Or maybe it was a kind word or an unnoticed task at home or at work that made you proud. It is the intensity that counts. Take a moment to reflect on your answer: Was this the best you could give? Is there any way you could have given something more?

I learned the essence of this mechanism from my grandfather Cooper. On Saturday mornings, when I was visiting or working at odd jobs around his house, he would ask, "What did you do this week that made you the proudest?" He would listen to my answer and we would talk about it. From time to time, he would also tell me about answers he got from asking the same question of recently arrived immigrants that he hired. What I heard was both humbling and inspiring.

"I saved a dollar this week for my little girl's first dress," one said. "My brother has polio and can't walk," said another. "The other night I carried him up to the top of the hill at the end of our street and we watched the stars come out." One man said, "My wife and I skipped a meal and brought it to our parents who have little. When they asked if we had eaten, we said, 'Yes, of course, we have had more than enough to eat.'"

That's the other thing this simple mechanism does: It provides a direct and unexpected way to notice and value the unseen but important efforts of others. Most of us never realize the number of times people lend a helping hand, go the extra mile, or perform some other act of kindness or initiative in the course of a busy week. Day after day, every one of us is capable of small yet exceptional acts of initiative and caring. When we live our lives in original ways such as these, we also come to realize that positive behaviors are a primary driver of positive attitudes, not the other way around.

At the end of our weekly conversation, my grandfather would say, "Next week, Robert, what can you do that no one else will expect from you?" He taught me what had taken him a lifetime to learn: Although we may dream about our future in splendid images, we must live our lives in practical everyday actions, one after another.

In all the times I have used this mechanism, I have never once encountered anyone who answered the two questions by saying that he or she had done nothing exceptional this week and would do nothing exceptional next week. Of course, no one wants to look stuck or unimaginative, but it's more than that. This mechanism stimulates a simple yet significant shift in the way we look at ourselves. It gets past good intentions and proclamations. It prompts a deeper way of recognizing the times you could reach for the exceptional.

If you ask yourself right now what you did last week that was exceptional, you'll probably have to think a while. When you establish the asking of the two questions—what did you do last week and what will you do next week—as an integral part of your life, it can change your approach to everything you do. It steadily raises your sights about what you are capable of.

On Tuesday, you may be thinking, "But I haven't done anything really exceptional yet this week." This may prompt an inner response, such as, "Then I'd better *think* of something exceptional to do!" This heightens curiosity about the possibilities for taking new actions. You'll be more likely to find yourself actively seeking ways to give the world more of your best, instead of just hoping for them.

Although studies indicate that people who regularly think ahead tend to experience more frequent leadership opportunities and career advancement, this mechanism is about something deeper than the external trappings of success. It keeps overriding the don't-grow-or-change instincts of the amygdala and clarifies what makes you original and sets you apart from the crowd. It serves as a reminder that it is up to each of us to keep finding practical and visible ways to leave a meaningful imprint on the world around us and on the lives of the people we care most about.

*D*eep within humans dwell those slumbering powers;
powers that would astonish them, that they never dreamed
    of possessing;
forces that would revolutionize their lives if aroused and
put into action.

—Orison Marden

2

Use Your Brains: All Three of Them

You Have More Hidden Intelligence than You Ever Knew

The dinosaurs of the future will be those who keep trying to live and work from their heads alone. Much of human brilliance is driven less by the brain in your head than by newly discovered intelligence centers—now called "brain two and brain three"—in the gut and in the heart. The highest reasoning and brightest ingenuity involve all three of those brains working together.

Take Richard as an example. As a young boy, he was dyslexic and "number blind"—unable to perform even simple mathematical computations. By his own admission, he was "pretty hopeless" in traditional learning, and he dropped out of school at sixteen. Yet a recent public survey ranked him as the most intelligent man in Britain.

Excited by life and its possibilities, he never allowed his lack of formal schooling to hold him back. He just applied other forms of brilliance to his endeavors. His first ventures involved no cash and lots of dedication, but he insists they were fun, as he believes all work should be. Today his business empire generates annual revenues estimated at nearly $4 billion from forty principal companies, almost all of which Richard started from scratch. His airline is one of the most profitable in the business, and his venture into the financial services sector has transformed that entire industry. He has provided more than 25,000 jobs for people along the way.

"We are Britain's largest private company, and I still can't work out the difference between gross and net," he says. "I look at a crossword puzzle and I just go blank." Yet Richard Branson stands out from the business crowd in large part because he keeps unlocking more of his hidden potential by using all three of his brains, not just one.

Richard Branson is not alone in applying that kind of multibrain brilliance. According to a survey that named the four hundred men and women who had the greatest leadership impact on the twentieth century, three out of five of them—including Edison, Einstein, Picasso, Henry Ford, Susan B. Anthony, Mark Twain, and the Wright brothers—had serious problems thinking in traditional ways or learning in school.

Outside the realm of the famous, "ordinary" people trusting all their brains are also changing the world. They are people like Gretchen Buchenholz, whose courageous action on behalf of the most vulnerable children in our society transcends everyday logic and the daunting power of the judicial system. She works to save the lives of babies born with AIDS—and overcame the resistance of the state of New York when it was refusing to identify infants with AIDS because it had decided that a mother's privacy was more important than her child's life.

Consider the story of seventeen-year-old Amber Coffman, who devotes many hours every week to feeding hundreds of homeless people. Who would do this for the past ten years, beginning at the age of eight, based solely on the rational thinking brain and not some added form of intelligence in the gut or heart?

On Saturday mornings, Amber, her mother Bobbi, and dozens of teenage volunteers gather to help others. They could be sleeping in, or going to the mall, or watching television, but their heartfelt commitment to the homeless leads them instead onto the streets of Baltimore carrying food, as they have done since 1993. They call themselves the Happy Helpers of the Homeless, and Amber says, "We have one of the largest families in the world." She plans to start a mentoring program for homeless and at-risk children, with an emphasis on homework and love. Each year on her birthday, instead of giving a party for herself, she gives a party for the homeless. It's unlikely that good thoughts, by themselves, would drive such an exceptional contribution from one individual. What other dimensions of intelligence may be in action here?

Neuroscience Has Turned Conventional Wisdom Upside Down

The old view of how "brain one"—the brain in your head—influences human behavior can be summed up this way: Whenever you have a direct experience—such as interacting with a person or facing a challenge, problem, or opportunity—it comes to you through the five primary senses and enters the nervous system. In this traditional model, each experience goes right to the brain and you think about it, responding with behavior. Everything happens in your head.

Reality, as we will see in a moment, is nothing like that. In fact, whenever too much brain activity is drawn off into thinking and remembering, not enough brain energy is left for feeling and experiencing the scope and depth of what's new right now. As a result, performance that could be ingenious and practical becomes clumsy and irrelevant.

There are times when reliance on the thinking brain is not only insignificant to the acquisition and expression of caring or expertise; it actually seriously interferes.

Everyday we're learning more about the mysteries of human intelligence and ways to keep expanding and deepening our inherent potential. Here are several highlights of the findings to date: First, we now know that intelligence is distributed throughout the body. When it comes to brilliance or insight, we cannot separate the body from the mind. Whenever you have a direct experience it does *not* go directly to the brain to be thought about. The first place it goes is to the neurological networks of the intestinal tract and heart.

The Brain in the Gut

Every contact point with life creates a gut feeling: you may notice it as butterflies in your stomach or a knot of intestinal tension or excitement. Or, depending on how intensely you have been trained to always stay in your head alone, you may not notice it at all.

But it is there. And it is asking a lot of questions, whether you know it or not. Not just asking them—answering them, too, in ways that will affect your actions. How important is this meeting or this challenge to this person? Is there an opportunity here? Is there a threat? Is my happiness or advancement at risk?

Known as the enteric nervous system, this "second brain" inside the intestines is independent of but also interconnected with the brain in the cranium. Scientists who study the elaborate systems of nerve cells and neurochemicals found in the intestinal tract now tell us that there are more neurons in the intestinal tract than in the entire spinal column—about 100 million of them. That complex circuitry enables it to act independently, learn, remember, and influence our perceptions and behaviors.

Whether or not you acknowledge your gut reactions, they are shaping everything you do, just as they shape everything that everyone around you does . . . all the time.

The Brain in the Heart

After each experience has been digested by the enteric nervous system, it's the heart's turn to ponder it. In the 1990s, scientists in the emerging field of neurocardiology discovered the true brain in the heart, which acts independently of the head. Comprised of a distinctive set of more than 40,000 nerve cells called baroreceptors, along with a complex network of neurotransmitters, proteins, and support cells, this heart brain is as large as many key areas of the brain in your head. It has powerful, highly sophisticated computational abilities. Just as the brain in the gut uses its neural circuitry to act independently, learn, remember, and respond to life, so does the brain in the heart.

In the fetus, the human heart develops before the nervous system and thinking brain have developed. The electrical energy in every heartbeat, and the information contained therein, is pulsed to every cell of the body. The heart is a muscle charged with energy, and every beat brings billions of cells firing in a perfectly synchronized rhythm. Recent studies on how learning occurs and how emotions are generated have found that the coherence of the heart brain's rhythms can change the effectiveness of the thinking brain, often dramatically.

With every heartbeat, there is instantaneous whole-body communication—a wave that travels through the arteries many times faster than the actual flow of blood. This creates another language of interior communication as pressure wave patterns vary with each intricate, rhythmic pattern of the heart. Each of your trillions of cells feels this pressure wave and is dependent on it in a number of ways.

Still another route the heart uses to communicate is through messenger chemicals in the hormonal system. One such chemical in the heart is atrial peptide, a primary driver of motivated behavior.

If we don't *feel* our values and goals, we can't *live* them. It's the heart, not the head, that plays a dominant role in moving us to excel.

In terms of human ingenuity and initiative, it also turns out that the heart is not only *open* to new possibilities, it actively *scans* for them, ever seeking new, intuitive understanding of what matters most to you in your life or work. The brain in your heart instantaneously searches for new opportunities to grow or learn, establishes a "reading" of what others feel, measures the coherence or congruence of that feeling state, and checks its own inner state of coherent values and passions. In this way, the heart seems to function as a far-reaching sensory system or personally meaningful radar for uncovering significant or creative opportunities.

And there's more: the heart's electromagnetic field is by far the most powerful produced by the body. In fact, it is approximately 5,000 times greater than the field produced by the brain.

The electrical changes in feelings transmitted by the human heart can be felt and measured at least five feet away and even ten feet away or more.

Just as your gut processes far more than your food, your heart circulates far more than your blood. Every single heartbeat speaks an intelligent language to your whole body, a language that deeply influences how you perceive your world and how you react to it.

It's no wonder that when people don't feel cared about and uniquely valued, they do not put their hearts into their life or work. After an extensive three-year study of the critical variables for leadership success, the Center for Creative Leadership recently concluded that the only statistically significant factor differentiating the very best leaders from the mediocre ones is *caring* about people. It's not that we don't need a foundation of other qualities and competencies to work well in a given field. It's that caring is the glue that holds all this together and enables people to shine.

The Brain in the Head

Third stop for nerve impulses is an area at the base of the brain known as the medulla. Several key things happen there. Inside the medulla is a vital link to the reticular activating system or RAS. The RAS connects with major nerves in the spinal column and brain. It sorts the 100 million impulses that assail the brain each second, deflecting the trivial, letting the vital through to alert the mind.

This part of the brain has evolved over millennia with an inherent tendency to magnify negative incoming messages and minimize positive ones. Although human beings today live in a technology-driven world of galactic voyages and virtual realities, we still face everyday life with deeply embedded traits of Stone Age hunter-gatherers.

Eons ago, amid almost constant life-threatening dangers, it doubtless served the human species well to amplify negative messages. In today's world, that ingrained reaction often tends to complicate things. A few well-intended words of criticism—not a life-threatening communiqué, to be sure—are nonetheless amplified by the RAS into a simple message: Danger! Danger! We bristle up and get anxious and defensive. Conversely, a genuine compliment is usually deflated by the RAS to not much more than a whisper. Which is why, at the end of a typical day when a hundred things have gone quite well and one has gone slightly wrong, nearly all of us become preoccupied with the one thing that went slightly wrong. That's the hard-wired instinct of the RAS, and if we don't learn to guide and manage its influence, it can dominate our perceptions and paralyze progress.

Given the choice, the RAS always interprets things negatively. "Better safe than sorry" are the words it lives by. So, for example, when a manager or family member behaves ambiguously—sending vague or mixed messages, avoiding you, or appearing to pursue a hidden agenda—the RAS almost invariably conveys this to the higher brain centers as a threat to your status, role, reputation, integrity, or relationship. If you have no clear understanding of where you or others stand on an issue or challenge, or what is rumor or fact, the natural tendency in the nervous system is to assume the worst. As a result, there is mistrust, second-guessing, gossip, and cynicism . . . withholding . . . no stretching to learn or grow . . . avoidance of initiative . . . waiting and watching . . . all killers of human genius and effectiveness. And the irony is that the more we hear exhortations to change those behaviors, the louder the RAS shouts its message: Danger! Danger!

In contrast, consider what happens when we take into account—and make an effort to actively manage—the RAS response. Here is an example: Let's assume you're getting angry at one of the many things that may cause you to become frustrated or off balance. It's likely that deeply set habits or patterns are at work. The RAS is primed to magnify feelings of impending threat or lost control, instantly priming you for an outburst or, if you manage to suppress that reaction, increased tension or resentment.

Stop the scene right there. Become clearly aware of both the irritation or problem and what you're feeling about it. Now consider what you think about this feeling. Is it useful right now? What is it telling you? Should you just go with it? How primed are you for a habitual reaction?

Then consider what response would serve you best right now. What reaction would fit with your values? If you could look back at yourself an hour or month from now, what current action would be most beneficial? This is a simple example of better facing what's in front of you right now by involving several of your intelligences, not just one.

Consider another example: Let's assume this is a particularly challenging day for you. Work is piling up, too many things have been going awry, you feel a headache coming on. (Or maybe this is an all-too-typical day!) Someone important to your life or work walks up to you. You look at her a bit anxiously, wondering to yourself, "Uh oh, what now?" Your gut is wondering that same thing, and—whether you're aware of it or not—those butterflies are holding a convention. Your heart has started sending some very distressing code to your cells. Dot dot dot; dash dash dash; dot dot dot. SOS.

Then this person says, "I'm just stopping by to tell you that the effort you made last week was right on target. While everyone else was getting defensive and arguing, you were the one who spoke up on behalf of Lee, the one new member of the group who raised a tough question and came up with a new idea."

"I know both of you got criticized," she continues, "but you handled the heat well and stretched everyone's thinking. I arrived late in the discussion and stayed afterward to talk with people. I can tell you that you saved us a bunch of problems down the line and won the gratitude of Lee, who has some other good ideas to give us. The whole group has a better focus and is making some solid progress this week. You are a real asset. Thank you."

Imagine how you would feel. Despite the rough day up to the point when your boss appeared, and despite the usual power of the RAS to muffle most positive comments, what would be the impact of such a genuine, specific message? In this case, whether by plan or chance, someone interacted with you about some specific idea you raised or action you had taken. On the commute home, my guess is that although you might still dwell on some of the negatives of the day you would remember, perhaps most of all, the genuine, specific message that you received from this other human being. And your whole body would feel much more at ease.

Leaving the RAS, in split seconds the neural communication travels to the limbic system, where we perceive the world and shape our response to it. The limbic system is also the seat of emotions in the brain. There is evidence that the limbic system functions 80,000 times faster than the thinking brain's cerebral cortex.

At last the neural cascade of impressions from your current experience reaches the thinking area of the brain known as the cerebral cortex. Prior to this, each experience has been sensed and interpreted by the gut, heart, and other brain regions. In other words, it appears that we think *last*, not first and foremost.

Whenever you over-rely on your brain in the head, needless extra struggles appear. One reason is that whenever your mind operates without being balanced by the gut and heart, the intellect exists primarily as an act of convenience. It can conjure up all kinds of ideologies, philosophies, theories, admonitions, principles, and beliefs, but even if these are eloquent and well-intentioned, they don't amount to much by themselves. We have to *feel* what matters in order to *live* or *lead* in ways that matter.

It turns out that the oft-heard call to "keep emotions out of it" ends up being a sure track to poor decision making. Yes, of course we must think as clearly and insightfully as we can. Yet without the active involvement of the brains in the gut and the heart, if you try to *think* your way to a decision or solution, you'll fall short of the best you can do.

Another way you might apply these insights about gut-heart-brain intelligence is to clear your mind from time to time so that it can't drown out the insights from your other sources of intelligence. This also helps you disarm the RAS from dominating you with negative or fearful worries or reactions.

Things on the mind create background chatter that can distract us from applying our full intelligence to what matters most right now. Whatever is being "held" on your mind consumes energy and attention. When there's too much on your mind the result is needless distress and tension. A lot of these thoughts and worries stay on our mind simply because we haven't faced them or clarified them, or have no trusted way to remember them or take action on them later.

This is where a day book or journal comes in. To test this, take a minute right now to clear your mind of whatever is nagging you: thoughts, ideas, or worries. Put them all on paper. Next to each concern or idea, jot out a single line that describes the best solution or outcome: What would be required for this to be dealt with in the most satisfactory way? Then add one physical action you could take next to make progress, and when would be best to do it, in reaching this solution. What commitments can you make? For things that matter most, put a specific action on your calendar. For others that are little more than background noise or distractions that are of little if any value today, cross them off or file them away for a future "worry time" or "new idea time" rather than letting them get jammed up with today's priorities. Once on paper, such thoughts tend to lose much of their power to nag or distract you.

Each time you pause to clear your mind, you increase your ability to get out of your head and more fully call upon your other intelligences. When facing the next challenge or opportunity, you can listen more clearly to what your gut and heart are adding to your mind's insights and make better choices in taking action.

From a practical standpoint, reaching the peak of your true potential depends on developing and applying an energizing, authentic level of intelligence and bringing it to everything you do. For this to happen, you must combine the perceptions and impressions of the gut, heart, and mind.

Start by learning to tap *all* of your sources of wisdom and insight. Each time you face an important moment during the day, ask, What does my gut say about this? My heart? My head? Then listen more clearly to each of those three streams of intelligence as you decide how to act or interact. With practice, this will not in any way slow your ability to make on-the-spot decisions; rather, it will deepen and improve such decisions. Many of us have learned to ignore the butterflies in the gut and feelings in the heart because doing so makes it easier to just charge forward with the head, bulldozing right past potentially superior choices that take into account your collective intuitive intelligence.

Make sure your words are consistent with what you feel inside. From up to ten feet away, and sometimes from halfway around the world via telephone, others can sense what you are feeling. Yet, according to popular thinking, it's smart to downplay the difficult stretches of life or work by trying to put a good face on things, pretending that you have an answer or everything's just fine. Similarly, there are those who would have you believe it's also wise to downplay the highs, by projecting that you're "doing okay" when you're actually extremely excited or doing great. In both cases, conventional wisdom is wrong.

When people hear something that seems to be at odds with what they're feeling from someone else, nearly everyone instinctively bets on the feelings, not the words. When you try to mask inner turmoil by saying, "Things are fine, don't worry. I have it all figured out and under control," there are two likely reactions by others. First, you're being dishonest: their heart and gut can sense that you don't have everything figured out or under control (who does?). Second, they tend to assume things may be even worse than they actually are. This can be the RAS magnifying the negative, prompting us to tell others, "He said things are fine here, but they're not; we're in trouble." Rumors and gossip get amplified and spread. Then other people may withhold their help, thinking, "If you're so smart and have such a good plan, go ahead and impress me with it." They watch and wait, never trusting you. In essence, you've lost twice: you're not believed and little if any help is offered. To say, "Things are fine here" when you're in turmoil inside doesn't fool anyone. That kind of "happy talk" theatrics undermines collaboration and stifles growth.

On the other hand, if the words you say are aligned with what you feel inside, there is often a very different outcome. I'm not advocating ruthless, tactless honesty here. Expressing a truthful sense of uncertainty or stress or inner turmoil is one thing. However, cruel or hurtful feelings are often best left unsaid, or transformed in a constructive way. And sometimes when we feel really upset, it's more a result of tension or tiredness than it is about the other person. If you're *really* upset about something or distracted by a sudden setback or dilemma, there are times when the best thing to do may be not to talk to anyone at first. Instead, go off to regain your bearings. *Then* talk to others.

When faced with a new dilemma, you might say, "I know you might think that I have this all figured out. The truth is, I don't. If we are to succeed in facing this latest challenge, it will take every bit of ingenuity from each of us." Watch what happens next. Instead of pulling away, many people will step forward, offering their own initiative and commitment. "You can count on me to help with this. It won't be easy but I have ideas. We can do this together." This is one of the uncommon yet simple ways we can better draw on the combined brilliance and potential of all three of our brains, not just one.

*T*he human heart is local and finite, it has roots,
and if intelligence radiates from it, according to its strength,
to greater and greater distances, the reports,
if they are to be gathered up at all,
must be gathered at the center.

—GEORGE SANTAYANA

3

No One Has to Lose for You to Win

As I was growing up, my family lived on a side street in a small neighborhood in Ann Arbor, Michigan. Every summer evening, the turnaround at the end of our block swarmed with kids. One of our favorite games was Capture the Flag.

As many as thirty players would huddle behind a stone wall or a fence while one player went out to conceal a red flag, leaving only a tiny corner of it in view. The hiding spot could be any of a thousand places on the block or on the hill behind. The goal was to be the first to find it.

With a shout, the game would begin. We raced to our favorite spots. We tripped each other. We made lots of noise. We gave false hints as distractions. We first searched the yards and alleys closest to the starting point, ever alert to clues from others. We worried about who might be getting closer to the flag than we were, and how could we stop others from finding it.

We took it for granted that using all our energies to beat the others was the best way for us to win. But a few did not compete in that same way, and they were the ones who almost always won. Not only did they win, they left us in awe.

Scott and Neil, two of my neighbors, were just-turned teenagers when I was midway through elementary school. After college, Scott went into the business world and became an executive. Neil joined the U.S. Army's 101st Airborne Division and was killed in Vietnam in 1968.

Scott and Neil taught me how to capture the flag. They showed me that it rarely mattered how big or fast you were (again and again, either of them would prevail over bigger and faster players). Or how high you could jump. Or what grades you got in school, how many friends you had, or how loud you could yell.

Instead, capturing the flag was about reaching inside yourself and entering the Game, sharpening your senses so you could notice—sooner and from great distances—a flicker of red from the exposed corner of the flag. Bypassing the human traffic jam at the starting point, it was possible to work inward from the outer edges of the neighborhood instead of racing about in helter-skelter search lines from the middle of the street. Doing so afforded the best viewing angles from fences, rooftops, and hills. It revealed foot tracks in little-used places on the lawns and alleys. Even as you ran, you could see in more directions, extending your awareness beyond the others who were bickering and shouting.

More often than not, Scott and Neil amazed us all. They used unexpected search patterns. They scanned for bushes with bent branches, gates left ajar, heel marks in the dirt of flowerbeds, and any other imaginable sign. They looked upward from garden paths and downward from the heights. Once, Scott climbed a porch trellis and ascended to the roof's peak on a corner house. He spotted the flag stuffed into a flower box at the end of the block—a great hiding place. That reconnaissance took him a whole minute. Then he walked calmly down the opposite side of the street before dashing across to retrieve the flag. The rest of us were still bumping into each other in the turnaround.

Neil once jumped from a fencepost to a carport roof and then ascended a triangular metal support structure for a television antenna that went twenty feet higher in the air. While several of us stood lead-footed, transfixed by his daring climb, he spotted the tip of the flag inside the back of a curb drain across the street while other searchers were running right past it, never seeing.

Something else stood out. When another person found the flag, Scott and Neil were always first to offer congratulations. They smiled at the exhilaration of the game. When they won, they didn't gloat; instead, they kept searching for ways to be more ingenious and to have more fun.

They made everyone around them feel more worthy and excited, too. When my two older friends talked, they sounded like adventurers with a friendly rivalry as they described some new way they had devised to discover where the flag was hidden and find it faster than their own personal records. If they fell down, or got turned around, they could smile at that, too—and they learned faster than anyone else. For them, Capture the Flag was a cool learning lab in its own right, not an endpoint. They made it count. Although I didn't realize it at the time, they were teaching me to excel, not compete.

Free Yourself from the Trap of Constant Comparisons

The grown-up game of life presents us with plenty of flags to chase after. Many of them are external symbols of our accomplishments: a promotion, degree, bonus, new job, new car, achievement milestone, or a special vacation. Others may represent new levels of internal growth we have been aiming for: contentment, friendships, a legacy in the world, vitality. A life with no accomplishments to aspire to—no flags to capture—would be dreary indeed.

But when the flag itself becomes the goal, and when we assume that we have to defeat others to reach the goal, things can turn bad for us. We might get what we're after, but inside we feel empty whenever we do just enough to keep someone else from winning rather than excelling in our own right. In many families, communities, and organizations, competition has become an immense distraction and a source of unproductive conflict. An intense focus on competing can become one of the principal barriers to excelling in life or work.

Here's what we know: zero-sum competition—that is, competition in which one person must lose in order for another to win—tends to undermine the best in most of us. It makes us wary and distrustful of others, causes us to withhold and distort information, inspires us to negatively caricature others, makes us intolerant of uncertainty and change, and it so narrows our focus that constructive creativity is practically shut down.

Competition inhibits learning and creativity because people in conditions of competition focus solely on the task at hand, paying too much attention to what competitors are doing, comparing themselves to others but not to greater possibilities, and trying to win the favor of those who are judging the contest. Even thinking competitive thoughts can interfere with best performance and increase the release of negative stress hormones. In studies on athletes, for example, competitive words caused more than double the levels of stress hormones such as norepinephrine. As a result of these studies, researchers recommend that people "abandon competitive thinking during exercise. Performance improves when you take pressure off yourself."

That's why—to choose just one example—W. Edwards Deming, the quality pioneer whose insights changed business around the world, vehemently opposed relative performance evaluations. He saw that comparative ratings—in which some people may "win" but many others have to "lose"—breed damaging competition, undermine motivation, and stimulate contempt for others in people who were, at first, excelling in their field. He contended that such ranking systems encourage leaders to label people as poor performers even when they are doing high quality work. Deming found that when people received negative comparative evaluations, even when not true or based on jealousy or politics, it left them "bitter, crushed, bruised, battered, desolate, despondent, dejected, feeling inferior, some even depressed, unable to comprehend or take action about why they are inferior."

Recent studies indicate that up to half of all work time may be wasted or compromised due to mistrust. In large part, this mistrust is prompted or worsened by competition. Remember, whatever our conscious good intentions, our ancient brain instincts have been programmed to assume the worst. "It's a war out there," the subconscious asserts. "Defend yourself. Smile, play along, cover your back, withhold information, put a good face on things but gossip about others."

This dark side of competition is so common that often we don't even see it, or if we do, we console ourselves that that's just the way things have to be. That's why so many individuals and organizations are unknowingly stuck in antagonistic comparisons and constant distractions that siphon off energy and preclude the biggest breakthroughs.

I win/you lose competitiveness is often personally painful, especially when it's against close associates or good friends. It's one of the main reasons it's so hard to feel good about the way we live our lives—even if we can count ourselves among the winners, we still may look around and ask, "Is this what it feels like? Is this what I knocked myself out for? Is this what I trampled other people to get? Is this what I neglected my loved ones for? Why doesn't it feel fun or satisfying?"

It doesn't have to be that way. The degree and spirit of competition in any society or group is largely a matter of choice, not the inevitable result of some characteristic of human nature. Many people erroneously assume that beating others and performing well or succeeding are identical. They are not. Dominating others in a zero-sum contest is only one limited measure of winning. Many other aspects of success require no one to lose in order for you to win. In fact, according to one study, "superior performance not only does not *require* competition; it usually seems to require its absence."

Don't Compete, Excel

Star-performing individuals make breakthroughs happen in any walk of life or field of endeavor by focusing on excelling while everyone else is just competing. Yes, such exceptional men and women may stand out from the crowd individually; but at the same time—like my childhood friends Scott and Neil—they are also fun to be around because they value others, too. Because no one else has to lose for them to feel valuable, they make it a point to acknowledge the distinctive attributes in others and draw such qualities to the fore.

To *compete* means to run in the same race, in the same way as everyone else, constantly comparing yourself to others and knowing that, in traditional zero-sum competition, someone else must lose for you to win. The goal is to get across the finish line first by any "fair" means.

To *excel* means to reach beyond the best you have ever given because doing so matters to you personally, for its own sake. It means to run your own race—as an individual, team, or organization. To excel is to know your greatest strengths and passions, and to emphasize them while honestly admitting and managing your weaknesses. To excel demands a willingness to pay exceptional attention and, paradoxically, to know when and how to think *less* in order to learn and experience *more*. To excel requires anticipating and exceeding expectations by fluidly and ingeniously working at the upper edge of your capabilities—not once in a while but hour after hour, frequently in the midst of stress, uncertainty, sudden changes, and high expectations.

Here are some strategies that may help bring out your best and the best in others, without trapping you in zero-sum thinking:

- *Every time you get competitive, lighten up—and focus on discovering new ways to excel.* Whenever you find yourself zeroing in on another person's shortcomings (or, more correctly, on your assumptions as to their shortcomings), or feeling that someone else must lose for you to win, catch yourself. Stop. Remind yourself of how debilitating such competitiveness can be. If it helps you gain perspective, think of something humorous. Get back into the flow of what was is most fun or challenging about what you're doing. Shift gears. Change your view. Surprise yourself.

  Often competitiveness comes from not wanting to stretch or change yourself. The failures of others can make it appear that you are just fine or are advancing when, in truth, you're standing still.

- *Whenever you notice you're comparing yourself to others, change the view.* How about comparing yourself to the best in yourself? When tempted to settle for what's common, ask, "I'm making an effort here, but *compared to what?* Am I stretching deeper inside myself for something new or different that might be possible? What could happen if I call on more of my best here?

Yes, there are times when the gold medal goes only to the winner. But not in the race of life, where the winners are those who are superior not to others but to their former selves. In excelling, you save time and energy that would have been spent comparing yourself to others and fighting others, and you apply that time and energy to being your best. At the same time, you maximize the opportunities of others by enabling them to build their success around your success. That's how submerged resources are brought into the open and individual growth blossoms. It's also how collaboration takes its wings.

What Happens when You Focus on Excelling: Grace Hopper and Lance Armstrong

When Grace Hopper entered the computer field in 1944, as she later recalled, "you could fit everyone who had ever heard the word computer into one small room." She instantly loved the challenges of this new industry; the pure intellectual joy of the endeavor stimulated her to keep stretching her imagination. In 1952, she created a new type of master program that enabled the computer to compile working programs from subroutines; that invention would become known as the compiler, a vital part of every computer today. In 1955, she developed the computer language that would be transformed into COBOL, the language that made large-scale computing possible. She is credited with so many breakthroughs that she is referred to as "the Mother of the Computer."

As if that wasn't enough, she also rose within the ranks of the Navy, becoming one of its first female admirals. When someone would try to stall a new idea of hers with the familiar phrase, "But we've always done it that way," she would respond with her personal motto: "A ship in port is safe, but that's not what ships are for." A skull-and-crossbones flag hung in her office, and the clock on the wall ran backwards. This, she said, was to remind people to excel through flexibility in their thinking instead of getting stuck fighting each other or holding on to old ways. When she taught at a university, she gave the final exam on the first day of class, so students would know what they were supposed to learn and could have fun going beyond it. She wanted her students to upend convention, make mistakes, get themselves and others to consider unexpected possibilities, and keep pushing back the boundaries. Most important, she wanted them to keep having a blast doing it.

Her willingness to sail into uncharted territories and see beyond the horizon was legendary. As early as 1954, she was predicting that software would soon be more important than the computer itself, and that computers would end up being the size of shoeboxes and going everywhere. Long after many others would have retired, she was working out new computer applications. She was the nation's oldest military officer on active duty. She remained a valued consultant to Digital Equipment Corporation until the day she died in her sleep at the age of eighty-five. President Bush awarded her the National Medal of Technology. She was the first individual to receive it.

Grace Hopper's individual passion for computing allowed her to excel in that field; her infectious commitment to stimulating the best in others elevated her to the Navy's top echelon.

Some people, like Lance Armstrong, seem at first to win by competing, but only learn later what it means to truly excel. Armstrong did fine on his own as a cyclist, winning individual championships, but he could never conquer cycling's most prestigious challenge, the Tour de France. The Tour de France requires not only individual initiative but teamwork, and Armstrong for a long time was too competitive to be a successful team member. When he won the individual World Championships, he screamed as he launched his attack, taunted other riders, and showboated across the finish line. He kept comparing himself to others, angry most of the time, determined to best them all and make sure they knew it.

Then he developed life-threatening cancer, and doctors gave him a 3 percent chance of surviving. As he battled that disease, he realized how unsatisfying his self-centered triumphs had been, and he vowed that, given another chance, he would not be the same person.

A medical miracle, he lived to ride another day, and to honor his commitment to excel as a person and as an athlete. He fell in love and got married. He and his wife, Kristin, had their first child. He saw the world through new eyes. When people ask him today, "How did cancer change you?" he answers, "How didn't it change me?"

When he began to ride again, not one racing group would sponsor him until the U.S. Postal Service team took the chance. And then he accomplished what he could never have done on his own. The Tour de France is called the Race of Truth, because its agonizing challenges reveal so much about a person's character.

Working as a team member, he won it the first year back on the race circuit. And then he won it again.

"I want to die at a hundred years old," he says, "with an American flag on my back and the star of Texas on my helmet, after screaming down an Alpine descent on a bicycle at 75 miles per hour. I want to cross one last finish line as my wife and ten children applaud, and then I want to lie down in a field of those famous French sunflowers and gracefully expire, the perfect contradiction to my once-anticipated poignant early demise."

*Independent of others and in concert with others,
your main task in life is to do what you can best do
and become what you can potentially be.*

—Erich Fromm

4

Be a Lighthouse Not a Weathervane

When I was a young boy, my grandfather Downing taught me about the lighthouses of Scotland. One summer weekend when I was nine or ten, I was staying with my grandparents and had just finished some yard work. I joined my grandfather in his small study. We sat together and talked about the day. As usual, he was quizzing me about what I most loved to do and what was ahead for me. I had been telling him about a book I had just read: *Kidnapped,* by Robert Louis Stevenson. I was glad it had a good ending. Some of the middle parts had kept me awake at night.

He smiled and reached over to turn on a small lamp as nightfall came.

"Do you know about the lighthouses of Scotland?"

"No," I answered.

He stood up and went over to the globe he kept on the shelf by the window. "This is Scotland," he said, pointing to the craggy shoreline to the north of England.

"There was a family in Scotland named the Stevensons . . ." He saw the look on my face and smiled. "Yes," he nodded, "the same family of the author of your book. For centuries, the seas around there were notorious for shipwrecks. At night the only light on all the coasts was a coal fire on the east, which was usually extinguished when it rained or stormed. Thousands of people drowned every year."

"But in 1786, the Northern Lighthouse Trust was established, with Robert Stevenson, the great-great-grandfather of the author of your book, appointed as chief engineer. For the next two centuries, four generations of the Stevenson family fought nasty weather, jagged coastlines, and government opposition to build lighthouses in some of the most remote outlooks on the coast and reefs of Scotland. It was amazing what they accomplished."

He drew a lighthouse on his prescription pad. As a surgeon, he always had one of these small pads in his pocket. Most of the time he used it not for prescribing medications but for sketching things about life; it was a way he learned and taught. "This is how the Bell Rock Lighthouse looks," he said, drawing a glass dome on top.

"The Stevensons designed the lighthouses to resist the gales of the North Sea and supervised the actual construction. Sometimes the conditions were desperate. They designed interlocking granite blocks"—he sketched two of them for me—"that tied the foundation to bedrock so strong that it could withstand the enormous waves that battered the pillars. They developed the lamps and lenses themselves. They wanted to send a gleam across the water for miles. When the lights came on, thousands of lives were saved on ships that would otherwise have foundered on the hidden reefs."

He looked at me intently for a few moments. "People are like lighthouses, Robert."

"How?"

"It's easy to act as if you are a weathervane, always changing your beliefs and words, trying to please everyone around you. But we were born to be lighthouses, not weathervanes. Imagine a vertical axis running through the center of your heart, from your deepest roots to your highest aspirations. That's your lighthouse. It anchors you in the world and frees you from having to change directions every time the weather shifts. Inside this lighthouse there is a lens and a light. The light represents who you are when nobody else is looking. That light was meant to keep shining, no matter how dark or stormy it gets outside. Robert, when you find that light inside you, you will know it. Don't let anyone else dim it."

"And one more thing," he added. "Remember to look for the light inside others. If at first you can't see it, look deeper. It's there."

Who Are You when Nobody Else Is Looking?

Every one of us has inherent qualities that anchor us in the world and enable us to shine. To live in that way, we must clarify our own values and understand those of others. It's one thing to be alive. It's something else altogether to live—and work—according to who you are, deep down.

People won't put their hearts into something they don't believe in. They might put their intellect into it, but not their hearts. When our individual values don't fit with the life we're leading or the direction we're moving, we withhold our best and feel empty or stressed. Like those around us, we may soon be likened to a weathervane, going whichever way the wind blows.

Know Your Individual Distinguishing Values

What are the five values that best describe or define who you are and what you stand for? Choose any word or phrase to describe each value. Jot them down. Think of who you are when no one else is looking, how deep your roots go and how high your aspirations extend. What words first come to your mind and heart? What words would you want others to think of when they think of you?

At first, you may be inclined to list words favored by your organization or church. Or words that are popular. But simply by asking this question about your individual distinguishing values, you start what I call an internal conversation. A sorting-out process begins. How deep can you get? I doubt that *productive* will be one of your words. Or *punctual*. Or *controlling*. Or *superior*. I have watched the surprise on the faces of people from all walks of life when completing this simple exercise.

Now take a moment to read the words aloud. Do they sound like a true and distinctive reflection of who you are? If not, find other words that are closer. When you're finished, copy these words on a three by five card. Carry the card with you to keep assessing these values whenever you have a spare moment here and there. Are there any other words that give a clearer glimpse into your unique spirit and deepest commitments?

I remember an executive who sat in stunned silence at his table long after other members of his group at a leadership workshop had left. When I walked over to talk with him, he said, "I can't believe it."

"You can't believe what?" I asked.

"I can't believe that a long time ago I lost these values. I climbed all the way to the top of this organization and my value words today—the ones that ring true in my heart—have nothing at all to do with what we do in this organization or the official value words we post on the wall for our employees. On the surface everything seems fine, but I don't fit in. No wonder it has been such a strain for me to be here."

Within a year, he changed jobs and moved with his family from a major city, big house, and large income to a small place in the countryside that is miles from the nearest town. He recently returned from doing humanitarian aid work in Eastern Europe. He is designing a one-of-a-kind business school course based on what he learned. He's happier than he's felt in a long time.

People ask whether they should specify current or future values. My answer is, it doesn't matter. This simple exercise is designed to spark a direct and soul-searching dialogue that links your heart and mind: the outer you talking with the inner you. If you chose words that describe you as you are now, then a voice in you will probably say, "Yes, but you could be more." If you select words that are aspirational—that represent more of what you wish to be than what you are today—a voice inside you will likely say, "Yes, but you will have to work hard to begin living these words."

Clarity of individual values is the gateway to commitment and initiative. In one study, researchers asked people about the connection between values and their commitment to doing exceptional work. When group or organizational values were unclear and the person was also unclear about his or her own personal values, the average commitment score was 4.9 on a scale from 1 to 7. When group values were clear but the individual's personal values were unclear, the commitment score was fractionally lower.

The second highest commitment score came when individuals had clarity on personal values but lacked clarity on group values. Here, the average commitment score was 6.12 out of 7. Keep the high clarity on personal values and add clarity on group values— and alignment with these values—the commitment score went to the highest measure of all, 6.26 out of 7. In this vital respect, knowing your individual values matters even more that shared group values.

Rate How Well You Are Living Your Values

A friend of mine, Nan Summers, who has worked for a number of years in management at Disney World, took the preceding exercise one step farther. She felt intently committed to weaving values into her daily actions. She listed her five top value words in the left margin of a page, and marked the days of the week across the top of the page.

Each evening, she took a few minutes to reflect on the day and rate herself from 0 to 10 for how well she had *lived* each value that day. She noted her reactions and observations. Then she looked ahead to tomorrow and planned how to better align her efforts with her values.

At week's end, she asked, "Am I satisfied with the results? If not, what can I change going forward?" This is a simple yet direct way to evaluate how well you are living your values. It is also a powerful reminder of the bridge that must repeatedly be built between knowing and doing.

Be Aware of the Distinguishing Values of Each Important Person in Your Work and Life

Consider taking a few minutes at an upcoming get-together to explore individual values with family members, friends, or coworkers. This is a way to shed new light on what matters most to you at the same time you learn more about others. Even in groups with an overarching shared mission or purpose, it is unusual when more than one or two of the five values are shared by the group or team as a whole. Nonetheless it is our individual values that bring each of us to life *inside* as a unique person; they cannot be implanted from outside.

What if someone you know happened to choose five value words that included money, power, and control? Your first reaction—assuming this wasn't what you thought this person valued—might be to say, "How could you be so selfish?" or "I can't work with you if that's what drives you." Don't be too quick to judge. Other people's values may not be the same as yours, but they are clarifying and real. I have observed how the very act of identifying individual values initiates a conversation—not only with others but an inner dialogue with your best self.

I know a man who listed money, power, and control among his five distinguishing values. The other people in his management team were stunned, but within a few hours a conversation was started that changed forever the relationships these individuals had. The leader talked about how his entire family had been killed in an auto accident when he was a small boy. Social Security had provided for him as he grew up in more than ten different foster homes. The reason, he explained, that money, power, and control were among the important words for him was his fear that he did not yet have enough savings or insurability so that if he were killed today his own children wouldn't be left where he was left.

You could have heard a pin drop in the room when he said that. None of these other individuals—some who had worked with him for more than a decade—had any idea about what he had been through. Their empathy and respect for him immediately grew. Those words meant something far different to him than to them. His experiences had shaped a deep and abiding drive to provide for his children and—for now—it factored in to his commitment to his work.

A useful variation on this exercise is to have others create a list of what they believe *your* distinguishing values are. You may be surprised by what they say—that is, by what your actions have been telling them are the things that really matter to you. Use this as a starting point for further exploration and discussion about what actually matters most to each of you. Then go out of your way to respect each other accordingly.

There was a great cartoon several years ago that showed a man in a business suit racing down the driveway. From the porch, his wife was calling, "Wait! You forgot to put on your facade!"

Keep demonstrating what you value. *Show* it in what you do and how you treat people. Lower the façade. Be more open and clear in inviting others to better understand what matters the most to you, at work and in life. Let them see you step up to new challenges and call upon your own values during tough times. Let everyone see your light, and let them know that you see theirs.

*D*well as near as possible to the channel
in which your life flows.

—HENRY DAVID THOREAU

5

Dare to Trust

When Daniel Boorstin, a noted historian and Librarian of Congress, was asked to name the most interesting thing he had ever found in the nation's capital, his answer was immediate—a small box containing the contents of Abraham Lincoln's pockets from the night he was assassinated: a pair of scratched eyeglasses, a very small amount of money, a pocketknife, and a tattered but carefully folded newspaper clipping.

"Rather pathetic," was the way Boorstin described that clipping, which was from the last year of the Civil War and contained direct and specific observations about how Lincoln struggled to make the best of the difficulties that beset the nation. It noted that he worked, often alone, late into each night at the White House, seeking ways to save lives on both sides of the battles that raged day after day. His goal, the reporter wrote, was that the country would be able to heal itself at war's end.

Lincoln endured four years of heartrending war. His 6-foot-4-inch frame withered from 185 pounds to 125. He worked long hours on war plans, especially following the defeats of 1861 and 1862, finding ways to deal with the difficult and pompous around him, such as General George McClellan. Bouts of depression tormented him.

Despite the pressures of his office, he made himself accessible to average citizens in a way no modern president would. Mothers with missing sons, wives with imprisoned husbands, and thousands of other people with personal tragedies petitioned this sensitive man. In his speeches, he constantly strove to convey an eloquence both anonymous and intimate: the plain weighty tonality of his expressions was meant to feel as if it spoke in a voice already inside each of us.

He was without relief or renewal at home. Two of his sons had died, which exacerbated the already fragile emotional and mental state of his wife, Mary, who would be declared legally insane after his death.

The soldiers of the Union Army came through experience to know Lincoln. They knew, for instance, that after formal reviews he could be counted upon to wander among them telling humorous stories, despite that fact that at many times, as one private put it, "every lineament of his countenance indicated a severe mental and emotional strain." In the final analysis, the soldiers realized Lincoln was not only their leader; he was also their fellow sufferer in a terrible war.

How ironic that a small, "pathetic" piece of paper was a key to sustaining a man as great as Lincoln. What set those specific, albeit modest, words of praise apart was that they spoke plain language about a distinctive effort Lincoln was making. Nothing grandiose—which was how he saw himself, an average human being committing everything he had to do a job well.

We all need a note like that in our pockets—or hearts. What similar kinds of small gestures—a note, an article, a simple gift, a few kind specific words—have served as the spark that allowed you the confidence to trust yourself at difficult moments during your life? How have you helped others trust themselves?

Trust is an emotional strength that begins with a feeling of self-worth and purpose that we're called to extend outward to others. The warm, solid gut feeling you get from trust—from counting on yourself and trusting and being trusted by others—is one of the great enablers of life. With it, we have the inner room to grow, to become emotionally fit, and to exercise and expand our capacity to build bridges from one issue to another, one idea to another, one person to another.

We trust others when two crucial qualities are present in the relationship. First, we must feel that they understand us: that they know who we really are and what really matters to us. Second, we must feel that they care about us, and that they will weigh our true needs, interests, and concerns when they make decisions.

Here are some ways you can build those qualities into your relationships.

Notice What Truly Matters to Others

Lincoln earned trust from soldiers because he did not view the world from behind his presidential desk, but through the eyes of those whose fears, hopes, and humanity were caught up in that terrible war of brother against brother. Such empathy not only helps build trust, it opens you to new understandings and new possibilities. The voyage of discovery, as Proust said, depends not on visiting distant shores but on seeing the world with new eyes.

You can use a day book or a small notebook to start seeing others with new eyes. Jot down the names of four individuals who are important to you, and then make an entry whenever you notice something distinctive about one of those people: a particular gift or talent, or something that makes their eyes light up. (FedEx founder Fred Smith says a mechanism like this, used by all supervisors, was a critical means of helping the company nurture the potential in everyone who works there.) Taking such notes encourages you to sharpen your observation powers. Before long, you will be noticing things that you would have missed in the past. When you notice exemplary qualities, make it a point to let the person know.

"Pretend you have x-ray vision," my grandfather Cooper would say to me. "Look beneath the surface of whatever is going on around you." However you do it, keep finding ways to look at the world, and the people in it, with new eyes—and take notes on what you find.

Slow Down to Show That You Care

We long for access to those people who are important to our future: friends, relatives, peers, and leaders. Each of these relationships provides us with a line of hope. How much easier, or necessary, it can feel today to turn away. Many of us are numb with rushing. We rationalize that we can't be all things to all people. That's true, but there are key moments when we must make a conscious effort to show that we value others. We must be more keenly aware of what happens each time we turn away from another person who is counting on us and, even if inadvertently, we weaken that person's line of hope.

Trust advances one brief interaction at a time. Each human point of contact either opens or closes a door. Even when you're rushed, you can still show that you care. There are three essential considerations for making the most of every moment in a brief interaction:

1. *Breathe before you speak.* A single breath slows the world down a bit, increasing empathy, patience, and curiosity. Pause for several seconds before you talk. Make kind, clear eye contact. At first this delay may feel like an eternity, but it prepares you to deliver the treasured gift to the other person of being genuinely listened to, even if briefly.

2. *Be clear about time.* When anyone says, "I only have two minutes," it can feel like nothing. Therefore, don't use negative presuppositions like the word "only." Instead, say, "I have two minutes to spend with you right now." Then, it's crucial to add, ". . . and if you need more time—or we need more time—we'll schedule it."

Sometimes—more often than you might expect—a brief interaction will be enough to reassure the other person that you understand his concerns. Your commitment to make more time if necessary shows that you're not just brushing him off. When you are clear about time and commit yourself to shared understanding, people feel valued and tend to be more effective than usual in making the best use of the limited minutes they have with you.

3. *When possible, sit down, don't stand.* Neuroscientists have found that in many environments where people feel rushed, the brain is programmed to perceive *standing* conversation as far less genuine than *seated* talk. One minute standing can feel like

nothing; one minute sitting can feel like ten. If you're talking with children, get down to their eye level. You'll both learn more. A related point: Try not to look at your watch. This common habit can make others feel devalued. Instead, listen intently. By instinct, guess when the time is up and *then* check your watch.

Do You Trust Enough to Be Trusted?

A small exercise can help you think about the amount of trust you have in your life. Draw a circle and write the names of the people you wholeheartedly trust inside the circle. Pause for a few moments after writing each name to ask your inner voice if you trust this person absolutely. You either trust or do not; on an emotional level, there is nothing partial or conditional about trust. Then ask yourself whether you are satisfied with the levels of trust you have created. Are there people outside the circle who you wish were on the inside? If so, what can you do to engender more trust in them? What about others' level of trust in you—how many trust circles of others would you be inside? Again: Are you satisfied, and, if not, what can you do to be more trusted by others?

Trusting relationships expand and extend our capabilities in so many ways that we can't afford to just wait for others to show that they are trustworthy, we must act deliberately to initiate and affirm trust. Have the courage to entrust others more than you have to. Do the unexpected: Give away some of your opportunities every day. Encourage others to take responsibility for pursuing such chances—first and foremost for their own advancement and, secondly and indirectly perhaps, for yours, too. Promise what you will do and do it. Keep coming through. Keep showing what it means to be counted on.

It is by your own initiative and example that trust grows in the world. In *Understanding the Mysteries,* Lao Tzu asks, "Do you trust enough to be trusted?" That's the right question.

A mong the most essential qualities of human spirit are to trust oneself and build trust with others.

—GANDHI

6

Honor the Greatness in Others

It was autumn years ago while I was hiking in Tibet that a small girl asked me a question that changed my view of what it means to honor the greatness in others. I was standing beside an old rutted path at the foot of a mountain. I watched a Tibetan family approaching me on foot, and nodded in greeting at a man, his wife, and five children, who walked past me on the road. "Pilgrims," said my guide, an older Tibetan.

After talking with the man, the guide told me the family had walked for several hundred miles from eastern Tibet to visit the historic landmark set high on the mountain slope above us. In Tibet, it is considered a blessing to make such journeys as a family.

But then, as I watched in dismay, they were turned away by Chinese army guards at a barricade that had been erected across the entrance road at the base of the mountain. Since 1959, the Chinese government and army have illegally occupied Tibet and have perpetuated what some human rights groups have called an attempted genocide of the Tibetan people.

As he turned to face me and my Tibetan guide, the army offi-cer took a step back and patted his holstered pistol, gesturing to the nearby guards armed with rifles. I offered to pay the entrance fee—the army's "toll," which I assumed, based on experiences in other parts of Tibet, the soldiers would pocket themselves—with my Chinese currency. "No," said the officer. "New policy. Tibetans cannot come here."

The family had been watching me during this interaction. They clearly did not understand what I was saying. But they were listening very closely, as if sensing beneath the words. Now they peered again up the mountainside before slowly turning away. I watched their faces. After weeks of hard travel, I knew their hopes must have been dashed, yet they were talking to each other very openly and honestly. There was an air of anger and disappoint-ment, to be sure, but it seemed to ease, or be consciously released, as they walked together down the slope. The father turned and motioned for me to come with them.

Near the river not far from the base of the mountain, the man and his wife spread quilts on the grass and prepared a meager lunch, asking me to join them. I shared the food I had in my pack. As we ate, I noticed that from time to time each of us turned to look up at the ancient landmark, outlined by the sunlight. I found myself thinking of how many times in life people arrive at their destination only to find a passage changed or barred because of the wrong currency, timing, or expectations. When that happens, how openly do we acknowledge our bitter disappointment and, instead of getting stuck in it, transcend it, moving on? Rarely. After the meal, I thanked the family and rose to leave.

"Wait," said the father. "My children wish to teach you a phrase in Tibetan." He motioned to one of the children, a girl, who I guessed was four or five. The little one stepped forward and, bringing her palms together in front of her heart with the fingers pointing skyward, she looked me straight in the eyes. She said happily, "*Tashi deley.*"

I nodded, repeating the gesture and phrase. She and the other children smiled from ear to ear. Standing there, I was struck with the thought that in so many families and organizations there are few people left with such brightness in their hearts or eyes. Where along the way did we lose this? And how can we get it back?

"In eastern Tibet," said the child's father, "we greet all people this way. For several years now, it is again allowed by the army." The man brought his palms together in front of his chest and with his wife and children, saying "*Tashi deley.*" "It means," said the father to me through my guide, who interpreted the words, "I honor the greatness in you. I honor the place in you where lives your courage, honor, love, hope, and dreams. *Tashi deley.*"

I brought my palms together in front of my heart and looked into the eyes of this family, people who, only an hour before, had faced a grave disappointment in their lives and had also been total strangers to me.

"*Tashi deley,*" I said. The children's faces beamed.

"Now please teach us a word in English," the girl said in Tibetan, pointing to me.

I thought for a moment. "In America, when we greet each other we say *hello.*" My guide repeated the words in Tibetan.

"Hello!" shouted the children, their eyes bright, practicing to get the pronunciation just right. "Hello!" "Hello!"

I smiled and nodded as I pulled on my climbing pack and headed down the road. In Tibet, on the top of the world, the altitude is so high and the vertical slopes so steep that when the sun goes down, it goes quickly. I wanted to cross to another valley before darkness came.

The young girl and one of her young brothers ran after me. She caught my hand from behind and pulled on it. My guide was beside me as I stopped and turned around to look in her eyes.

Then something happened that I'll never forget. She asked me a question that changed me. This is a little girl who is growing up in a part of the world where there is little hope, especially for young girls. The terror inflicted on them by an occupying army and government from China has been well documented. But she already knew she had some qualities deep inside her that no one else could take away, no matter how hard they might try to restrict her life or harm her.

"In America," she asked expectantly, "when people say 'Hello,' do they honor the greatness in each other?"

The question struck a chord in me. I peered into her earnest, bright face. "No," I said, and then I added, "but I wish they did."

Every step I took through the mountains that rimmed that valley in Tibet, I realized that so many of the problems we face begin when we fail to honor the greatness in each other. Rarely had I ever felt anything when I said hello to others. What was the price I had paid, that we all pay?

The Tibetan girl sensed the truth. Every human being has greatness inside, somewhere. No exceptions. Those who look for, and honor, this greatness in others are already growing. In some small yet vital way, their star is rising.

It's not always easy, but there are several things you can do to get more of the respect you deserve, and to show that respect to others.

Ask for the Recognition You Deserve

Many people have come to tolerate the absence of respect and to expect poor recognition, or none at all, for the efforts they make. One of the main reasons why people end relationships in life or work is that they get "limited, if any, genuine praise or recognition for their contributions."

Take a few moments to remember the best respect and recognition you have ever received—a time when you made an effort and someone else noticed and genuinely acknowledged you, saying something like, "Thanks for what you did. I saw you making this (specific) effort. You made a difference."

When you don't get enough of that kind of recognition today, or others seem to be taking you for granted, you must ask to be valued—clearly and respectfully.

Let's say you worked long and hard on something. However the "Thank you" received isn't at all like the best form of respect and recognition you hoped for. A key person didn't seem to value your effort or contribution. What then?

Here's an approach to consider: Arrange a time to meet with this person. During this interaction, emphasize four things:

1. *Acknowledge the other person's effort to recognize you.*

2. *Describe your best form of recognition.* "I'd like to tell you about the one time I felt the most respected and recognized . . ." Describe it. Be specific. When was it in your life? How did it feel? What did it mean? How did it inspire your next efforts? Other people need our help on this. They're not mind-readers, no matter how much we expect them to be or how hard they try. They need your insights to know how best to value and respect your efforts and get more of your best one-of-a-kind contributions.

3. *Align direction.* Say something like, "I am certain that you hope that I will keep contributing more of my best to every effort that's needed."

4. *Help shape new behavior.* "To help me keep giving more of my best, I would really appreciate it if the next time you thank me for my efforts you would make the recognition more like the kind I just described." I've never known a boss or spouse or peer to say, "No, I won't do that." Instead, they are likely to be responsive to this request and more aware of your next efforts. In a specific and significant way, you have become more visible in this person's eyes.

Give Recognition with the Honor It Deserves

Pause for a moment before thanking others. Keep several things in mind:

- *Make it genuine.* Samuel Johnson said, "He who praises everybody praises nobody." He was right, sort of. When praise is generic and shallow, it ultimately fails. Instead, learn all you can about what another person is most excited about and what their favorite work is—and the direction it's taking, the possibilities and obstacles it offers, the way the individual is dealing with the pressures and progress.

- *Personalize your comments.* Be specific. "Here's why I believe in you . . ." When people listen to comments from another person, they weigh how well this person knows who they really are and what they're capable of. Consequently, whenever you value or recognize another person, make it as individualized and specific as you can. Don't make assumptions. Ask and observe. Margaret Mead once said, "Always remember you are absolutely unique. Just like everyone else."

- *Individualize your remarks for members of a group.* Whenever you thank more than one person, single out each individual.

Most people give praise to the whole group. Yet no matter how sincere they may be, they inadvertently make every one of these individuals feel devalued. Each individual knows that he or she contributed something that the others did not. And you missed it.

Before thanking a group, learn at least one specific contribution that each individual has made to the project's success. Assemble and thank the entire team. Say, for example, "We couldn't have accomplished this without each of you. I wasn't there for the entire effort but I have learned at least one specific thing that each of you contributed to produce this great result. Then, one by one, mention something specific and distinctive about the contribution of each individual. Watch people's eyes. It's amazing the difference this can make.

Acknowledge Others Eye-to-Eye

Throughout our lives, we assess much of our value and meaning to others by the look in their eyes. Those looks are more powerful than words—they speak to the brains in the heart and gut, not just the head. All it takes is an instant to make kind, clear eye contact. And then to sense something of the hidden genius or greatness—known or unknown—in the other person. This has nothing to do with doing. It is warranted simply by a person being present or showing up. It is one of the simplest and most vital ways to honor the inherent worthiness in others.

Lift your head. Take off the blinders. Whenever you walk past others, especially at home, in your neighborhood, or at work, acknowledge them with a kind glance and a nod of your head. Yes, in some places and cultures around the world, direct eye contact is not positive. But in every neighborhood or setting there is some respectful way that people need to be seen and valued. If you can learn what it is, you can provide such valuing.

Whenever You Hear Someone's Name, Take a Moment to Sense Something of the Greatness Behind It

Our names are not labels. They are the cover of a human story. Beneath and beyond the name, yet tied to it, is a unique person's life, with love, loss, laughter, dreams, hardship, and some vast measure of still hidden possibilities. From the moment you meet another human being and first hear their name, no matter how brief the interaction, your story is touching theirs. How might we better acknowledge this humanity in ourselves and others, even for a moment?

Respect Every Request You Make

Whenever you call on someone else to help you face a challenge or take on added responsibility, my guess is that, like me, you usually go through some intense consideration. You ponder talents, attitudes, and past actions of a number of people you could call on, and then make a choice. You contact this person, and ask him or her to take action to handle the problem or pursue the opportunity.

However, many of these requests get conveyed in some form of shorthand, without explanation for *why* we are asking this other person to help.

The recipient of such a message often feels it's a case of "If you do contribute a lot here, they dump extra work on you," which isn't fair. That perception is confirmed when this person looks around and, sure enough, it seems others are leaving work early or heading off to do something fun and he or she has to stick around to get all this extra work done. In addition, the request for added effort gets perceived—with no little ire—as a compliance maneuver. The recipient thinks, "If I speak up or say no, I'll face some kind of sabotage or be ignored. So I'll just do it anyway. You expect me to do everything around here—and I resent it."

Each time you make a request of another person, make it a point to:

- *Explain, "Here's why I'm asking you . . ."* Be specific about why you need this other person's energy, talents, and time. With every request or assignment to solve a problem or pursue an opportunity, explain *"Here's why . . ."* Take a minute on the phone or in person, or an extra paragraph or two in a written message, to let the other person know why you have chosen to ask him or her to handle this, and which strengths and experiences make this person the best choice. Be clear, genuine, and specific. In addition, use this as a two-way process. If someone calls you with a request or assignment, ask him or her to briefly explain why you have been selected.

   Note: If this happens to be a "just do it" assignment or "because I said so" request, then acknowledge it honestly and handle with care. "I needed someone to help with this and you're the first person I ran into." It doesn't feel great on the receiving end, and many people won't believe it was random, but sometimes it's necessary to just do something and move on.

- *Acknowledge, "I know you're busy . . ."* and let the other person know that if they'll help with this request you'll reciprocate in some way that's valuable to them. "I realize how busy you probably are right now. Please let me know what I can do to help take something off your plate so you can free up the time to accomplish this." Who do you know who doesn't feel swamped with things to do? None of us believe we have much time to take on anything more. That's why this step is so crucial. Acknowledge time constraints in others when asking for something. Whenever you can, find a way to lighten their workload in exchange for coming through on your request.

Every Week, Use Handwritten Notes to Acknowledge the Efforts of Others

Messages that come from the heart tend to go to the heart. It was my grandfather Downing who first showed me the power of such a small commitment. He was a quiet man who practiced medicine and helped pioneer advances in surgery. On Monday mornings, he would go in to his small office earlier than usual, carrying a handful of clippings about people he knew who happened to be mentioned in last week's newspapers, along with notes of remembrance he had jotted down. He wrote personal messages. To my grandfather, such notes were an essential part of caring made visible and real.

What one or two people have made the biggest difference in your life this week? Who would benefit most from some words of encouragement from you? Have you ever saved a special note or letter from someone? Why did it mean so much? What was said?

Not long ago after teaching a seminar in Seattle, I received the kind of note that one cherishes through the years. It read:

Dear Robert,

When your children ask if having their father leave home and come to this city was something worth doing, here's what you can say:

"There was a 50-year-old woman who attended my leadership program yesterday. Her name is Katharine. She is intelligent, creative, and passionate. Until yesterday, she doubted she was any of those things. She came early. She hung on every question I asked, every story that was told, every new skill we worked on through the day. She laughed and cried. She reflected and wondered. She found new ways to discover more of what matters most to her and to live better, not just work better. She also found a few of her biggest dreams again. When she left, she was 50 years young."

May you be fortunate enough to receive such notes from time to time. And may you be generous enough to send many more!

SECOND KEYSTONE

ENERGY

7

Be Quick
Without Rushing

I remember drowning. It was a Saturday in mid-summer 1960. I was nine years old. My Grandfather Downing and my mother had taken my younger sister, brother, and me to go swimming at an old gravel pit that had been converted by the town park board into a swim area.

It was early afternoon and the pond was crowded with people. I was practicing my stroke in the deep water. Behind me, a man was teasing some friends on the diving raft. He jumped off without looking and landed on my neck and back, knocking the wind out of me. His weight drove me deep toward the bottom of the murky water. Choking and disoriented, I struggled to turn myself around and kick upward toward the surface of the churning brown water filled with swimmers. I almost didn't make it. There was a moment when my chest knotted up with panic and my arms and legs weakened. The feeling of the water in my nose and lungs was terrifying.

For a long string of dark moments I was lost. To this day, I don't know what saved me, other than Providence, but I remember that all of a sudden I broke the surface, coughing and gasping for air. I heard the lifeguards blowing their whistles and screaming for everyone to get out of the water. The body of a teenage boy had just been found on the bottom of the pond.

Minutes later we stood shivering on the beach, watching as my grandfather waded out to meet one of the lifeguards who handed him the boy's limp body. The mass of people backed away from the water's edge as my grandfather, the city's senior physician and surgeon, set the boy on the sand, checked for signs of life, and then at once began trying to revive him.

We squirmed through the crowd to get up close. I wanted to watch him bring the boy back to life. I was sure that out of the corner of his eye he saw me. For what seemed a very long time, he worked to restore breathing and a heartbeat. Many in the crowd were crying as they watched. An ambulance siren wailed in the distance, drawing closer.

But it was too late. The boy had died.

The large crowd broke up. About half left. Not long afterward, the lifeguards reopened the pond for swimming. Some people headed back into the water, others milled around. Not long after that, my grandfather came up beside me on the beach. I was standing off a ways from my brother and sister who were splashing their feet in the shallow water. Unable to get the image of the dead boy out of my mind, I didn't want to go back in. Grandfather put his hand on my shoulder. "What are you feeling right now?" he asked me.

"Nothing . . ." I started to say, stammering. "Afraid," I admitted at last, "afraid to go in."

"Because you might drown like that boy did?"

"Yes, and _I_ almost drowned, too." I told him what happened.

"A lot of people are feeling upset or afraid right now," my grandfather said. "They—"

"But I could *die* out there" I interrupted, pointing to the water.

"Yes," he answered. "But 'out there' in the water, Robert, is no more dangerous than 'out there' on the highway." He swept his arm toward the two-lane road in the distance. "The truth is, people can die anywhere. Sooner or later, all of us die. But a lot of us don't ever really *live*."

"What do you mean?"

"What I mean is not very many of us have the courage to take risks and do things we want to do but we're afraid of doing. So we resist. We keep coming up with excuses. We make things even harder. When you first learned to swim, Robert, you needed faith to go in the water. It was hard, too, when you first went into deeper water. You needed to face your fears and listen to your teachers. You had to stick to it and learn. But then you began to excel at it, and it seemed to get easier and, sometimes, more fun. Many people who could be very good at things in life, like swimming, give them up. Something feels complicated or difficult or frightens them and they don't go back into the water. Your fear is nothing to be ashamed of."

He then told me about the best swimmer he ever saw, an Olympian who had given a demonstration at a pool in a city not too far away. "Even though he was going faster than any swimmer I had ever seen, he made it look so easy," my grandfather said. "Compared to him, the others were flailing and thrashing through the water. They were not only going much slower, they were struggling a lot more."

"How did he do it?" I asked.

"He used streamlining. That's when you glide through the water with almost no resistance. But no one else can do it for you. You have to learn it yourself."

"I don't know if I can . . ."

He looked me straight in the eyes. "How are you going to find out? Your swimming instructors can help you but then it's up to you. You'll never be able to learn how to streamline if you don't go back into the water."

Many times since then I've heard his quiet voice echoing in my mind and felt it in my chest. He knew that we all have to face our fears, sooner or later. I went back into the water that day. Years later I went on to become an All-American swimmer. Through it all I learned that streamlining isn't just for the water. It's for life.

We have the greatest access to current capabilities *and* our untapped potential when we keep our energy high and streamline our efforts. Each of us needs a variety of practical ways to outwit the ancient brain's tendency to react to rising stress by doing more of the same, only harder, longer, faster, and louder. What's required is a form of streamlining that can be likened to having an overdrive gear in a car, still moving quickly but with less strain and greater capabilities. That's where *calm energy* comes in.

When Less Is More

It is possible to have many things to do and still function with a clear mind and a positive, creative sense of relaxed control. No matter what the circumstance, there is a way to be quick without rushing. This distinction is vital. When I was a boy, I loved to skip stones across the quiet surface of a pond. I still do. The water does not overreact or underreact. It matches the incoming speed and weight of the stone, distributing the force of each skip on its surface, and as the ripples fade, the water returns to calm. Similarly, this is the feeling of reacting perfectly to challenges by being calm and energized.

Think of a time when you were doing a great job accomplishing things that were meaningful to you but you weren't feeling stressed out or uptight. Chances are, it felt easier to make solid progress, even when what you were doing was hard. That state of peak productivity and relaxed control is the focus of this chapter.

There are two primary energy states, *tense energy* and *calm energy*. Most of us are ensnared by tense energy, a stress-driven state characterized by high muscle tension and an almost pleasant sense of productivity and power induced by emergency stress hormones such as adrenaline and cortisol.

You may awaken tired and stiff in the morning but after several cups of coffee and some heavy tension—struggling to get the kids off to school on time, cursing in morning traffic, worrying about all the work you have to do—you may soon feel energized. That kind of energy is fueled by a nearly constant sense of pressure and anxiety that compels you to push yourself toward one objective after another, never pausing to rest or reflect. Minor irritations and small stumbles loom up as major frustrations and poor-old-me obstacles. Your efforts also get infused with a moderate to severe level of physical tension which, after a while, becomes only barely perceptible (or even pleasing) to you.

All that psychological and physical energy is costly: Underneath the stress-hormone-induced buzz, the billions of messenger chemicals that connect your senses and heart with your brain are being depleted. Before the end of each relentless day they may be all but gone, leaving you with only the stamina required to veg out in front of the television. In the longer run, you can suddenly find yourself aging prematurely, at the edge of burnout and exhaustion, facing serious health disorders.

The alternative state, *calm energy,* is characterized by low muscle tension, an alert, more optimistic presence of mind, peaceful and pleasurable body feelings, and a deep sense of physical stamina and well-being. It is essential to—and sometimes even synonymous with—the ultimate record-breaking state known as "flow" or "the zone," in which your mental and physical reserves are high, and you have the best combination of healthy vitality and increased creative intelligence. With calm energy, you make far more progress in causing the right things to happen throughout the day because you can focus on the things that are important to you without getting consumed by details.

The highest levels of thinking, feeling, and action come as a natural expression of the "flow" state, the place within you of relaxed alertness and of streamlined actions. With high levels of calm energy, we are more likely to feel happy and optimistic. We see things more realistically, and less dramatically. Molehills are molehills. With tense energy, molehills appear as mountains, and frustrations rise, thwarting our creativity and stamina.

When you develop the ability to enter and maintain a state of calm energy, you distance yourself from life's noise and distractions, its rushing and anger. You promote increased clearmindedness and sustained vitality. You streamline.

At Every Energy Downturn, Stop Rushing and Think *Less*

To increase calm energy and begin to accomplish more with less strain, start with heightened self-observation. Take a few moments right now to map your typical energy waves during a 24-hour period. First, imagine that you have no caffeine, tension, anger, urgency, or deadlines. Okay, that's fantasy, but it's very useful. Imagining this energy state helps you get a truer reading on your distinctive biological vitality patterns.

Next, use the chart on this page to fill in the blanks for each two-hour time period. Put an "x" at the approximate energy level you naturally have at that hour. Here are some simple guidelines: If you're usually awake during the time noted, 0 is maximum tension, distraction, or tiredness, and 10 is maximum energy, alertness, and attentiveness. During times when you're normally asleep, 0 is insomnia or awakening every few minutes to see if you're still at work, and 10 is sleeping like a baby. Go ahead and map out your natural energy wave:

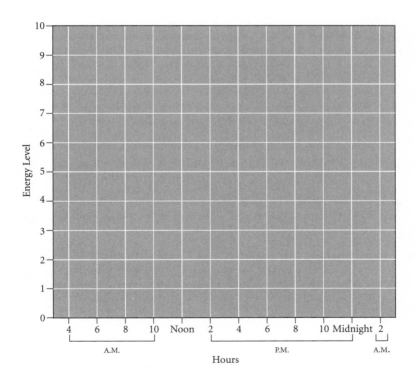

When finished, connect the "x"s to reveal your natural energy pattern. Use this to help you manage each of your normal individual downturns in vigor and focus.

Human energy is powerfully affected by the biology of time. An intriguing field of scientific exploration known as *chronobiology* has been mapping and measuring the energy rises and falls that we each experience throughout the day. Those are called *ultradian rhythms*. They occur in cycles of activity and rest every hour and a half to three hours. The ultradians coordinate complex patterns of messenger-chemical communication between and among the mind, heart, senses, and body. These messenger chemicals help us regulate energy levels. At the natural downturn of each ultradian rhythm, Nature has provided each of us with a series of revitalization signals that prompt us to take a few minutes to rejuvenate our mind, body, and spirit.

Few of us heed these signals, and this costs us dearly in escalating energy-drain and health stresses that can turn, over time, into constant fatigue and illness. Instead of shifting gears or slowing down, we keep going, overriding the need for the messenger chemicals to replenish and restore our full energy. The body becomes flooded with fatigue toxins and stress hormones which—when triggered by anger, caffeine, or urgency—can give us the illusion of a "second wind" when in actuality we're just being driven by tense energy.

To begin increasing your calm energy, notice each natural downturn in your vitality or focus power, and whenever these occur make a conscious effort to disengage from tension. You can still be moving quickly, but stop rushing yourself mentally. Chances are, you'll begin to think more clearly almost at once.

I also suggest developing your own version of what I call *strategic pauses,* which require 15 to 30 seconds, and *essential breaks,* which take 2- to 5-minutes at mid-morning and mid-afternoon. Although many people assume there's no need for pausing or stopping during the day, dozens of scientific studies show that the opposite is true. Introducing short breaks actually *speeds up* work and increases energy, yielding greater total accomplishments per day, with less distress and fatigue. Moreover, the illusion that by working nonstop we will "catch up" is just that, an illusion. By one estimate, each of us will have at least 35 hours of unfinished work in front of us our entire life. In short, we'll never catch up!

The most important thing you can do to streamline your efforts is to take strategic pauses and effective breaks and to start your day by giving your calm energy the chance to rise above your tense energy. Here's how you do those things.

Take Strategic Pauses and Essential Breaks

It's a paradox of modern life: To get ahead, we have to know when—and precisely how—to pull back. When you learn to take strategic pauses, you experience natural, powerful rises in your biological energy. This energy influences thoughts, feelings, attentiveness, and actions—giving you a clear boost. But if you skip the next break, your energy level will fall unavoidably.

Taking pauses is at odds with how most of us are accustomed to living and working. We get up earlier and earlier. We drive ourselves—and others—harder and longer than ever, all in the name of keeping up or getting ahead. What we're missing is smart pacing. We must learn to go through our days less like bulldozers and more like tennis champions—the men and women who've learned to deeply relax for a few key moments between shots, even in the middle of a difficult set. If they wait to rest until the end of the match or day, it's too late; they overeffort and underperform, giving less than their best.

According to some reports, impaired alertness has become one of the great dangers of contemporary life. Part of this is numbness brought on by widespread sleep debt—we don't sleep nearly as well or long as we need to. But it's also due to the fact that so many of us are pushing nonstop all day, every day. When we work for longer than twenty or thirty minutes straight on a single task, our problem-solving time increases by up to 500 percent and we find ourselves short-tempered and ill-mannered.

The difference between pauses and breaks is one of frequency and time required. A strategic pause of no more than a half-minute is ideally taken every half hour all day long. Essential breaks require as little as two to three minutes, two or more times a day. A revitalizing pause or break has seven elements:

1. *Deepen and relax your breathing.* How you breathe has a lot to do with how much energy you can generate and sustain all day long. Oxygen interruption—brief, frequent halts in breathing or chronic underbreathing—is a common contributing factor to tension and tiredness. Conversely, whenever you deepen your breathing you increase calmness and vigor.

2. *Change your view and catch some light.* Eyestrain is a common but overlooked cause of tension and fatigue—especially late in the day. Hour after hour, the tiny muscles in the human eye use more energy than any other muscle fibers in the body. Without a brief rest every half hour or so, they become tired and produce headaches, fatigue, and tension in the neck and shoulders.

If you've been doing close-up work, take a few moments to blink your eyes and look at more distant objects, such as a picture or poster on the wall, or the scene out a nearby window. If you've been scanning faraway scenery, switch to focusing on something nearby. These easy actions help provide a brief and vital rest for the most active eye muscles, prompting a healthy exchange of fluids in the eyes and providing increased oxygen and other nutrients.

There is evidence that even brief exposures to a natural scene can also be an excellent antidote to mental fatigue. In studies of workers with desk jobs, access to a view of natural scenes nearly doubled satisfaction ratings. People with a view of nature felt less frustrated and more patient, found their work efforts more challenging and interesting, expressed more enthusiasm for their work, and reported greater overall life satisfaction and health.

Increased brightness can also boost energy, sometimes dramatically. More than half of your body's sense receptors are clustered in the eyes. Because of this, the eyes need regular changes in images and brightness, acting as light-harvesters—firing nerve impulses to the pineal gland and the higher centers of your brain. This process can powerfully influence biological sleep-wake cycles and provide invigorating antidepressant effects.

During each strategic pause or essential break, step to a window or glance at a bright indoor light. Many people report a lasting sense of calmness followed by a surge of energy after looking at a bright outdoor scene or glancing at indoor light (even at the intensity level of normal room lamps).

3. *Re-balance your posture and loosen up.* The longer you sit still, the less energy you have available to get up and get going. In this step, begin by standing up—tall, loose, and at ease. For those

of us who spend long periods of the day sitting down, there is evidence that simply standing up every half hour or so increases alertness and energy by up to 30 percent.

Poor posture—even a slight slumping of the shoulders—depletes lung capacity by as much as 30 percent. According to researchers, the key to ideal posture begins with frequent awareness check-ins about the position of your neck—the goal is to keep your chin slightly in, head high. It's a very relaxed feeling of being taller. Imagine a beanbag on top of your head and gently use your neck muscles to push it toward the ceiling. Next, loosen and realign your shoulders so that they are as relaxed and wide as they can be. This immediately increases oxygen flow to the brain and senses.

Physical movement is another key to your vigor and focus power. Every time you get up and move, you increase your energy and alertness. Every time. A few seconds here. A half-minute there. You get an energy boost and, as a bonus, increased clear-mindedness.

Most any exercise helps raise energy. Even just getting on your feet—a good thing to do right now as you're reading this—can make a difference: standing produces more energy than sitting. Therefore, make it a point if you have a sit-down job to get up often, to stand while you talk on the phone, for example. How about walking around for a minute or two every hour? Or going up and down a flight of stairs or heading out into the hallway or outside for some fresh air?

4. *Sip ice water.* One of the most overlooked reasons for lack of energy is a lack of water. Water provides the medium for nerve impulse conduction, the transmission of other biochemical processes, and the muscle contractions that stimulate metabolism and generate energy.

Even a slight dehydration—not enough to make you thirsty—can measurably deplete energy. What causes this invisible fluid loss? Dry, energy-efficient homes and workplaces. Stress. Caffeine. Alcohol.

By sipping extra water every 20 to 30 minutes during the day, you not only improve your overall health and resistance to illness but also provide a clear, repeated signal to your metabolism to keep your energy and alertness levels higher. This effect may be even more pronounced when the water is ice-cold, because when ice-cold water reaches the stomach it stimulates increased energy-production throughout the body and raises alertness in the brain and senses.

Beyond these benefits is the compelling suggestion that you may "maximize calorie burn by keeping the water ice cold," suggests one researcher. "A gallon (128 ounces or eight 16-ounce glasses) of ice cold (40 degrees Fahrenheit) water requires hundreds of calories of heat energy to warm it to core body temperature. Water may be one of the simplest, most powerful keys to increased energy and loss of excess body fat."

5. *Enjoy a moment of humor.* Too much seriousness can interfere with energy and make it more difficult to streamline your efforts. By pushing nonstop and staying relatively glum and intense about work or life, we lose out in a number of ways. First, we miss the forest for the trees. The small pleasures and momentary wonders of being alive pass us by. In contrast, every time you have a hearty laugh, a whole series of biochemical events occur. Energy increases, brain wave activity changes in positive ways, and hormone production re-balances.

In many situations, the best light-heartedness is known as "cosmic humor"—finding the funny things that arise in the midst of life's paradoxes, difficulties, and uncertainties. Sometimes the best humor of all is the ability to laugh at yourself—taking yourself lightly as the day goes forward. What did you see or hear recently that tickled your funny-bone? Any antics of children? A great—and nonhurtful—joke? What about a quick glance at a favorite cartoon?

6. *Finally, add some inspiration.* Steal a glimpse of where you're headed. Remember one of the mentors or teachers who helped shape or guide you. Recall a genuinely supportive word or note you have received lately. Or stop to gaze into a favorite memory or photo of your loved ones, for whom your sustained energy may matter the most of all.

These six steps are shared in every strategic pause and essential break:

- Deepen and relax your breathing.
- Change your view and catch some light.
- Re-balance your posture and loosen up.
- Sip some ice water.
- Enjoy a moment of humor.
- Add some inspiration.

There is one additional step when taking an essential break at mid-morning and mid-afternoon:

7. *Eat smart.* Millions of Americans have learned to starve themselves between meals, assuming it is a weight-control habit. It's not. Eating low-fat snacks between meals can actually increase your energy and metabolism. Here's why.

Whenever you skip between-meal snacks, blood sugar falls and you are likely to experience increased fatigue and tension. Eating smaller, nutritious meals and snacks helps to stabilize blood-sugar levels, which in turn optimizes memory, learning, and performance. When you go for four or five hours at a stretch without eating, your blood-sugar levels drop and your energy wanes. It may take a strong dose of willpower just to get out of your chair, let alone do some daily exercise. Research suggests that spreading out your food intake helps increase levels of energy and alertness, lower blood cholesterol levels, reduce body fat, enhance food digestion, and lessen the risk of heart disease.

In recent years, one of the surprise findings in nutritional research has been the discovery that, in a number of cases, eating carbohydrate-rich snacks can actually help reduce feelings of impatience or distress. The best between-meal snacks are those that taste great to you and also happen to be high in complex carbohydrates and fiber and low in fat. This matters for two reasons: high-fat foods promote body fat gain and high-fat foods drain energy and can be a significant cause of fatigue. What you choose to eat may also influence the production of brain messenger chemicals called neurotransmitters, which affect your mental alertness, concentration, attitude, mood, and performance.

Just a few bites of high-protein food may contribute to increased energy, greater attention to detail, and alertness lasting for up to three hours. Options include a sandwich with chicken breast, turkey breast, low-fat cheese, or fish; a cup of bean or lentil soup; a small serving of nonfat yogurt, cottage cheese, cream cheese, or skim milk—with fruit. When you're on the run, try a small handful of almonds, raisins or figs, or a whole-grain cracker with some salmon or thin slice of low-fat cheese.

In contrast, one of the simplest ways to reduce mental distress and tension is by, first, avoiding over-stimulating yourself with caffeine (in coffee, tea, and soft drinks) and, second, eating something that is low in fat, low in protein, and high in carbohydrates. This kind of snack influences the production of neurotransmitters and may help produce a calm, or more focused state of mind and relaxed emotions. Options include low-fat cookies or a low-fat muffin, bagel, or English muffin; cooked whole grains (rice, wheat, oatmeal, corn, buckwheat, barley, etc.) eaten with fruit or a sweetener but without milk; low-fat pasta salad with fruit or vegetables; or some whole-grain bread, low-fat (baked) chips, or rye crackers topped with your favorite all-fruit preserve.

Test it yourself. Your success in choosing the right combinations of foods that help you manage your energy and focus largely depends on careful observation of your body's responses and habits. Over the next few weeks, take notes on your state of energy and mood 10 to 15 minutes before meals and snacks. Do you feel alert and motivated? Calm and focused? Tense and irritable? A half-hour after eating, reassess. Create a list of the food choices that seem best for you and use it as a helpful tool in managing your day-to-day eating patterns.

Start the Day Right—*Without* a Bang

Many of us have gotten into the habit of setting our alarm as late as possible, keeping the lights dim, avoiding morning exercise, and leaping out of bed in a hurry to begin the day. All of that adds up to a tension-producing shock to the system. Blood pressure soars. Stress hormones pour into the bloodstream. Yes, you may feel awake, but it's a survival signal, not a sign of true vigor, and it won't last long. Caffeine adds a short-term chemical boost to the brain and senses, but this varies from person to person, and it's neither natural nor lasting energy. Add some rush hour anger and you have plenty of tension-producing ingredients for the proverbial starting gun that begins the day for millions of people.

There's a better way.

From the moment you get out of bed, your brain cues the body's metabolism to match current and anticipated physical, emotional, and mental demands. Researchers can predict how much energy you will have in late afternoon and evening by how you get up in the morning and what you do, or don't do, in the first hour or so after arising. In a sense, your metabolism adjusts itself for the day, trying to anticipate how much energy, and what kinds of energy, will be needed.

With four simple steps, you can start your day primed for increased calm energy:

1. *Awaken without a jarring alarm.* Ease, don't leap, out of bed. Where possible, awaken to pleasing music, which tends to be much more invigorating *and* relaxing than the traditional alarm. Keep the volume low. By easing out of sleep you retain more of the invigorating power of sleep.

While still in bed, take a few moments to be still. Blink your eyes. Take several deep breaths. Open and close your hands. Loosen your shoulders and release any tension you notice in the neck, jaw, back, or arms. Remind yourself why you're getting out of bed to provide for your loved ones, keep learning, and make more of a difference in the world. When you rise from the covers, do it slowly, giving your muscles a chance to ease into action. These start-the-day actions are generating calm energy.

2. *Turn on the lights.* On sunny mornings, do you step outside for a breath of fresh air and soak in the brightness? Many of us do this on vacations but not during the rest of the year. We should. The brain responds to many signals but few are more powerful than light. The body has hundreds of biochemical and hormonal rhythms, all keyed to light and dark, and the mind and senses are powerfully affected by exposure to bright light with an intensity between 7,000 and 12,000 lux, which is comparable to daylight just after dawn. According to the scientists, there is a neurological link between the retina of the eye and the *suprachiasmatic nuclei* in your brain, which play an important role in attention-focus and energy production. In most cases, the more light, the more focus and overall energy.

Test this tomorrow when you step out of bed: Progressively turn on three or four times the number of lights you'd usually turn on. Switch on the bedroom nightstand light and overhead lights, the hallway lights, *both* bathroom lights and all three kitchen lights. That's the idea. Leave these lights on for the first 15 minutes that you're awake. Or, best of all, step outside for a minute or so to flood your eyes with daylight. Feel the difference in energy. For many people, the added light boosts mood and shifts your metabolism away from sleep and toward calm energy.

3. *Get at least five minutes of relaxed physical activity.* No, pulling your clothes on doesn't count as enough physical activity, in case you're wondering. However, even just a few minutes of moderate exercise increases calm energy and reduces tension.

Before or after eating breakfast, go through a gentle warm-up and then do a few minutes of light physical activity such as going for a walk, slowly climbing and descending a few flights of stairs, or pedaling at a relaxed, moderate pace on a stationary bike or outdoor cycle. For variety you might do some moderate muscle-toning exercises. As little as a minute or two of light physical activity sends a signal to the brain to reduce tension and increase alertness and calm energy.

4. *Enjoy several bites of a great-tasting breakfast.* More than any other food we eat all day, breakfast may matter most. When you start the day with a low-fat, high-fiber breakfast—say a bowl of oatmeal with low-fat or skim milk and a piece of fruit, or a slice of 100 percent whole-grain bread with nonfat cream cheese and salmon or all-fruit preserves—you switch *on* and turn *up* your energy. When this food reaches the stomach it triggers responses in the brain and senses, shifts in messenger chemicals that are essential to alertness and calm energy.

A breakfast rich in carbohydrate, protein, and fiber stimulates the sympathetic nervous system, revving up hormones and neurotransmitters in the brain for an active day. In fact, the right kind of low-fat breakfast helps set your energy level for the entire day.

The world belongs to those with the most energy.
—ALEXIS DE TOCQUEVILLE, in
Ralph Waldo Emerson's journal, 1862

8

An Ounce of Emotion Is Worth a Pound of Repetition

Nothing brings out hidden qualities like passion does. Passionate birdwatchers find themselves enduring physical hardships beyond what they thought they could handle, just to spot another rare creature; passionate cooks discover new tastebuds and devour new information; passionate sports fans learn that they have a capacity for understanding and memorizing statistics that had eluded them before; passionate lovers are thrilled by new depths of feeling and unexpected reserves of energy.

Passion's effects are always profound in the sense that they come from places deep within us. So much has been made in contemporary America of toiling along—of relying on repetition or toeing the line in order to get ahead—that many of us have lost touch with the zeal that can bring out our best. First thing Monday morning, do you wake up envisioning—"Another week of stress and strain at work"—or "Another chance to do more of the things I love"?

You might consider how much of your potential for greatness you are losing by worrying about the infrequent dark side of passion and thereby not trusting your better self. Nelson Mandela, who has seen plenty of ugliness as well as plenty of beauty in his life, challenged us all to face up to our untapped capacity in his stirring inaugural address. "Our deepest fear is not that we are inadequate," he said. "Our deepest fear is that we are powerful beyond measure. It is our light, not our darkness, that frightens us."

Name a person from history whom you think of as having lived passionately in accordance with his or her ideals. It may be Martin Luther King, Jr., or Joan of Arc, or Pablo Picasso, or Mother Teresa, or Jesus of Nazareth, or Nelson Mandela, or your favorite painter, teacher, poet, mentor, activist, or jazz musician.

For the most part, these people came from humble beginnings. Yet they accessed capabilities and inspiration that most of us do not reach. It's also true that many of these men and women suffered more than the rest of us do, and experienced doubts at times about the wisdom of following their passions. Yet I think you'll agree that most of them would not have traded their lives for more ordinary ones. As Hegel observed, "We may affirm that absolutely nothing great in the world has been accomplished without passion."

Even if you don't aspire to Hegelian greatness, but only to using more of your untapped capabilities, passion is a practical necessity. It is a driving force of heart and soul. It engages your excitement for activities that matter most to you and that lead to inner happiness. Daily life involves very hard work, and some of it doesn't contain much excitement or joy. If we're not careful, before long it may lack not just excitement but even enthusiasm, not just joy but even enjoyment. And that's a straight track to numbness and regret.

One of the things that makes children so fascinating to us is the passion with which they undertake so many things. It's fair to say that we would probably never learn to walk if something in us didn't call forth a passionate commitment to master that complicated, scary, and often painfully learned skill. But how many of us, as adults, are quick to give up when we're faced with a similar challenge? From time to time all of us have had dashed hopes and have lost touch with our enthusiasms in the crush of school, jobs, and marriages—reality.

When do we begin trading passion for comfort or routine? Maybe it's when we're taught that even the most honest tears— which appear as a passionate expression of loss, disappointment, pain, or even joy that is beyond words—are "for babies." Yet, when the eyes moisten, that often expresses a profound awareness of life that is deeper than words—that's why so many people experience tears at major moments of life transition, not only in grief at funerals but also at joyous occasions such as births, graduations, and weddings.

Of course, you have to be blasé about some things. Otherwise, you might die of overexcitement. Yet your individual passion about a direction or a dream can see you far. Consider the example of Albert Lexie, who lives in Pittsburgh. For the past forty years, Lexie, who is mentally retarded, has supported himself by shining shoes.

Since 1981, he has shined shoes two days a week at the Children's Hospital of Pittsburgh—donating all of the tips he earns to the hospital's Free Care Fund. Those donations now add up to more than $40,000. He has become the very soul of this medical center. He remembers people's names. Through the years, his open heart, ready smile, hard work, and constant desire to shine shoes to help "his" kids has touched thousands of lives. His personal contributions have made medical care possible for hundreds of children.

I'd like to tell you about someone else who didn't give up, someone who's not famous and who has had more sadness in his life than anyone ought to. His name is Steve Perkins. As it happens, Steve does have a Harvard degree, but unlike many of his classmates he hasn't used it as a passport to wealth. He has always been committed, passionately, to social justice. He's worked for twenty years now at a nonprofit-community-based economic development organization in Chicago. His best friend was Chicago's leading civil-rights advocate, Albert Raby, and Steve worked tirelessly alongside his friend as Raby managed the political campaign that led to Harold Washington's momentous election as Chicago's first African-American mayor. Steve was deeply hurt when Washington died suddenly in office, and even more so when Raby also died suddenly, a year to the day after Washington's death. Not long after that, Steve's own son, twenty years old, died in a tragic accident.

Would you or I have given up? With each of those terrible events, Steve rededicated himself to honoring the others' memories in his own work. When the top executive position became open at the organization that Steve had served for so long, he applied for it. He thought he could do the job, and he felt that he had earned it.

The board of directors didn't see things Steve's way. They decided an outsider was needed for the position, and hired one. Steve wondered where all his dedication had gotten him and where his organization's loyalty to him had gone. Hurt and feeling discounted, he even briefly considered quitting. Instead, he thought hard about what he would most like to do with the rest of his career.

There was a project he had begun but not been able to devote much attention to: bringing together faith-based organizations and helping them understand and shape the "total ecology" of their communities—the relationships among the people, the environment, the physical qualities, transportation networks, job opportunities. To help people view their communities in a comprehensive way through their diverse faith traditions, and then make those communities better.

He asked for authorization to focus more on this work, which encompassed so many of his passions and commitments. Granted that authorization, he put his whole heart into it. It's extraordinary work that values the human intellect and the human spirit. It draws out untapped capabilities in Steve and in many others each and every day. It has flourished and changed whole communities, and now its latest extension is nearing fruition: the creation of an Academy of Environmental Justice on Chicago's south side, named in honor of his friend Al Raby.

Today Steve can say, "It was great to go after the CEO job. It was even better not to get it and to move on to roles and projects that fit me better." Recent studies confirm what Steve recognized in a happy story and what many of us have learned from sadder observation and experience: A poor fit between your passions and your work may be more detrimental than a poor fit between the demands of your job and your current abilities.

This new research confirms an older study that I have always found compelling. In 1960, a researcher interviewed 1,500 business-school students and classified them in two categories: those who were in it for the money—1,245 of them—and those who were going to use the degree to do something they cared deeply about—the other 255 people. Twenty years later, the researcher checked on the graduates and found that 101 of them were millionaires—and *all but one* of those millionaires came from the 255 people who had pursued what they loved to do!

Now, you may think that your passion for Icelandic poetry of the baroque period, or butterfly collecting, or golf—or social justice—might consign you to a permanent separation between what you love and what you do for a living, but it isn't necessarily so. Vladimir Nabokov, one of the great novelists of this century, was far more passionate about butterfly collecting than writing. His first college teaching job, in fact, was in lepidoptery. Research on more than 400,000 Americans over the past 40 years indicates that pursuing your passions—even in small doses, here and there each day—helps you make the most of your current capabilities and encourages you to develop new ones. It can also help keep you feeling younger throughout life!

MAKE AT LEAST A LITTLE TIME FOR WHAT YOU LOVE

Art Tatum was born in 1909 in Toledo, Ohio. He was African American and born partially blind. As an adolescent, he was beaten by other kids and became totally blind. He had perhaps the most exuberant love of music of any child. He wanted desperately to learn to play the piano.

But he faced two problems. First, he couldn't see. Second, although Art had learned some violin at music school, his family lacked the money for a private piano teacher. So Art learned to play the piano the only way he could—in the honky-tonk saloons of Toledo in the early 1920s.

Even on days when he was tired from schoolwork and part-time jobs, he would make at least a little time for what he loved. He would get a friend or family member to walk with him to one of the honky tonks nearby, on Indiana Street, and he would ask to sit at the player piano while it played. By placing his fingers lightly on the keys, every time the player piano pumped and the keys dropped, Art could follow the motions. It was complicated—yet he loved it. There were so many keys involved, at times it felt nearly impossible to follow them with his fingers. But his passion kept encouraging him to try. Far into the night, song after song, his heart willed his hands to master this art. In this way, he learned to play.

But what Art Tatum didn't know—because he didn't have a piano teacher to tell him it wasn't possible—was that when the player piano manufacturers of the late 1800s and early 1900s made player pianos and made the rolls of paper music to play them, they used *two* pianists, not one.

Because he didn't know what he tried was impossible, Art Tatum did it anyway. He became the first pianist in history to play *four* hands of piano music with his two hands. Even the most renowned pianists were in awe of his capacity. At one point when Art Tatum joined Fats Waller, another legend of jazz piano, for a concert, Waller said to the audience, "I am just a piano player. But tonight, God is in the house."

From that point on, until his death in 1956, Tatum changed the entire field of jazz and influenced the world of music. To sample his genius, listen to "Tiger Rag"—recorded in 1934—in Jazz Archives Masterpieces.

Art Tatum didn't shrink from what he most loved to do. He grew into it, a little more every day in whatever ways he could. I'm convinced that whether or not he had become famous, the pure joy he personally felt—and, in turn, conveyed to others—when playing the piano would have been gift enough by itself.

What Are Your Most Compelling Life Interests?

One of the simplest ways to increase passion is by noticing where it's hiding in the midst of your busy life. What do you love enough to do for free? What gives you so much enjoyment that you yearn to do more of it? What were your childhood dreams? What do you get the biggest kick out of doing—even if you're not great at doing it? What makes you feel the best about yourself? When you daydream, where does your heart go? What brings the biggest grin to your face these days or puts a spring in your step, a hum in your voice, a sparkle in your eyes, or gives you the goosebumps?

Write down five of your top passions. Once you start looking more closely for those things, what you love is usually easy to uncover. By focusing on passion, you can begin to put it at the center of your life and work, instead of losing it around the edges. By the way, do you know the most compelling interests for each of the people closest to you? That's important, too.

Put a Dose of Extra Passion in Your Daily Routine

Make some small changes in your daily schedule. Increase your chances to do more of the things you love. An early morning walk. Mentoring a child. Gardening. Writing. Making music. Deepening a relationship. Rekindling your romance. Pursuing an art. Playing a sport. These are new routines worth creating—but only if you keep a degree of flexibility, and fun, in them.

It's important to note that whenever a routine become tedious or dull it not only thwarts excitement; it can also begin to produce tension and negative emotions. Take gardening, for example. In small, enjoyable doses, it can be invigorating for many people. But there comes a point where you might let the garden get too big or grow tired of the same plants each year, and then the tedium of tending to it may outweigh the enjoyment. You'll know it because you'll find yourself feeling tension or frustration—not joy—when you think about it. That's when a change is called for. Otherwise, these negative emotional states may cause more erratic heart rhythms that can diminish brain-wave coherence and adversely affect intelligence.

It's not just a question, however, of knowing what you love to do; it's about doing it, often. It turns out that the happiest people are the ones who weave many simple pleasures into their lives, rather than waiting around for the big enjoyments. Research also indicates that every single dose of affirmative emotion—a few moments of excitement, caring, enthusiasm, and enjoyment, for example—can produce positive changes in cardiac rhythms, brain waves, the immune system, and hormonal balance.

Because of this, do whatever you can to keep shifting your attention toward whatever excites you or makes you smile. It's a simple antidote to stress and a renewed call to capability.

Carry a Day Book

Whatever we focus on tends to grow stronger. A day book is a journal that's small enough to fit in your purse, pocket, or briefcase. My favorite has pages that are easy to insert and remove. John F. Kennedy carried one. He kept it with him to write down thoughts, new ideas, quotations from his readings or travels, and anything that struck him as funny, interesting, meaningful, or poignant in some way.

Jotting down notes is a good, consistent way to keep passions in sight. Studies also suggest that a pen in hand connects to the human heart far better than a keyboard. Therefore, when it comes to uncovering or exploring passions—all the things you truly enjoy doing, whether you're good at them or not—a small journal in hand can be very valuable in day-to-day life. If you don't have an eye out for new passions, you'll only keep repeating the old ones.

After his brother was assassinated, Robert Kennedy continued his brother's day book and expanded it, calling on its entries for many of his speeches. DaVinci used a day book to enter his sketches, ideas, and questions. Einstein, Gandhi, and Edison carried day books. Richard Branson, founder of the Virgin Group, has filled more than one hundred such books with his observations, perspectives, and dreams. Consider this a running record of your own impressions and exciting ideas. Feel inspired? Explore why. When did people's eyes light up today? What surprised you? What touched or moved you? Wouldn't it be cool if . . .? Feel. React. Wonder. That's how to bring passion into sharper focus and to find new ways to weave more of what you love into what you do.

We are shaped and guided by what we love.

—GOETHE

9

Launch That Rocket in Your Backyard

When he was a young boy, his friends called him Sparky, after a comic-strip horse named Sparkplug. School was all but impossible for him. In the eighth grade, he failed every subject. In high school, he flunked physics with the lowest score in the school's history. He also flunked Latin, Algebra, and English. He did poorly in sports. No one seemed to care about him. He remembers being astonished when anyone even said hello.

He, his teachers, and classmates all knew he was a loser by every conventional measure. He resigned himself to the bottom rung of mediocrity, or worse. But, against all doubters, he believed in his heart that he had one natural streak of genius or talent: drawing. He was proud of his sketches, even if no one else thought much of them. In his senior year of high school, he submitted a series of cartoons to his high school yearbook. They were rejected.

After high school, he completed a correspondence course in art—his only art training. Then he wrote a letter to Walt Disney

Studios, hoping to be a cartoonist there. He got a request for draw-
ings, and he worked many hours on them before mailing them to
Disney. His reply from the studios: a form letter turning him down.

But Sparky sensed he had been endowed with a unique talent
that was of value, if only to him. So he reacted to the rejection from
Disney by drawing his autobiography in cartoons about a chronic
underachiever, a boy whose kite would never fly and yet someone
the whole world would come to know: Charlie Brown. Sparky was
Charles Schultz, and his "Peanuts" cartoon strip that began in 1948
went on to become one of the most popular cartoon strips in history, ending in late 1999 at a time when it was appearing in 2,600
newspapers in 21 languages. Through the years, he made an estimated $55 million. He had his own star on the Hollywood Walk of
Fame. And he drew every cartoon himself by hand.

Each of the Peanuts characters became household names for
an estimated 350 million readers in 75 countries. Those characters
had strong, distinctive personalities and a willingness to think and
act on their own, even when surrounded by life's pitfalls, just as
Schultz did in counting on his truest hidden talent and developing
it into his greatest strength.

Each of Us Is Gifted in a Unique Way

Vast amounts of human potential get overlooked or lost because
we fail to grasp the truth that Schultz sensed: He was gifted in a
one-of-a-kind way. Even when no one else seemed to value or
even appreciate his talent, Schultz worked up the courage to find a
way to develop it into a defining strength. Against the odds, he
championed this strength and eventually touched the world.

Like Schultz, every one of us is gifted with natural and enduring talents along with a strong inner drive to turn them into strengths and apply them in pursuit of something that is meaningful to us. In most cases, a glimpse of these talents can be seen very early in life.

Imagine slipping into the back of a preschool class during one of the free times when the children can immerse themselves in anything they want to do. If you look carefully, you'll see that each child is revealing something special about what he or she is instinctively great at and feels most excited about or satisfied in doing.

A little girl is reading a picture book to another child, telling the story with much enthusiasm. Nearby, two little girls are building a tower of colored wooden blocks. One is piling them skyward, caring little about how the blocks fit or look, while the other girl keeps straightening up the edges and standing back to admire the symmetry and form.

Not far away a boy is arranging a neighborhood out of tiny snap-together pieces, shaping the streets so that his toy cars can move easily along them. Behind him, another boy is fingerpainting the sun and stars, enjoying the feel of the paint oozing between his fingers. He pauses to dab a bit on his nose and then mixes more colors together to see what happens. One of his friends has settled down at the worktable by the window with bins of colored clay. Knowing he can't go outside to play in the mud, he starts building his own mountain range, positioning it right in line with the sunlight streaking in.

A tall girl is hunched over a drawing table, using colored chalk to sketch a picture of a house and with a bright but very orderly flower garden in front. A few feet away a boy in baggy sweatpants and an oversized shirt is pretending he's on stage, making funny faces and improvising as he acts out a story.

Another boy is watching and enjoying the scene. A girl is running back and forth nearby, trying to get someone to play hide and seek with her. Three children are unpacking a storage box of costumes, talking about their own roles in make-believe, giggling and grinning from ear to ear. Behind them, along the wall, others are doing somersaults and juggling foam balls. One of the boys has gone to the refrigerator and is nibbling on a snack, looking out the window. Another sits alone on a chair, oblivious to the din around him, ignored by others yet content in a world of his own.

More is being revealed here than random scenes of children playing. Passions and talents are bubbling up through the mosaic of play opportunities. Each free and spontaneous immersion in an activity can provide a glimpse, however small, of each child's giftedness into the future. Patterns of inherent drives and talents emerge. Some of them will hang on through an entire lifetime. We catch sight of several of the distinctive ways that each child most naturally behaves, learns, reasons, interacts, decides, and is motivated. Such yearnings and tendencies reveal the presence of talents, especially when they are felt early in life.

No, none of these children can become anything he or she wants to be. That's a popular myth that has been proven wrong. Yet each of us can discover and apply our own unique talents and, through the years, keep building new strengths—and becoming more of our one-of-a-kind best.

Four decades of global research on nearly two million people proves that we cannot do anything well just by setting our minds to it, yet each of us can do one or two or three things better than any other 100,000 people. Those things are our individual talents. We each need to discover them, develop them into strengths, and then apply them as fully as we can. On some occasions, talents and passions are one and the same, but often they are not. Sadly, we have become so focused on trying to "fix" our weaknesses—which can be likened to pulling weeds—that we fail to grow a great garden or, as I see it, launch the rocket that's waiting in our own backyard.

Consider the story of Homer "Sonny" Hickam, Jr., from Coalwood, West Virginia, a small company town where for generations the only things that really seemed to matter were coal mining and football. The introspective second son of the mine's superintendent and a mother determined to push her son to a better life, Sonny fell in with a group of misfits for whom the future looked uncertain, even bleak. They weren't talented in football and rebelled from becoming miners.

After watching the Soviet satellite *Sputnik* streak across the Appalachian sky in 1957, Sonny and his teenage friends took their paths into their own hands. They used their keen mathematical curiosity, love of constructing models, and a dream of building rockets to the stars in ways that changed their own lives and altered the view of their entire community. With the help—and often hindrance—of the people of Coalwood, the boys taught themselves how to turn mine scraps into rockets that soared miles into the skies. Their uncanny talents and hard work produced defining strengths that touched not only those around them, they eventually influenced the entire aerospace industry.

Hickam went on to become a distinguished engineer with NASA and has left his one-of-a-kind imprint on space exploration. Talents, and streaks of genius, are waiting within every one of us. Although such compelling life interests may not take us into space or fit the expectations of those around us, that should not be enough to stop us. Each individual's greatest chance for growth is in the area of greatest talents and strengths. Whenever we find a chance to shine at something in our own right, even when brief or fleeting, we must take it: There are times in every life to aim our rocket for the sky and let it fly.

What Is Your Natural Pattern for Getting Things Done?

Think back across the activities and pursuits in your life. What has felt the most natural? Where, exactly, have you shined the brightest?

Talents are instinctive, naturally recurring patterns of thought, feeling, or behavior that can be enhanced by new knowledge, skills, and experience. Skills, for example, reveal if you *can* do something whereas a talent reveals how well and often you do it. Your talents are innate and enduring, whereas knowledge and skills—which combine to turn talents into strengths—can be acquired through learning and application. Over time, a talent can be developed into a *strength*—a consistent near perfect performance in an activity. The consistency, the ability to shine repeatedly, is vital.

Before his death in February 2000, Charles Schultz drew the same cartoon strip, Peanuts, for over 41 years. How did he do that? Not from willpower or luck; it was one of his defining strengths. He was able to excel under intense constraints that were formal (typically four cartoon frames, except on Sunday), thematic (kids only, no adults), geographic (the kids stay in their neighborhood), and visual (heads will be round; a vigorous scribble across half a face will signify humiliation; three rings around a head with a smattering of stars above will convey that a kid has just fallen or been knocked silly). He mastered covering a vast emotional territory using joyful constraint. In book form, the complete 18,250 Peanuts cartoon strips would compromise 5,000 pages. In his own unique way, he was a gifted artist indeed.

The one sure way to reveal your greatest potential for strengths is to carefully observe yourself. Try an activity and notice how readily you pick it up. Notice how satisfying it feels and whether you keep saying to yourself, "When will this end?" or "When can I do it again?" Observe how quickly you can skip past steps you haven't been taught yet and see if you get so absorbed in doing it that you lose track of time. This growing awareness of self is vital. If you watch yourself carefully, your dominant talents will reveal themselves across time and you can then cultivate them into powerful new strengths. The same powers of heightened awareness can be used to better understand the unique talents and strengths of others, too.

Whenever you apply talents and strengths, there is a sense of commitment to using them well and a feeling of satisfaction at your level of contribution. There's another distinction, too: Unlike passions, every once in a while a strength or talent is *not* something you love to do even though you're good or even great at doing it.

For example, one of my good friends is exceptionally talented at editing. But he doesn't find it pleasurable, and never has. He likes the satisfaction of doing a good job in his own distinctive way, and he's very talented at helping worthwhile writing projects reach a wide readership and prompt soul-searching and positive change, but the actual practice of writing and editing is very hard work for him and rarely much fun at all. He has stopped trying to force himself to like it.

Even so, by knowing how to apply his strengths—in this case, something he's great at but doesn't love: editing books and articles—he is able to launch work projects effectively, and with less resistance, knowing he may be able to finish sooner and, because he's good at it, get great results. This can then free up more of his time and energy for pursuing other things that he loves doing far more.

Studies indicate that individuals can double, and even triple, their effectiveness and productivity by focusing on identifying talents and developing them into new strengths and doing whatever they can to fully apply *all* of their strengths, while spending relatively little time managing weaknesses.

An example of this comes from my work over the past decade with partners at international professional services firms. I have learned that a great accountant has an innate and compelling drive toward precision. She can focus intently—and very naturally and well—on creating a business plan or accounting system that will be highly effective. Ask an exceptional accountant when she feels best at work and she will say, "When the books balance" or "When the business plan works well." This may seem a little strange to people who aren't great with numbers, but if you consider it, for a person blessed with an inherent drive toward precision and ultimate resolution in solving a mathematical equation, accounting can be a great job. An exceptional—and quite natural—grasp of mathematical and analytical solutions is more than a skill. It is more than memorized facts or knowledge. And it requires more than passion. It is a talent that, with knowledge and skillful development, becomes a defining strength. Without such a talent, no one will be exceptional at this pursuit, no matter how hard they try.

There is evidence that these inherent talents are something we can sense in many different situations. It may also be readily evident from our experience that, no matter how hard we try, we cannot fit someone else's view of what we should be able to shine at doing. My most vivid memory of this comes from an experience when I served in the Marine Corps during the Vietnam War. Throughout basic training and advanced infantry training, one Marine in my unit kept saying, "This is not me." Many of us tried to work with him, to help him find some role where he could excel. Yet, we felt his frustrations growing.

One night after some intense combat survival training with hundreds of Marines, he returned to camp, dowsed himself with lighter fluid, and set himself on fire. I was the first one to reach him. I will never forget the look on his face, his eyes wide with terror, engulfed in flames, screaming "This is not me! This is not me!" We got the fire out. He was rushed to the burn-trauma center and he survived.

The rest of that night, I sat awake in the dark. I wondered how many other people I might meet in my life who were trapped living at the brink of setting themselves on fire because—for reasons the rest of us might not understand—the effort they were called to make was at odds with their inherent capacity or the voice of their spirit.

What Are Your Natural Talents and Defining Strengths?

Most of us spend too little time identifying our innate talents or developing them into distinctive strengths that we apply day after day. One of the best ways to change this is through heightened self-awareness. To get you started, you might use the following lists to begin identifying some of the activities or approaches where you believe you shine:

- *What is your natural style of approaching a task that really matters to you or working to accomplish an important goal? What takes precedence:*

  - *Details:* Descriptions, data, numbers, or measurements

- *Structure:* Design, models, physical elements or materials
- *Sensory experience:* Sights, sounds, colors, textures, lighting, form, or movement
- *Human aspects:* People and interactions
- *Ideas:* Philosophy, principles, theories, or concepts being used
- *Process:* Strategies, mechanisms, techniques, or procedures for accomplishing the goal

- *What is your natural style of learning?*

  - Visualizing or conceptualizing the subject
  - Memorizing facts
  - Determining why it matters
  - Understanding how it links to what you already know
  - Reading everything available about it
  - Making notes or diagrams
  - Observing
  - Experimenting
  - Asking others
  - Discussing things

- *What is your natural style of influencing others?*

  - Listening very carefully to the feelings and priorities of others
  - Negotiating
  - Empathizing with the challenges that others are facing
  - Analyzing the facts or data for making a choice

- Suggesting and weighing alternatives
- Conversing and talking things through
- Serving as a test case or personal example
- Conveying excitement or persuading by motivation
- Measuring the benefits of doing something
- Encouraging others to learn more or try a different approach
- Counseling others along their own path
- Referring others to a reliable source of knowledge
- Writing or diagramming the possibilities or problems
- Establishing a logical sequence of reasons for action or nonaction

Review these notes. They will help you learn more about your own distinctive pattern of talents. What can you do to include more of these talents during the day, so that you bring out more of your best? Talk about this with others. Find new ways to understand— and make the most of—talents and strengths in yourself and every person who is close to you.

Emphasize Strengths, Manage Weaknesses

We live in a weakness-focused world. Based on the erroneous belief that good is the opposite of bad, for thousands of years humanity has been fixated on faults and failures. True, we are each imperfect, but our weaknesses reveal little about our strengths— which we must cultivate from instinctive talents and champion in our everyday lives rather than letting these gifts languish while we spend most of our time trying to "fix" weaknesses.

This issue becomes all the more vital in light of the fact that the brain's reticular activating system is primed to magnify negative incoming messages—including perceived faults—and to minimize positive. Criticisms and weaknesses tend to be amplified in the higher brain centers; in other words, they are blown out of proportion. Therefore, they must be managed with care. We are far better served by focusing most of our energy and attention on positive activities and pursuits that bring us vigor and satisfaction.

As you sharpen your self-observation powers about current strengths and talents, you increase your chances for greater success (on your own terms) by:

- Finding new ways to apply your defining strengths
- Knowing the difference between weaknesses and nontalents (which you can ignore)
- Managing weaknesses out of your way

Find New Ways to Apply Your Defining Strengths

Notice how much—or how little—time you spend developing or applying your strengths. How can you improve the fit between what you do from day to day and what you shine at doing?

Many of us get so caught up being busy that, looking back, we realize we've spent much of our time gridlocked or just plodding along instead of lining up more of our best work and getting it done sooner. One of the gifts in using your strengths is how much you can accomplish in an hour, and thereby gain more time or money for doing other things you may love more—such as pursuing your passions.

Know the Difference Between a Weakness and a Nontalent (which you can ignore)

As one research project summed it up, "Each of us is a couple of talent cards short of a full deck." That makes sense. In view of this innate imperfection, let's consider the difference between a weakness and a nontalent. A nontalent is a behavior that is perpetually a struggle. You might have a nontalent for remembering names or thinking artistically. Should you spend time trying to fix this? You could learn a way to memorize names. You could take art classes. But chances are not much will change. The best thing to do with most nontalents is ignore them. They just don't matter in the big picture of things.

But a nontalent can become a weakness if you find yourself in a role where success depends on it. If you are working on a neighborhood council or in a service business, your nontalent for recalling names becomes a weakness because other people want you to recognize and value them by name. If you are trying to plan ahead, then a nontalent for strategic thinking becomes a weakness because you can't seem to guess what lies just around the bend. It is wise not to ignore weaknesses.

Manage Your Weaknesses Out of Your Way

The first question to ask yourself about something you don't do well is: Does this require additional knowledge or know-how? Every one of us has experienced the benefit of developing insights or skills that help us handle certain situations. Let's say you can't keep up with your schedule because you're being driven crazy by a difficult software program that you just can't get the hang of. So you take a class or get some coaching on making this software run smoothly, and the weakness vanishes.

There are several other primary ways to deal with a weakness: Create a support system, find a complimentary partner, or find another role.

In many situations, the most expeditious way to manage a weakness is with a support system that works around the shortcoming so it doesn't get in the way. If you struggle with remembering names, buy a name-filing system and refer to it often. If you are a terrible speller, use a spell checker every time you send a letter.

The next choice is to find a partner whose strengths complement your weaknesses. If you tend to be visionary but impractical, then, when you sign on for a project, make sure to enlist the help of someone who is exceptionally practical. Few people who excel in life are well-rounded in a literal sense. It's the working partnerships that are well-rounded. These individuals do not turn their weaknesses into strengths. They accept that they are not perfect and realize that this would take far too much time, energy, and effort, and it would distract them from making their best contribution. The key is to match one person's valleys with another individual's peaks.

If you find yourself spending most of your time trying to manage around weaknesses, then stop doing it. Instead, when training, or a support system, or a complementary partnership doesn't work out for you, search for an alternative role. Everyone is great at something. The key is to keep searching until you find the right fit for what you do best, what you are naturally talented or highly skilled at doing. But don't stop there . . .

Use an Hourly Check-In to Apply More of What You're Best At

Once you have a heightened awareness of where you shine, devise ways to weave in your strengths during the day. For example, take a moment at the top of every hour (or during your essential breaks) to ask: "How can I apply more of my best?" Pause before agreeing to take on any new effort and be certain it involves doing some of the things you shine at.

You might also ask, Is this the most exceptional work I can do, the very best effort I can make? Am I drawing on the utmost of my capabilities? Am I providing the greatest value per minute of effort? Can I bypass, minimize, or delegate some of the upcoming tasks that I have no talent or skill for, or that feel like drudgery? Do I notice and reinforce the best in other people, or am I staring at their blemishes and weaknesses? Can I take on from others more of what I'm best at and, in turn, ask them to lighten my load of the things I'm not great at or don't love to do?

Without such questions, it's easy to keep rushing ahead, with lots of motion but not much enthusiasm or satisfaction. When you do work you're best at, it flows.

Keep Developing Hidden Talents into New Strengths

A cartoon I love shows one cat saying to another, "Maybe I could've done more with my life if I hadn't been so focused on tearing up the sofa!" Just because you may have certain strengths doesn't mean that's there aren't other hidden talents inside you waiting to be found. No, we cannot be everything we want to be, but we can further develop our natural talents. One of the practical tools for this is to take a few minutes each week to reflect on ways you did new things or tried to face old challenges in new ways. Then for each of these activities rate from 0 (least) to 10 (most) your response to the following:

1. Did it fit my values?
2. How natural or easy was it to learn?
3. How proficient was I at doing it?
4. Did I get a "kick" out of doing it? How satisfying was it?
5. How valued or valuable did I feel in doing it?
6. Did I get so absorbed in doing it that I lost track of time?
7. How much recognition or reward might I receive for doing it?
8. Do I want to give this more of my energy and attention?

When a new activity scores high, ask yourself an additional question: Do I have access to the knowledge and practical skills required to turn this talent into a new strength? Once you identify work you're best at, it's a natural tendency to hesitate before trying anything else, particularly anything new, because you might not be as good at it. But if you never try it, you'll never know. You'll just keep tearing up sofas. The best of life depends on a willingness to stretch beyond your current capacities by exploring, testing, and reflecting. That's where much of the fun is, too.

T hings which matter most should never be at the mercy of things which matter least.

—Goethe

10

Let Your Life Speak

Years ago, a speech therapist worked tirelessly to invent a device that would enable deaf people to "hear" by making sound waves visible. Unfortunately, the machine failed to achieve its purpose, but it was not altogether useless—it became the telephone. The man who inadvertently invented it was Alexander Graham Bell, and he never would have sustained the energy to make that revolutionary discovery if he hadn't been driven by a deeply embedded sense of his own accountability to help the lives of the deaf.

Two women were very important in Bell's life: his mother and his wife. His mother was a teacher. She guided Alexander's attention to acoustics and the study of speech. Through the full range of his youthful pursuits, she was always there to encourage him. She knew that Aleck would have to find out many things in life for himself.

Aleck and his brother invented a machine that could talk. It had lungs and vocal cords. Its first word was "Mama." In Boston, Aleck met his future wife, Mabel Hubbard, who had recently returned from school in Germany. She was beautiful, smart, and kind. He was brilliant, tenacious, and poor.

But it was more than the love and devotion of his mother and wife that drove Aleck to make his greatest mark on the world. Alexander Graham Bell's primary talent was in speech and speech therapy. He was driven by a promise he had made to himself to help the two most important people in his life, his mother and his wife—they were both deaf. His commitment carried him forward through the years and led to discoveries, including the telephone, that benefited millions of others. His efforts are an example of accountability.

There is an old Quaker saying, "Let your life speak." That's what happens when you come through on your promises, time after time. There are four essentials for making this happen:

1. Believe you can make a difference.
2. Promise what you will do.
3. Do what you promise.
4. Hold yourself responsible for your commitment and efforts, even when you can't control the outcome.

This timeless advice holds much common sense yet it is far from common practice.

Believe You Can Make a Difference

The more we feel we have the ability to change something for the better, the more obligated we feel to do whatever we can to make that happen. In an election year, for example, if you believe that your vote won't matter, it's likely that you won't vote and will feel justified in not doing so. Whatever we believe we can't affect, we generally take little or no responsibility for, and we tend to down-play or minimize our lack of involvement.

Alexander Graham Bell believed that he could find a way to help deaf people hear. He felt accountable to turn that belief into action. The critics and obstacles did little to deter him because he believed he *could* find a way to make a difference, he accepted the responsibility of doing so.

Promise What You Will Do

Once you believe you can make a difference, it's necessary to get crystal clear about what you're going to do about it. When you commit, be as clear as you can so there are no hidden ifs, ands, or buts. Although we cannot always guarantee the results of what we promise, we must enter into each commitment with every intention of fulfilling it. When we give voice to our commit-ments, we feel more accountable for them. Promise clearly and humbly while committing yourself to doing more than anyone else may expect.

Do What You Promise

This is a very simple, difficult, and powerful determinant of who you are. It is only when we honor our promises time after time that we win the trust and loyalty of others. What you imagine and hope for are manifested through keeping your word.

Taking even the smallest step to turn words into action gets us moving in the right direction. Jot notes to others describing what you're embarking on or following through on, "As promised, . . ."

Don't worry if at first others don't seem to notice. Do whatever you're doing primarily for your own sense of honor in contribution. Over time, people accord genuine respect to others based almost wholly on doing what they promise, not promises alone. Demonstrate an unwavering resolve to do whatever must be done to accomplish the best long-term results, even when this is very difficult.

Hold Yourself Responsible for Your Commitment and Efforts, Even When You Can't Control the Outcome

None of us is guaranteed tomorrow as we wish it to be. Today, with all of its complexity and beauty and sadness and possibilities, is all we have.

When you commit yourself to doing what you promise, you let your life speak in the most compelling way—by example. Accountability rarely depends on a specific outcome—which may be beyond our control—but on the quality of the effort we made and how honored our commitment along the way. For example, what you learned in class at school, or didn't learn, is most important, whether or not the grade reflects this. Look in the mirror, not out the window, to assign responsibility for poor results. It's rarely justified or useful to blame others, external circumstances, or bad luck.

If what you're trying to do doesn't work then it's best to own up to it—but such shortfalls can't happen too often if you're to maintain your credibility. There are times when circumstance may block you from coming through with the specific outcomes that you or others had hoped for. When you see that happening, say so earlier rather than later. Enlist help. And be willing to help others. Don't give excuses; be clear about where you are. In that way, others will be more likely to be committed and also honest with you in return. Sometimes we overestimate our available time or energy. When that happens, own up to it and learn from it.

When an effort has been made, if something goes wrong, or it doesn't turn out as you had first hoped, acknowledge your part in it. "I was there. I gave my best effort in doing what I promised. . . . It didn't turn out the way I'd hoped, but here's what I learned . . . and these are my ideas for going forward from here . . ."

Rarely is any disappointing outcome created by plan, and neither is it "all my fault" or "all your fault." Everyone involved has a piece of accountability to uphold. What's called for is honesty and new learning, not blame or denial. We must keep in mind that our best is never going to be the same from minute to minute. Life is alive and evolving. When you give your best to doing what you promise, there's less pressure to keep judging yourself, and you're less likely to get defensive or feel down or distracted by pointless guilt when mistakes happen or a setback occurs.

From time to time, all of us miss a mark we were aiming for. But when we are willing to keep our word and give our best effort, and then speak as truly as we can about the results of that effort and what we learned along the way, we are worthy of respect.

We Must Keep Reaching for Our Best—One Person at a Time

You are the only person on earth who has sole custody of your life—your one-of-a-kind life, your entire life.

At the same time, we all have a natural instinct not only to know ourselves but to help others know themselves, too. When we hold ourselves accountable to our best effort and truest self, we can ask that others who know us well—and care about us—do what they can to hold us accountable, too. They can encourage us and support us where needed. They can help us work through disappointing outcomes. In many cases, they may also ask us to get to know their best effort level and to hold them accountable to that as well.

This is the Brother's Keeper Principle, which dictates that once I have come to know you well, I must say and do what I believe is in your best interest and in line with your commitments, regardless of how that makes you feel about me. In other words, in many situations life is more about trying to make a constructive difference than trying to be liked.

In his essay, "Self-Reliance," Emerson writes: "I've been reflecting recently on why I don't have any followers. A lot of other people who have written less than I have, have all kinds of followers. I decided the other day that it is because the other people were trying to bring people to them while I've been trying to bring people to themselves."

An understanding of this principle is deepened through Nobel laureate Albert Schweitzer's writings following his journey to build a hospital in Africa. In answer to the question he kept asking himself, "Am I my brother's keeper?" He answered, "How could I not be? I cannot escape my responsibility." He insisted that all human beings counted as brothers, and his obligation was to respect them, to help those in need wherever he found them, with every medical and human means at his disposal, and to learn about them and hold them accountable to their own best effort, whatever that was.

Even nearing the end of his life, Schweitzer would finish his long day's work in the hospital and then sit writing at his desk, reflecting on what he had learned and writing others to beg for more supplies, his face almost touching the paper, his bristling moustache moving with his eyes, slowly, as he wrote with painstaking care. As darkness came, his pet ants would climb the desk and cross his pages. He wouldn't even hurt the smallest of creatures, so strong was his commitment and sense of responsibility to care for them, too. In these and many other daily ways, Schweitzer used accountability to look more deeply for the hidden capacity in himself and others.

Above all, and beneath all, accountability is generated from within your heart; it cannot be "given" from outside. It is conscience—and more. It prompts you to forgo excuse-making and instead to sense emerging problems and opportunities early on and accept a role in responding to them in new ways with commitment and ingenuity.

*B*lame *or finger-pointing and lack of personal responsibility*
Keep the gloomy game going.
They keep stealing your hidden genius and potential wealth—
Giving them to a dimwit on the sidelines with
No leadership, heart, or financial skills.
Dear one,
Wise
Up.

—HAFIZ, fourteenth-century Sufi poet

11

Sweat the Right
Small Stuff

When he became president of Centennial Medical Center, Bill Arnold announced an open door policy. Nobody came. Everyone just assumed it was another meaningless slogan.

Then he had his office door removed and hung in the lobby as a monument to the end of an era. His number one focus was what he called "golden gripes." He realized that every day most of us are robbed of energy and resourcefulness by chronic frustrations and small yet unresolved irritations. Such pet peeves, although often ignored by peers and managers, are among the most important causes of the death of individual initiative in families and organizations.

One of the first people to walk through Arnold's open door was a machinist who said he had complained several times because some of the most sophisticated tools he worked with were not being cared for properly and were difficult for him to locate when he needed them. He felt misunderstood, believing his supervisors thought he selfishly wanted to keep the tools only for his own use. He eventually gave up the griping, but not the gripe. Arnold listened and took action. Eventually, he addressed hundreds of other "little things" that were in the way of his individual employees giving their best. Among the results: After Arnold began paying close attention to golden gripes, employee turnover at Centennial was cut in half while earnings increased by 33 percent.

This highlights one of life's simple truths. In most cases, it's not the major difficulties or disasters that undermine our capabilities or kill off our exuberance and initiative. It's the unattended little things that, over time, bring out the worst in us and drive our relationships to ruin. The toilet seat left up. Clothes thrown on the floor. The top left off the toothpaste tube. Not getting home on time for dinner, again and again. Dishes left unwashed in the sink. Forgetting to say thank you for another person's efforts, or failing to search for that special surprise on your anniversary or a loved one's birthday.

These and a hundred other "little things" often become the big things that, over time, generate overwhelming resentment. Such small irritations have the power to cloud our view, diminish our sense of hope, drive wedges into our closest relationships, and poison our attitude.

Begin to Notice Which "Little Things" Really Matter

Okay, a lot of trivia in life doesn't matter, and worrying about it is a waste of time. But some of it counts. Knowing the difference is crucial. That's because an enjoyable and healthy life depends far more on the frequency of happiness than on the magnitude of happiness. That means we're usually better off having many small positive moments than waiting to be happy all at once when we win the lottery, receive the next promotion or raise, or can afford that special vacation or car.

The pioneering psychologist Abraham Maslow set forth a hierarchy of human needs and a path he called self-actualization. Yet, he also emphasized that there is a hierarchy of grumbles that has great influence over us. These individual irritations need to be brought into the open rather than being ignored or denigrated as not being important. Energy and attention that get bound up in small frustrations get wasted.

Maslow would tell us to listen not for whether people were complaining or not, but instead to notice *what* people were complaining about. In a family or organization in trouble, you can expect to hear lots of common grumbles.

"Why didn't you call and say you'd be late?" "No one asked about my day," "Who left clothes by the door?" "No one noticed the work I did to clean up," "What was all that commotion while I was trying to talk on the phone?" "Who left the lights on?" or "Why didn't someone else notice that the dog needed to go outside?" These are signs that people are distracted from giving their best. Even if we could force ourselves not to talk about such irritations, that doesn't mean they aren't still a problem or that, if left unattended, they won't grow into something major.

Know What Small Things Bug You and Which Ones Boost You

Identifying and attending to the important little details of everyday life can go far in freeing up the energy and focus required to discover or develop more of your capabilities. It also makes it easier for others to learn how to help you make the most of your time. Begin right now with a simple checklist of the things that leave you gritting your teeth or fuming—and, conversely, laughing or smiling. Every one of us gets bugged or boosted by certain small things. What are these for you?

"Little Things" That Bug Me	*"Little Things" That Boost Me*
1. _____	1. _____
2. _____	2. _____
3. _____	3. _____
4. _____	4. _____

Next, make it a point to focus on better managing these irritations out of your way at the same time you weave more of the little boosts into your day. Talk about this with loved ones, friends, and co-workers.

Develop a similar listing to identify the little things that annoy the individuals important to your well-being and future. And then don't do those things anymore. In your relationships, no matter how rational you try to be, you cannot survive inattention to the little things that, over time, annoy you to distraction or drive others crazy.

Get a Bit of Inspiration Here and There

Several years ago, it was nearing dusk as I crossed the arched wrought-iron footbridge over the River Liffey at the center of Dublin, Ireland. The breeze was brisk and many business people were hurrying home or to the pub. Everyone was moving fast. But there at the center of the bridge was an old man, leaning on the railing, staring out across the water, seemingly oblivious of the throng scurrying past him. I slowed as I neared him. Out of the corner of his eye he must have caught the look of curiosity on my face. He motioned for me to step to the edge beside him.

"How's the view?" I asked.

"Good," he murmured, gazing intently into the distance. "I'm getting another bit of inspiration."

"What do you mean?"

He answered with a question: "What about you, have you had a bit of inspiration here and there throughout the day?" He smiled and, before I could reply, he added, "You know it's better not to wait in hopes of having it all at once."

He was right. Now and then throughout every day, we need little glimpses of pure inspiration. Such moments change how we see things and keep calling us to savor life and give more of our best to it. When it comes to removing the barriers to hidden capacity, it turns out that some small stuff is well worth sweating, after all.

Nothing can bring you peace but yourself.
—RALPH WALDO EMERSON, "Self-Reliance,"
Essays, First Series, 1841

12

Get a Life

"Just as soon as I catch up on my work, *then* I'll relax," we say. Then I'll be there for you. Then I'll make it up to you. Then I'll show you how much I love you. Another time, another place, a different environment, a better situation, a more golden opportunity. Just as soon as . . .

Years ago, I lost part of my extended family in an airline crash. When search teams found the five bodies in the wreckage, the two parents had their arms around the three little ones. The passengers who had survived the crash must have quickly realized that the smoke and flames sweeping through the aircraft gave them no chance to survive. Trapped, the parents held the little ones until the end. "Just as soon as . . ." got taken away.

In my grandfather Cooper's musty tool-shop beside the driveway, he had a grinding wheel. One day while I was working for him, we were sharpening a grass whip for cutting weeds. I was trying to talk to him but it was hard to be heard above the noise. He kept saying, "What?" Finally, seeing how frustrated I was at not being able to have my voice heard, he pulled the plug on the grinder. It slowed to a stop.

"That's a good lesson to remember," he said, pointing to the now-silent machine. "When something is grinding you down, you have to know when to pull the plug."

What do your loved ones miss the most about you in recent years? What part of you isn't coming home at the end of the day? It's likely to be something small but significant, such as the sense of humor or playfulness you used to have before you got so busy. That's the part of you that people who care about you the most miss the most. You used to be much more fun to be around even when you didn't have money. It's time to get some of that spark back.

Put More Life in Your Days

As Emerson put it, "We're always getting ready to live but we never truly live." These days, we find ourselves doing too much and living too little. Here are seven practical ways to begin putting more of your best self back into your life beyond work:

1. Synchronize your calendars.
2. Call home at key times.
3. Come home first in mind and heart.
4. Change the way you walk through the door.
5. Eat a snack before you eat dinner.
6. Get up and move after the evening meal.
7. Remember the funniest thing that happened today.

Synchronize Your Calendars

Households that synchronize their schedules make life easier for everyone. When each household member can glance at a shared calendar—in our house, it's on the refrigerator door—it's easier to make future plans, accommodate the prior commitments of others, and plan ahead to spend time together. No matter what form of scheduling you now use—a day planner, electronic organizer, or other—test this approach.

Select a central spot for a traditional wall calendar. Have each household member take a few minutes to enter their personal plans over next month or two. List appointments, community or school activities, special events, and more. When you're making new plans, refer to this calendar to make sure you don't inadvertently conflict with other people's priorities and preset obligations. This is a simple way to help everyone in your home know that you are more aware—and respectful—of their time obligations. I have also found that it frees up more moments to have fun and enjoy being together.

When we overschedule family time or keep asking loved ones to defer the pleasures of daily living or their own aspirations until we make it in the work world—to hang on because things will get better—it assumes that the rewards of our work will justify the neglect of self and family. Pure fantasy. Therefore, it's a good idea to keep tabs on your family's goals. As individuals and together, what matters most? Take these priorities into account as you review your weekly schedule. Is anyone being left out? You might also ask others, Is there anything I'm doing that—whether I realize it or not—is getting in your way? When we invite such conversations, we grow closer in a world that keeps trying to pull us apart.

Call Home at Key Times

In many families, loved ones don't see much of each other. When individuals spend a large proportion of their time away from home, they may come to feel that others don't care enough about all that they're facing out there in the world. This may be based on misperceptions caused by a lack of regular, heartfelt communication.

One of the simplest ways I know to help prevent this misunderstanding and deepen your connection with loved ones is to check in with them regularly. Perhaps several times during the day. (Of course, a spontaneous check-in here and there can be great, too.) This might mean a quick phone call at lunchtime, or after school, or—if you're away overnight—last thing in the evening and first thing in the morning. What would be most appreciated by those closest to you?

Come Home First in Mind and Heart

Early evening is the time when energy plummets and vulnerability to tension and tiredness is especially high. This is also when more mistakes happen and molehills become mountains. In many cases, this is a family danger zone, because there's evidence suggesting that over half of the most damaging arguments are started or magnified within 15 minutes of people greeting each other at the end of the day.

If you work away from home, arrange for a brief transition time or decompression period at the end of your work day. These final minutes might include returning selected phone calls (picking through your messages and dialing only those numbers where the person on the other end is likely to be supportive and positive), cleaning up your work area, finalizing tomorrow's schedule, or organizing upcoming projects. Make it a point to clear your mind of as many work-related thoughts as you can. Write down your day's end concerns, ideas, and issues that pertain to tomorrow or some time in the future. The act of jotting down these thoughts helps to free you from overfocusing on work. You can come back to them later instead of trying to remember them all in your head. This transition time—and the ride home or minutes spent transporting your children or waiting for other family members to arrive home—are a golden opportunity to unwind and slow your pace a bit, to think ahead and give your mind and heart a boost. Here are several suggestions:

- *Catch some extra afternoon light.* As you wrap things up in your work, turn on a few extra lights and, if possible, step outside for a minute or two of late-day sunlight. From either outdoor or indoor sources, light offers an ancient and powerful way to lift your late-day energy and mood.

- *Free up your shoulders, free up your energy.* In just moments, by stretching your muscles and joints, you can also stretch your mind. Gentle physical movements—such as neck rotations, shoulder shrugs, and wrist circles—bring increased blood flow throughout your body and make it easier to loosen up and shake off the mindset of work.

- *Catch a glimpse of the big picture.* Make it a point somewhere between ending your work day and arriving home (even if you work at home, there's a necessary transition into being "at home" again) to take an extra few moments to look at something beautiful: a flower, a green plant, a row of trees, or the cloud formations in the sky. Even brief exposure to a natural scene is an antidote to fatigue, promoting a more positive mood, increased energy, and better health.

Change the Way You Walk Through the Door

No matter what your job, the rhythm of your work efforts is probably very different and perhaps far more intense than the rhythm of being at home. Yet many of us rush home and never let go of our work intensity. Instead, we hurry to prepare dinner, flip through the newspaper, eat quickly, and then either collapse in front of the television or plunge into another round of scheduled activities—errands, parental duties, catching up on paperwork, preparing reports, or paying bills. What's missing is a brief "time out" period to shake off stress and tension and start the evening with a dose of extra energy and excitement.

Like my family, yours probably is in the habit of meeting at day's end and sharing your rendition of "Here's what happened for me today." Little do we realize that this is a prime time for dumping complaints on each other and triggering fatigue-driven arguments.

Consider an alternative: Negotiate in advance with family members a different kind of greeting whereby you each express your pleasure in seeing the others in a warm, caring way but limit your first comment to just a few words, such as: "What a hectic day! It's great to be home"; or "Things were *crazy* at work, but I'm really glad to see you!" And then, without ignoring your partner or other family members, delay talking about your day (or hearing about your partner's day, or what the children argued about, which household appliances broke, who needs more money, and so on).

After a warm greeting for your loved ones at the door, take advantage of a few minutes of "personal wind-down time" to change clothes and go through whatever brief, relatively quiet interlude that helps put your day to rest and your life back in proper perspective: a hot shower or bath, a relaxing set of exercises, a calm-down time for a beverage and favorite snack. For some families, there may be days when this is actually the best time to employ a babysitter. The key is to make sure that, even if it's only for a few minutes, you make a clear shift away from work—to go for a stroll with your partner, step outside for a few minutes, putter in the garden, give each other a back rub, turn on some great music, or sip your favorite cup of tea.

Eat a Snack Before You Eat Dinner

Here's something you may find surprising: To rev up your evening metabolism and vitality, it's essential to eat before you eat. Low blood sugar levels and simple hunger-related tensions contribute to fading energy, negative emotions, and late-day arguments.

It's a good idea to choose a beverage such as hot tea, juice, or a healthy iced drink, and then enjoy a small, low-fat appetizer such as some fresh vegetable pieces with low-fat or nonfat cream cheese, or bean dip and a whole-grain cracker or two. Or you might try several whole-grain low-fat cookies with a half-glass of cold skim milk or a half-cup of yogurt.

For some people, the best choice may be a cup of tomato soup with a few whole-grain crackers, say researchers. This can be an energizing and satisfying appetizer. The least invigorating and satisfying? Surprisingly, it may be cheese and crackers. Experiment to find what works best for you.

Get Up and Move After the Evening Meal

What you do or don't do in the first half hour following your evening meal sets the stage for how much vigor and fun you will likely have throughout the evening hours and how well you will sleep. A few minutes of light physical activity at this time of the day elevates your energy level and metabolic rate just as it's winding down. Walking after a meal may speed up energy-boosting and fat-burning heat production by up to 50 percent.

Test how this works for you. Push back from the table after tonight's meal and go for a brief walk. If you walk with your romantic partner, it may very well improve your love life by helping to synchronize biological rhythms of energy and attraction. If, on your post-meal stroll, you include other family members or friends, you may also gain an ideal chance for some good old-fashioned talk and light-hearted fun—the kind that keeps you closer together rather than drifting apart.

Sleep researchers at the Mayo Clinic say a light evening exercise session can measurably deepen sleep. "If you can increase your body temperature with exercise about five or six hours before going to bed," explains Peter Hauri, director of the clinic's insomnia program, "the temperature then will drop most as you are ready to go to sleep . . . and sleep becomes deeper, with fewer awakenings."

Remember the Funniest Thing That Happened Today

I remember how much I loved to laugh in elementary school, and how my kindergarten teacher, Miss Robinson, would react to my moments of wit by glaring at me and sternly saying, "Well that's very funny, Robert, but you can't joke your way through life." If she was still alive, I'd give her a call and say, "Yes, in some important ways you *can* use humor to make the most of life!"

Every single day, humor is a gift of energy. It startles us out of our routines. It puts things in perspective. It brings us closer together. It helps us face difficult times. I remember how much one of the maintenance men in my high school loved levity and seemed to find something humorous in everything he did. For three years, every day when I arrived well before the school bell to participate in athletic workouts and study time, in one way or another he made me smile. Once, when I asked him how he managed to be light-hearted when nearly everyone around him seemed so serious, he said, "Things are almost always funny when you stop to look at your life from the other side of the street."

He was right. When we're mired in details and duties, it's easy to get lost in immediate concerns and lose our perspective and humor. But if we pause for a moment to mentally cross the street and look back at ourselves in the context of what really matters most, we can smile more often, and find new reasons to lighten up and laugh out loud.

At dinner time or while you're going for a walk following the evening meal, include some of the day's best humor. For example, you might encourage each household member to describe the funniest thing that happened today. If you live alone, you could do this on the phone with a friend or outside on the sidewalk with a neighbor. In one study of 50 married couples, psychologists found that humor accounted for 70 percent of the difference in happiness between couples who enjoyed life and those that didn't.

Even just a few minutes here and there of playtime in the evening can really pay off. Instead of speeding up and losing sight, you can slow down and take a good look, shaking free of the mindset of exhaustion and reclaiming more of your life.

How many people are trapped in their everyday habits: part numb, part frightened, part indifferent?
To have a better life we must keep choosing how we're living.
—EINSTEIN

THIRD KEYSTONE

FARSIGHTEDNESS

13

Align Your Life with Your Biggest Dreams

Photographs taken from spacecraft in the 1960s revealed, for the first time, the full sweep of ancient ruins in the Middle East, including the pattern of roads leading out from the sites where cities and temples once stood. None of these features were discernible from the ground: archaeologists had walked the terrain and examined it in details for years without ever seeing the patterns there.

It is much the same with life. When we focus too intently on our immediate situation and surroundings, we perceive less and less.

We orient according to the reach and clarity of our vantage point. That's why we need great goals to lift our gaze to possibilities that exist beyond daily habit. When I was young, my grandfather Cooper began teaching me about the power of Big Dreams by telling me the story of Padraic Pearse.

Born in Ireland, Padraic Henry Pearse was named after Patrick Henry of the American Revolution. In the early 1900s, he served as headmaster of St. Edna's, a small private school in the countryside south of Dublin. Today, St. Edna's would be called a character-based school. Pearse encouraged his young pupils to *live* what they learned. With every subject, the students were provided opportunities to apply what they had learned in the everyday world of nearby farms and in the neighborhoods of Dublin.

Pearse cared deeply about the heritage of Ireland and feared that its language, culture, and history were being eradicated by British domination. He wrote and spoke passionately about this. His biggest dream was for Ireland to have its freedom once more.

Pearse was by nature far from militant. Few would have imagined him as a revolutionary. He was too gentle. His students knew that he could not bear to see even the smallest creature harmed. Yet his conscience drove him to become one of the leaders of the Easter Rising, the Irish Rebellion of 1916. He had spent his life helping his students emphasize big dreams and the time had come for him to pursue his own great goals that, in his words, "were dreamed in the heart and that only the heart could hold."

Within the year, he led the Easter Rising. Following days of intense fighting in the streets of Dublin and surrounding countryside, the British Army prevailed against the revolutionaries. The leaders of the revolt were imprisoned. On May 3, 1916, Pearse and a number of those considered to rank among the best people of their generation were executed in Stoneyard Square of Kilmainham Jail in Dublin. The commanders of the British Army believed they had silenced their voices. But this did not happen.

The poor people of Ireland, most of whom had been afraid to support the Easter Rising, began to talk about the headmaster of St. Edna's, the school teacher and poet who had tried to live the words he believed in his biggest dream. Across the hamlets and countryside, people in Ireland began to ask their children, "What dream are you willing to give your life for?"

My grandfather took Pearse's words more literally in asking, "Which of your dreams are so big that only your heart—and not your head—can hold them?" Nearly all children know the difference between dreams of the head and those of the heart. So do the rest of us, when we pause long enough to notice.

Big dreams are mobilizers of human spirit. Think of the ancestors who left their homelands penniless, scorned, victimized, or persecuted for their faith or ideas. Some of them had to marshal the courage to cross an unknown sea to a new land. They had to start over. They heard people saying, "You'll never make it." But they did anyway. And many of those who arrived on our shores endured harrowing times beyond imagining.

Through darkness and uncertainty, what kept many of them alive and carried them through were big dreams: less of riches than of freedom for themselves and their loved ones. In their own unique ways and through the most trying circumstances, they held to great goals, and in so doing they discovered a central source of human capacity.

Big dreams keep us engaged with life's possibilities so we don't sink from sight in the quicksand of old habits and ongoing fears or frustrations. Such great goals are vital in work as well as in life.

However, there's a barrier to overcome. "Don't be so idealistic," we caution each other, falling under the risk-aversion spell of the ancient brain. "It's not wise to be too daring. Beside, you'll only be disappointed. And what if you fail? No, shrink your dreams down to size. Make them so small they most assuredly will come true. Settle for that. It's enough."

If we accept this rationale, we abandon great goals. We go for being comfortable, keeping our heads down, staying busy, going along, making do, getting by, and playing it safe. And we're wrong.

By the way, what if you fail at a noble task or big dream? Even then, the chances are good that your great goal will leave some kind of positive mark on you, your family, or community. On the surface, Padraic Pearse failed. The rebellion was ended in 1916 but not long afterwards the spirit of freedom was again advanced in Ireland.

Although a 1920 decree of the British government separated Northern Ireland from the remainder of the country and named it a distinctive part of the United Kingdom, the rest of Ireland declared its freedom in 1921. That freedom was secured in a truce with England. Despite tensions and bloodshed through the years between Protestants and Catholics, and the north and south, today there is peace. As much as freedom, Pearse dreamed of ending the exodus of people from Ireland. This, too, has come true: for the first time in over a century more people have been moving into Ireland each year than have been leaving.

Which of Your Dreams Are So Big That Only Your Heart Can Hold Them?

My grandfather Cooper once said to me, "Little plans have no power to stir your blood." He was right. People make a lasting difference in their families and communities when they align their lives in the direction of something that stirs their blood. A great goal lifts the spirit and ignites in the heart a compelling sense of direction and purpose. Even when big dreams don't come true— and many of them don't, at least not literally—they almost always change us for the better. They focus our daily actions and stretch us to learn, grow, and serve.

Consider one of the dreams of Mother Teresa: to do everything she could—singlehandedly if necessary—to help lift the spirits and fortunes of the poorest of the poor in India. In response to this dream, she worked tirelessly to help those forgotten people have enough food, hope, health, and a chance for work or education. For Martin Luther King, Jr., the great goal was to win freedom and equality across America. This dream mobilized his energies and efforts through many difficult years.

One of the big dreams of a woman who lives not far from my family is spreading the beauty of nature to everyone in a local nursing home. She grows flowers and brings them from room to room, letting their blooms brighten the days of those who are otherwise in a closed-in world. Twenty years ago, the great goal of Terri Crisp began when she tried to keep dogs and cats from drowning during a flood in Alviso, California. This experience opened the way to creating a team of 3,500 volunteers known Emergency Animal Rescue Services (EARS) dedicated to helping animals survive catastrophic events.

Keep Clearing Your Mind to See the Big Picture

From time to time, one of the best ways to achieve a sense of calm control in life is to get everything out of your head and onto paper. This frees up new energy to focus on great goals and enables you to notice and eliminate whatever is unnecessary and distracting. When there's lots of stuff on the mind that has nothing to do with what matters most, we lose the big picture.

Go ahead and try it: Reach for a pad of paper or your day book or journal. With pen in hand, jot down whatever thoughts, ideas, or concerns are running around in your head. These could be any of hundreds of things that, at this moment, are vying for your attention: a project deadline, a backlog of correspondence or e-mail, your child's grades or future, a thank-you note you need to write, bills to be paid, errands to the drugstore or cleaners, up-dates to your grocery list, an angry boss or customer, worries about your job, resources or promotion prospects, a messy garage or closet that you've been meaning to clean, your latest bank state-ment, an overdue oil change for the car, a new person you must hire or orient at work, interest rates or the stock market, your aching back, your next dental exam, wondering when you'll ever squeeze in some exercise time, the flowers drying in your window box, what gift to buy for a loved one, your lack of sleep, how to find more time for volunteer work, the appointment you missed this morning. All of your unfinished obligations, concerns, and upcoming needs must be recorded in some trusted way outside of your head so they can't keep distracting you.

Jot them down in a list, leaving writing space to the right of each item to clarify your exact commitment: Is this concern truly important and, if so, what you can do to finish it and by when? Some things can be delegated or let go. Others belong on the cal-endar or errand list, not your head. Others can be forgotten until month's end, not now. By putting these things in writing you free yourself to keep your sights on what is most important of all.

We Must Be Dreamers as Well as Doers

The gap between what can be imagined and what can be accom-plished has never been smaller. But it takes great goals to lead us out of our everyday limits into accomplishing more than we ever thought we could or would.

Consider starting with the extreme. Draw a line down the cen-ter of a piece of paper. At the top of the left column, write: *My biggest, boldest wish is* . . . Your answer may be as wild or far-fetched as you can imagine: To grow the rarest orchid, fly an airplane, climb a mountain, save a life, end hunger, protect an endangered species, hit a homerun in a major league ballpark, shield the environment from harm, cure a disease, perform at Carnegie Hall, care for a lost child, rescue animals, or fall in love forever.

Then at the top of the right column, put the heading: *I can't because* . . . Now fill in the reasons you won't be able to make this biggest, boldest wish come true. What's in the way? And why? In too many cases, we let habit and rationalizations block us from advancing in the direction of our deepest aspirations. When that happens, the one thing that is certain is that we will wake up one day and regret it.

There are as many bold wishes as there are people willing to discover them and commit to them. To begin clarifying your big dreams, complete these statements:

- When I imagine making the two greatest contributions to my family, they are . . .
- When I imagine my two greatest contributions to the neighborhood or community, they are . . .
- My skills and passions could change the world if . . .

Align More of Your Actions Around Your Big Dreams

On a day nearing dusk, a six-year-old boy hurried out with the crowd from the small town of Weil, in Germany, and found a place to stand at the edge of an open field. A hush fell over the gathered crowd as a vast canopy of starlight covered the entire darkening sky. A streak of cosmic fire stretched across nearly half of the heavens as the Great Comet of 1577 fired the spirit of little

Johannes Kepler. His mother had no idea that he would upend conventional thinking and seed the modern age.

He was an introspective loner, a sickly, spindly child, chronically covered with boils, scabs, rashes, and sores. Raised by an extended family that Arthur Koestler describes as "mostly degenerates and psychopaths," he had a "childhood in hell." Yet he had an irrepressible spirit and a big dream—of space flight—backed by an avid imagination and a ceaseless drive to comprehend, in his own independent way, the nature of the cosmos. Kepler's laws of planetary motion rescued the Copernican system from obscurity and paved the way for the law of gravity, upon which Newton constructed the modern universe.

"Let us create vessels and sails adjusted to the heavenly air," Kepler wrote to Galileo. "In the meantime, we shall prepare forthe brave sky-travelers maps of the celestial bodies." From Kepler's work came the telescope and the science of optics. Kepler charted the stars and planets despite being ostracized by the ignorance and provinciality of his time and relegated to miserable poverty and homelessness for most of his life. Kepler wrote his *Harmony of the World,* believing that the world that so mistreated him was nonetheless beautiful. "Kepler was one of the few who are simply incapable of doing anything but standing up openly for their convictions in every field," wrote Albert Einstein, who greatly admired this man who liberated himself from the rigid intellectual traditions into which he was born.

Keep Asking "Why Not?"

Think about the people closest to you. What are they saying is impossible? How do you respond to their doubts? Ralph Mosca is a cardiac surgeon who successfully pioneered a new kind of lifesaving repair of the heart's aortic arch in preterm and low birth weight babies. For years it had been a big dream. While others doubted that such a procedure would ever be accomplished, Mosca's ingenuity grew, along with that of his colleagues at the University of Michigan Congenital Heart Center in Ann Arbor, as he felt compelled to do everything he could to make it possible. There were so many tiny children who might have the chance to live if this procedure could be developed. That's the mobilizing power of a great goal.

Many big dreams involve much simpler things than heart surgery, and many are based on vivid personal experience. At age eight, Anna Kokmeyer decided she wanted to find a way to help babies in the Holden neonatal intensive care unit at the University of Michigan Medical Center. She was one of the unit's most dramatic success stories eight years ago, when she was born weighing one pound five ounces—about as much as four Beanie Babies. Doctors gave her less than a 20 percent chance of surviving as a healthy child.

An enthusiastic and healthy third grader, she sat down with her mother and looked at a scrapbook of pictures and stories detailing the four and a half months she spent in the neonatal unit, cuddling against a brown teddy bear, half a dozen wires, and the food and oxygen tubes that kept her alive. She still sleeps with that bear. She decided she wanted to give something back. To her it's a simple goal: "I like babies," she says, "and I want to help those who have a rough start in life."

It became her goal to give a cuddly toy for every one of the neonatal unit's 37 infant beds. "The babies need something small and soft to love, like my bear. They don't have their moms and dads around all the time." So Anna chose to forgo her usual birthday party and ask guests to bring Beanie Babies, blankets, and lullaby tapes, and put them in a pile on her dining room table. To raise extra money, Anna collected returnable cans and bottles, earning about $75.

There's another hallmark of a great goal here. Anna's patience and creativity at this pursuit have been exceptional, and her moments of helping the little babies transform her in some rare and marvelous way. A big dream awakens hidden capacity and drive. Throughout our lives, many of us have a number of big dreams, not just one. Some lose power over time. Others grow.

Ask others about their best projects and efforts. Imagine you're riding on a airplane or commuter train and the person beside you says, "What's *your* story?" or "What gets you the most excited about life these days?" As Tom Peters puts it, "I don't want an epitaph on my gravestone that says, 'He would have pursued some big dreams in his life, but other people wouldn't let him.'"

In your day book or journal, keep several pages for your notes on great goals—your own and those of the people closest to you. Possible headings: *My big dreams are . . . Here is how I am advancing them: . . .* On another page: *Here are the great goals of the people closest to me: . . . Here's how I'm supporting those dreams instead of criticizing them: . . .*

"Build Your Castles in the Air . . ."

When I visited my grandfather Downing, we would often sit in his study and talk. The topic was usually life. He always expressed a keen interest in my experiences and whatever I was looking forward to doing in the weeks or months ahead.

One of his favorite questions was, "Is that—or was that—worth giving a piece of your life to?" He challenged me to clearly weigh the value of time and energy. He was encouraging me to listen to what I cared about most deeply and to keep shaping my behavior accordingly.

Such questions serve as inner compass points for unlocking more of our hidden capacity. When you keep aligning your life with big dreams, you are in a far better position to *use* this newfound capacity. Thoreau said it well: "If you have built your castles in the air," he said, "your work need not be lost; that is where they should be. Now put the foundations under them."

We must not be afraid of dreaming the seemingly impossible if we want the seemingly impossible to become a reality.

—VÁCLAV HAVEL

14

Keep Glancing Ahead

Whenever the night sky was clear, my grandfather Downing would search for Sirius, one of the brightest and most distant of the planets we can see from Earth.

"Why is Sirius your favorite star?" I would ask him.

"Because it draws my gaze the farthest away from where I'm standing right now," he would reply. He had been touched by stories of the pioneering stargazers of the past, like Kepler and Galileo, who demonstrated an irrepressible mix of spirit, mathematics, and wonder, and who dared to dream of traveling into the cosmos.

I remember summer evenings when I was a boy and my grandfather Cooper and I would stand together outside as the darkness came, gazing at the heavens with a feeling of wonder. He believed that the light of the stars helped trees grow, or maybe that was just a story he told me because he loved trees.

From the time I was very young, I was his tree-planting helper. We would make our way around the edges of the nearby parks or the hillsides behind his home. It was an effort for him to walk with his cane, but that never deterred him. Together, we would pick a good spot and I would dig a hole. Then we would plant the small tree.

He loved to plant those trees that took the longest time to mature, such as certain varieties of walnut trees. Each time we finished setting a seedling, we would stare at it for a few moments and he would say, "Robert, a hundred years from now when this tree is all grown up and gnarly and filled with walnuts, who will be here staring up at it? What will the world be like then?"

Even if we can only guess what the world may be like a few years from now, not a century, such a view compels us to change in ways that will meet such a world or, better yet, to help shape it.

Many of us say we wish we could see into the future. But to see into the future means we have to see more deeply into ourselves, to know what our history has been, what choices we have made or failed to make, how much of life we have lived or failed to live, and what changes we have the courage to enact as we shape what is to come. If we let ourselves get lost in the shuffle of daily life, as we hurry along we end up knowing more about our shoes from looking down than about the stars—or life's unseen possibilities—from pausing for a few moments here and there to gaze upward and beyond . . . and adjust our course accordingly.

My grandfathers taught me that glancing farther ahead—not just once a month on a planning calendar, but years ahead, and doing it every single day—is one of the keys to awakening our hidden potential.

Create a Long Time Horizon

One of the persistent obstacles to unlocking human capacity is the vagueness or narrowness of our view of time. If we let ourselves get swept along in the all-consuming rapids of now, there is little chance to ponder what came before or envision what's yet to come. Or—we may get trapped in the past with its regrets and fond memories, unable to think forward into today or tomorrow. Or we may spend most of our time wishing for the far-off future.

To live life to the fullest, none of those views alone will do. Instead, we must learn to wisely devote most of our attention to the present while always holding it in light of the past's lessons and the future's possibilities. The ideal time horizon centers on making the most of today's reality while also devoting some time and attention to remembering the past's teachings and glancing farther ahead—toward desired results five years or more into the future.

Individuals who do this are most likely to demonstrate leadership, thrive under pressure, earn higher incomes, and have happier and longer lasting relationships. In contrast, the evidence shows that those who have a short time horizon—those individuals who rarely, if ever, think very far into the past or ahead into the future by more than a few months—tend to be the most rigid and rule-anchored, struggling with change of any kind.

Time Horizon

The Past's Lessons	The Present's Actions	The Future's Possibilities
Remembrance	Current Reality and Today's Potential	Desired Results

- *The past's lessons: Remembrance.* History and memory are vital factors in unlocking human potential. Therefore, it's vital to spend at least a few moments each day recalling something about where you come from and the experiences in life that have had the greatest influence in shaping what you have become. Remembering family traditions, blessings, and adversities from the past, and the gifts and challenges you have received throughout your life serves to sharpen and deepen your perspective. Many of the people who have had it the hardest in life, or whose ancestors had it the hardest, may have greater access today to hidden capacity. Think of your ancestors, teachers, and mentors. Think of the sacrifices they made so you could have freedom and a better life. Reflect across the generations of births, family rituals, and funerals you have been part of and know about. What were the most powerful feelings you have experienced when part of these moments of remembrance? What did you vow then to do more of—or less of—going forward?

■ *The future's possibilities: Desired results.* When we finish saying the word "future," it already belongs to the past. That's a simple example of why it matters to glance as far ahead as you can: What's coming next is already almost here. A long-term view—going forward five to ten years, for example—is vital for creating a strong bearing along which today's energy and actions will flow. But it's not just how far you can see but also *what* you see. Ask, "When I glance farther into the future, what do I want to create?" Creating is altogether different from reacting or responding to whatever situation you happen to be in. Creators start by envisioning their desired results. How clearly do you know what you want? Is it a big dream or a small, specific change or contribution? Only you can answer.

My grandfather Cooper served for a number of years as a school superintendent. One of his approaches to learning was

summed up when I would visit him in the early weeks of a se-
mester and as we talked about my classes, he would say, "Go
ahead, give yourself an A." How, I would ask. "Imagine it's the
end of the year," he explained, "and you have done exceptional things to learn more than you have to. What will it take
to do that?" That would encourage me to dig deeper for
things that excited me about a new subject or resources I
would otherwise probably not have found. It also gave us
more chances to talk about it along the way. That's another
thing that a long time horizon helps you do.

■ *The present's actions:* This is where most of your time and
energy must be devoted each day:

—*Current reality.* This is where you are right now: What's
going right, what isn't, and why?

—*Today's potential.* This takes your honest appraisal of the
spot you're in today and how it can be aligned with your
desired future. Compared to where you were yesterday
and where you want to be five years from now, what actions, however small, can you take today to create movement and momentum? This focus helps liberate us from
old habits and conditioned reactions to daily pressure.

Consider scheduling several opportunities each day to extend
your time horizon:

■ *Morning: Navigation time.* One of the most effective ways
I've found to link the past and future to the present is to commit a few minutes to doing it every morning. To do this, get
up five minutes earlier than usual and find a quiet spot to sip
your morning beverage and reexamine your schedule for the

upcoming day. Spend several minutes reflecting on significant experiences in your past. What have you learned? Are you applying these understandings today? Next, envision the future at least five years from now. What do you want to create? What kind of life and work? Look over today's to-do list and ask how important those tasks are in the long run. Does your upcoming schedule contain some activities of long-term value to you as an individual or to your family or work? If not, what changes can you make right now so you don't end up feeling victimized by your calendar? Finally, take a few moments to imagine where you'll be five to ten years from now and what the world might be like. What are you doing today that may help you be happier or make more of a contribution when that day arrives?

- *Afternoon: Reflection time.* By applying the strategies in Part II of this book, your evenings have already become more energized. This can be the best time to take stock of what happened during the day and to put things into perspective. What progress was made? What difficulties did you encounter? What new possibilities appeared? What was the most exceptional thing you did? What was the funniest thing that happened? When did people's eyes light up? What surprised you? What did you learn? Then adjust tomorrow's schedule with this in mind.

- *Weekends: Far-future time.* It can be very useful to invest a few minutes each weekend to peer even farther into the future. You might involve family members in this. Can you imagine the world twenty or even fifty years from now? If you keep doing what you're doing today, where will you be? How will you have shaped this future and specifically touched the lives of the people you care about most?

Every Half Hour, Pause to Get Your Bearings and Adjust Your Course

When my grandfather Cooper and I planted trees, he would stop every half hour or so. Reaching into his pocket, he would take out a small compass he carried. I always knew what he would say next: "Robert, let's stop and get our bearings."

He taught me that with a compass you determine your relative position: Where you are right now compared to where you were and where you are going. Are you closer right now to where you want to be than you were a half-hour ago? If not, how can you correct your course to make better progress? You might build some variation of these compass readings into your strategic pauses (discussed in Chapter 7). It is in this way that you keep closing the distance between where you are right now and where you most want to be.

Many years ago I spent some time doing volunteer work in the Southwest. There was an old man I came to know who had endured much in his life. Now penniless and finally sober, one windy evening he had slowly made his way toward the top of a nearby butte to watch the sun set. A storm was coming and I happened to meet him on my descent as I hurried down to avoid the bad weather. I glanced at the darkening sky and suggested he return with me to the shelter below. He shook his head and went on.

Before long, the rain came and the air turned very cold, as if it might snow. Muttering under my breath, I turned around and went back up the trail after him. I had a flashlight in my pack and he had no light at all. I found him on the edge of a rock outcropping, dangling his feet in the air. It was a daring perch even with no wind. Gusts of stinging rain pelted us as banks of purple-red clouds rose through flashes of lightning far off in the sky. He was shivering with cold but there was a look of utter peacefulness and wonder on his face. I couldn't understand it. My attention was limited to getting us back down to safety.

"Why?" I asked him.

He looked puzzled.

"Why did you take this chance?" I said as the wind died off. "Why didn't you return to the shelter with me and then wait to come up here another time?"

He stared far off at the horizon, reveling in the majesty of sky.

"I didn't want to miss the view."

That was all he said.

Many times in all the years since then I have recalled his words and tried to apply the wisdom of his example. I don't want to miss the view.

Time is the substance I am made of.
Time is a river that sweeps me along, but I am the river;
Time is a tiger that can rip me apart, but I am the tiger;
Time is a fire than can consume me, but I am the fire.

—Jorge Luis Borges

15

Face the World
Straight On

In the twentieth century, one black-and-white historical image was reprinted more times than any other. It shows six U.S. Marines raising the American flag on Iwo Jima. By their own admission, these were not heroes; these were young men who were called to duty and rose to meet the challenge.

One of my mentors, Charles Eastwood, was an Army officer who commanded a unit that relieved the Marines on Iwo Jima after the island had been secured. He told me that his most vivid memory of that time was of seeing the remnants of the Marine's 2nd Battalion, 28th Regiment, marching toward him along the beach. It had been a month and a half since these men fought their way ashore. Of the 250 Marines in that unit, only 27 were left alive. Among them were the survivors of the group of six who, after battling to the island's highest peak through a landscape of hell, raised a flag.

Eastwood told me that what he remembered most of all was their posture. "I'll never forget what I saw and felt that day," he said. "Their features were darkened with gunpowder and severe strain. Many were injured. They had prevailed against 20,000 defenders who fought to the last man. In watching the Marines, we sensed their courage and commitment by how they carried themselves: with spirit and strength. They faced the world straight on."

I have always remembered that description: They faced the world straight on. Exceptional posture is more than just the manifestation of physical balance or standing up straight. It expresses mental and emotional balance—and, indeed, reveals something of the human spirit.

Good Posture Is Unlocked, Not Forced

"Stand up straight!" was an admonition many of us heard from parents and physical education instructors. And we *tried*—with our head up, shoulders broad and pulled back, buttocks tucked, back ramrod straight, stomach sucked in. But by tightening muscles we ended up feeling stiff and braced in a tiring, unnatural position that couldn't be maintained for very long.

Think about the times when you feel inundated with stress, discouraged, or exhausted. What happens to the way you sit and stand? Do you end up slouched over, with shoulders rounded and tension in the neck, jaw, shoulders, chest, back, or arms? Many people do. In fact, that crummy posture has a name: somatic retraction. It restricts breathing and reduces blood flow and oxygen to the brain and senses by up to 30 percent. It also adds excessive strain to the spine, slows reaction time, and can magnify feelings of panic and helplessness.

Great posture isn't something you can force; first you must unlock it. When you do so, you also free up hidden capacity. With a bit of practice, upright, relaxed posture can produce greater energy every hour of the day. We're not born knowing how to do it right. No reflex system sets up good posture. We have to learn it. Excellent, natural posture relies on five key muscles—out of nearly 700 in your body—to almost effortlessly hold your chest, shoulders, neck, and head in balanced alignment.

Five Keys to Staying Upright with Energy and Ease

Over the years I have asked a number of specialists on neck and back pain about the most practical and proven ways to sit, stand, and move with ease instead of effort. I have found that there are five keys to balanced posture, which combine to free up hidden capacity in ways most of us have never imagined. With a bit of regular practice, these techniques will become easy, and even automatic, to apply. Share them with the people closest to you. Few other gifts that can touch so many aspects of life and work.

Hold Your Head High

We live in a head-forward society. Look around you. Notice how many people have their shoulders slumped and chins forward as they collapse downward toward their computer screens and phones. Notice the number of people studying their shoes as they walk down the street. Whether you're pushing a shopping cart, sitting in front of a computer or television, driving a vehicle, standing behind a counter, working on an assembly line, or cooking, cleaning, reading, or sitting at a desk, chances are your head and neck are off balance.

Reminding yourself to "Keep your chin up" only makes things worse because it tilts the head back and puts added pressure on the neck. Instead of lifting the top of the head upward to straighten the neck, nearly all of us slump our shoulders and let our chin slide forward as the head tilts back. It's amazing that we survive this poor posture. The resulting stress contributes to tension headaches, vision problems, and jaw and neck pain.

Your head weighs between 10 and 15 pounds. To avoid placing undue stress on the neck, shoulders, and spine, your head must be in a comfortable, centered position. To experience what this feels like, take a moment right now to sit comfortably and breathe naturally. Imagine that a five-pound weight is on the top of your head. Gently push up against the resistance of the weight. Feel your posture immediately improve by better balancing and stabilizing of your head and neck. You might also imagine that a sky hook is gently pulling the top of your head upward.

Whenever possible, the head should lead your body motions. For example, as you stand up, reach, or turn, move your head upward and then into the direction you are going and let your whole body follow smoothly in that direction.

Align Your Neck

One of the least known and most effective ways to reduce strain on the neck, shoulders, and back is to tone a small but vital muscle at the crest of your spine called the rectus capitus anterior. This muscle is involved in flexing and rotating your head and is essential to good posture. When strengthened, it helps keep the head in a balanced position over your neck.

To tone this muscle, use a gentle "head nod" exercise. Starting in a comfortable sitting or standing position, let your neck lengthen, gently extending upward as if lifted by an imaginary cord attached to the top of your skull. With your head and neck in this slightly elevated position, nod your head as if in agreement, bringing the forehead a little forward and chin slightly in. Repeat this head-nod exercise a dozen times a day.

Next, find the best alignment of your neck beneath your head. Lengthen your neck and let the top of your head move upward, chin slightly in, shoulders broadening, lower back flattening. Now gently lean your head to the left and then to the right, returning to the most central, balanced spot you can sense. Next, move your head slightly forward and then back, finding the precise center once again above your neck. Be certain to keep your chin slightly inward and feel an upward lift at the top of your head.

When talking on the telephone, bring the handset up to your ear and mouth; don't bend your head and neck down to the phone or cradle it between your ear and shoulder by forcing your neck to the side. When you read, bring the book up to you with an armrest, bookstand, or pillow, and adjust your reading lighting accordingly.

Begin to "think taller," to encourage your head to move upward into a balanced position. Don't push or strain your neck; simply bring your head back over your shoulders, with your chin slightly in. You'll sense the difference and you can see it in the mirror.

Level Your Shoulders and Open Your Chest

With your head and neck balanced, the next key to excellent, effortless posture is to level and relax your shoulders and then open your chest. This makes it easier to sit, stand, and breathe.

A number of the muscles of your respiratory system are connected to cervical and lumbar vertebrae, and how you breathe literally affects the position of your spine.

The serratus magnus and serratus anterior muscles are designed to assist breathing and posture. These muscles are positioned like long fingers that connect from the spine and shoulder blades around your rib cage. When the serratus muscles are weak, it is easier to collapse your chest as you sit or stand. When that happens, it hunches the shoulders farther forward, exerting 10 to 15 times as much pressure on your lower back than sitting up straight does. By design, the serratus muscles help balance the shoulder girdle to the chest, taking strain off the spine and making it easier to breathe deeply and stay upright yet relaxed.

One of the simplest ways to strengthen and tone the serratus muscles is with a modified dipping exercise. Perhaps you remember holding on to the parallel bars in physical education class, lowering your weight toward the floor and then pushing yourself back up: That's a dipping exercise. It's no fun. You can perform a much easier and safer exercise sitting in your chair. First, sit upright with your feet shoulder width apart and flat on the floor. Bend your elbows outward to the sides, away from your body, and position your hands beside your hips as if you are holding on to a parallel bar that runs from back to front parallel to the ground next to your right and left hips, respectively.

Slowly and smoothly raise your hands upward toward your armpits, keeping your elbows out to the sides, until the insides of your wrists almost touch your armpits. Now tense your arms and the muscles at the sides of your chest as you slowly push your hands back down while imagining that you're pushing yourself upward on the parallel bars. Continue slowly until your arms are almost fully extended downward at your sides. You will feel the serratus muscles tensing. Now relax. Repeat this simple exercise several times every other day.

In addition, make sure each time you sit down that you take a moment to choose the most balanced, comfortable sitting position, with your shoulders level and your chest open. To do this, first, seat yourself squarely; don't slump. Center your buttocks and upper legs on the seat. Leaning to one side or becoming off-center in any other way shifts the line of gravity and causes tension and restricted circulation if you stay in that unbalanced position for very long.

Let your chest and shoulders come forward as you bend at the thigh/hip joints (*not* the lower spine). This ensures that your buttocks and lower back are centered and far back in the chair. Then smoothly bring your upper body back against the seat back (once again, "hinging" the movement at your thigh/hip joints, *not* your lower spine). Whenever possible, place your feet flat on the floor.

Tone Your Lower Abdomen and Flatten Your Back

There is evidence that the abdomen and lower back are the centers of all strength in the body. The abdominal muscles are sustainers of energy. They flatten your waist, help hold the internal organs in proper alignment, and stabilize the lower back at its most vulnerable point—the lumbosacral angle of the pelvis.

Unfortunately, America's most popular abdominal exercises—traditional sit-ups and leg-lifts—don't work even if you do 5,000 a month. These exercises may actually cause or aggravate lower back pain by pulling on the front of the lower spine. When this happens, your back is swayed inward and the lower abdomen is pushed outward—creating a "pot belly" appearance and contributing to overall tension, tiredness, and back pain.

Two specific muscles, the transversalis and pyramidalis, are designed to strengthen your lower abdomen and help level and protect your lower your back. These muscles are toned by a simple breathing exercise I call the "Transpyramid." This is the single most important abdominal exercise you can do.

To do it, sit in an upright, comfortable position. Take a normal breath in, breathe out, and then forcibly blow out as much air from your lungs as you can, allowing your *lower* abdomen (which is where the two key muscles for this forced exhalation are located) to come in and up as much as possible.

Now try the exercise again. Slowly exhale and, as you reach the place where you normally finish breathing out, smoothly and forcefully breathe out *more,* using the power of your *lower* abdominal muscles. At first, you might use your hands to gently push inward and upward on the lower abdomen during the exhalation part of the exercise. Work up to doing a total of ten or twelve of these exercises each day. Fit them in wherever you can, such as doing one or two upon arising in the morning, before each meal, at every stop light when running errands or commuting to work, or each time you step up to the kitchen counter or sit down in your car or at your desk.

Neutralize Tension Spots

Among the most common saboteurs of energy and posture are tiny irritated nerve receptors, known as trigger points, in your muscles and tendons. If unnoticed and untreated, they tend to worsen and spread, leaving us feeling older than we need to feel, even debilitated or immobilized.

Trigger points are part of life, caused by bumps, bruises, twists, and strains; imbalanced posture; chronically tensed muscles;

fatigue from overwork; emotional distress; poor sitting or sleeping positions; or a lack of sleep. Once formed, they tend to remain in your muscles unless treated and released. They cause you to hold tension in and "guard" muscles by limiting their motion. In addition to producing pain, stiffness, fatigue, and restricted range of motion, trigger points also restrict circulation and can cause weakness and loss of coordination.

In many cases, the discomfort occurs at or near the trigger point. But there are times when the actual tension or pain show up at a site in the body far distant from where the trigger point originates. For example, a hidden trigger point in the shoulder muscles might cause neck pain or headaches. This is called *referred pain.*

You can easily locate and relieve these tiny trouble spots. First, be certain your muscles are warm and relaxed. Otherwise, it's difficult to distinguish tense bands of muscle—where trigger points are usually located—from adjoining slack muscles.

In most areas of the body, you can gently press the muscle against underlying bone using your fingertip or thumb. Try using the pad of the thumb or knuckle of the index or middle finger. In the temple areas of the forehead and the hinge joint of the jaw, the pad of the index finger can be a good choice for applying pressure. Reach up and press on the muscles at the base of the skull. Press on the outside of the jaw joint. Squeeze the muscle between your neck and shoulders. Apply pressure to your forearms. Once you've located an area of tense muscle fibers, press or squeeze it with light to moderate pressure until you feel a spot of tenderness—the trigger point.

With practice, you can learn to readily notice when trigger points are aggravated and then take immediate action to relax the affected area by re-balancing your posture and relaxing tight muscles. If necessary, you can also use simple direct pressure to help relieve trigger point areas and reduce tenderness or stiffness in the muscles. Of course, all persistent or severe pain requires medical attention.

Once you have located a trigger point, apply pressure that is gentle enough so that it creates only mild discomfort. Hold the trigger point for six to ten seconds and then release. Go on to another trigger point, treat, and then release. And so on. You may repeat the therapy at each trigger point twice in one day if desired. Most trigger points respond well to this brief pressure.

One of the areas to explore is the base of the skull—the site of trigger points that cause many headaches. Gently place the pad of your right thumb—or, if you have weak thumbs, use your index finger reinforced or covered by your adjoining middle finger—on the back of your neck just to the right of your spine. Glide up to find the natural "notch" at your hairline at the base of the skull. Apply moderate pressure upward against the bone to locate any trigger points.

Search the area from right next to the spine outward along the base of the skull to just behind your ear. Relieve any trigger points by applying pressure for six to ten seconds, and then release. Repeat the process for the matching area on the left side of your neck where it meets the skull.

Another area where trigger points are commonly found is the trapezius muscle that attaches from your shoulders to your neck. Using your thumb on one side of the muscle and index and middle fingers of the same hand on the other side, squeeze the uppermost muscle midway between the crest of your shoulders and the sides of your neck. Apply pressure with your thumb on the front side and your index and middle fingers on the back side of this muscle. Squeeze slowly and firmly. If you find a sensitive area, hold the pressure on that spot for six to ten seconds and then release. Move a finger-width at a time toward the sides of your neck and then out toward your shoulder crests, locating and relieving any trigger points along the way.

Few simple actions can provide us with this much added energy and ease. In the words of Heraclitus, the renowned Greek philosopher and author of *On Nature,* "One's bearing shapes one's fate."

H old your head high.
Look the world straight in the eye.

—HELEN KELLER

16

Hope Irrationally

People have been known to survive for more than an hour without oxygen. Without water, humans have lived almost a week. Without food, a few have remained alive for nearly three months. Yet without hope, no one can survive. And the hope of this world depends most of all on what we demand, not of others, but of ourselves.

That's something I learned as a boy from my grandfather Downing. As a surgeon, he devoted much of his time to details. The stakes in his work were life and death. Because he helped pioneer a number of new forms of surgery, he was often trying to save patients who would otherwise not survive. He had come to understand that, even more than air, fluids, and nutrients, every person needs as much hope as possible.

As busy as he was, my grandfather made it a point to walk a bit more slowly than others. When I asked him why he did that, he said it was because it gave him a chance to stop chasing after details and slow down enough to expand his perspective and keep hope alive. I remember how he attended outdoor band concerts during the summer, marked the growth of flowers in the gardens and window boxes of town, and served as a volunteer in civic groups and on the parks board. Long after his own children were grown, he attended school plays, athletic events, and concerts just to keep reminding himself of the magical hopefulness and remarkable perspectives of young people. "That spirit is something none of us should lose," he said.

We Must See Past the Flyspecks on the Window of the World

When I was twelve, one summer morning he came home after hospital rounds and volunteered to drive me to a ballpark across town where I was planning to meet some of my young friends. On the way, we stopped for gas.

As we pulled up to the pump, a woman was yelling at the lone attendant. "I still see bug spots on my windshield and on my driver's window! I will not leave until you remove every last one of them!" The teenager went back to spraying and wiping the glass, scrubbing hard. The scowling woman followed right behind him, complaining as she leaned forward to inspect the remaining bug spots while my grandfather and I waited.

At last, in obvious disgust, the woman got into her car and drove away, never thanking the station attendant. Her car bounced over the curb and the front tire plowed through a flowerbed. She didn't seem to notice, busy as she was staring at every last smudge on the glass.

"When she speeds up, there'll just be more bugs on her windshield," I said. "Doesn't she know that?"

My grandfather nodded. "If she stops to think about it, she'll realize it's true. There's a good lesson here about what's important and what isn't, and how easy it is to get them mixed up. Some people end up spending most of their lives staring at the fly specks on the windows of the world."

He reminded me that by nature we're quick to notice blemishes—in life, in circumstances, in others, in ourselves. We're masters at locking our gaze on little imperfections and then magnifying them way out of proportion.

I'll never forget what my grandfather did next. The attendant finished filling our car with gas and spent a minute doing a passable—but far from great—job of cleaning our windshield. He was obviously still distracted by the harangue the woman had dished out. My grandfather smiled and gave him a very good tip.

The teenager looked confused, staring at the coins in his hand. "But why . . ." he said, turning to look with some embarrassment at our windshield.

My grandfather said, "That's for how hard you tried to do a great job cleaning that woman's windshield."

As we drove through town toward the ballpark, I kept staring at all the bug spots and smudges on our windshield. "Why the tip, grandfather?" I asked. "He sure didn't do a very good job."

"Not on our windshield, but he did on the woman's car. In money, there's not much difference between no tip from the woman and what I gave him. But that young man has a bit more hope now than he would otherwise have had about the value of working hard. I could have given you the money, Robert, to buy an extra soda or candy bar with your friends. But I feel better about using it here where I believe it made more of a difference." Hope is like that. It comes from the big picture of life more than the blemishes.

Bypass the Brain's Tendency to Focus on the Negative and Small

If you had a few minutes every week to step outside your usual realm of personal concerns and tasks, how much hope could you muster for the future of life and the larger world? The unconscious pattern of the brain is to get stuck on blemishes, irritations, and the negative. To hope requires a deliberate choice.

For example, it is widely assumed that there are stringent limits to human inventiveness and growth. That assumption is profoundly wrong. The only true constraint is our imagination and optimism, one person at a time. So irrational hope may not be irrational after all—it just seems that way when viewed through our false sense of limitations.

What happens when you hope more than you have to? Consider the story of Edwin Land, who ignored the teasing criticism from others when they called him *Blue Skies* for his endless hopefulness. He also refused to accept the scornfully dismissive reaction to his ideas by the highly educated people around him. From his self-taught boyhood to his first jobs as an adult, Land brought a daring and optimistic spirit to his small business pursuits.

In his pioneering of modern technology from the late 1920s onward, he was eventually second only to Edison in the number of patents he received (535). It was Land who created the first polarizers and instant cameras, high-speed and X-ray film, 3D and instant movies, and military devices for aerial reconnaissance and night vision.

One of the approaches that Land was said to use during interviews was to give the applicant a Polaroid camera and an assignment: "Come back tomorrow with three pictures that will change the world."

If you were given that assignment today, what pictures would you take in the next 24 hours? My grandfather Cooper said that once he tried Land's technique when interviewing prospective new teachers for the public school system.

One applicant came back with three pictures of the faces of children on street corners in a major city. "What do these photographs mean?" said my grandfather to the would-be teacher, who replied, "These three children are leaders of the future." My grandfather said, "How do you know that?"

"First, I looked in their eyes with the camera," said the applicant. "I could see that, like all children, they are geniuses in hiding. Second, I aim to make teaching so much fun inside and outside my classroom that no parent will want to allow any child to miss school." That's an example of irrational hope and a willingness to work to make the "impossible" come true.

At Least Once a Day, Shift from the Microscope to the Telescope

As a young boy, I remember waiting for the darkness to settle in at the edge of a lake we visited now and then on warm summer days. As the air turned cool, I would warm my feet in the sand that still held heat from the sunny day. My friends and I would stretch out on our backs and gaze up at the sky filled with stars. Usually full of revelry and a bit of mischief, we would grow still and quiet. The immensity of the heavens awed us with its brilliance. One by one, those of us who knew constellations called them out, and the others squinted to see. We were humbled and inspired by the beauty and mysteries of the cosmos.

In part this may be because the invention of optics and, in particular, the telescope marked the birth of modern scientific method and cleared the way for a dramatic reassessment of our place in the universe. My grandfather Downing knew that the microscope was of great value. It symbolized that there is always much more to life up close than is available to our unaided senses.

But because he used microscopes in his medical practice, when he came home at night he sought to balance his perspective by using a telescope to look at the stars. It was his prized possession. Through it, he could glimpse the miracle of the universe and this helped him renew his perspective.

I always looked forward to summer nights when, after evening hospital rounds, he would come home and, if I was already asleep, would gently wake me up. Together we would go to the upstairs door that opened onto a small section of the rooftop above the kitchen. Waiting there were two chairs and the telescope. He and I would take turns looking at the stars. He knew all the constellations. "This is the best way I know to keep renewing my hope and perspective," he would say.

On the final summer of his life he asked me to make a promise to him.

He told me that his work life was devoted to seeing things through microscopes and painstaking analysis. In short, it was about details. His work was about people, too, and that's what he loved most, people and their lives, but he kept finding that, if he wasn't careful, the details took up nearly all of his time.

"Robert," he said, "whatever job you have someday, you will probably find that it's mostly about details. Promise me that you'll notice the days when these little things threaten to overwhelm you. Whenever that happens, promise me that you will stop, even for just a few minutes, and look up at the sky and contemplate the stars."

"Many people think that life somehow automatically gives us back our hope and perspective," he added. "But it doesn't. We have to take them back."

Looking at the stars was a way he taught me to do this.

Years later I learned that the prime motive for Thoreau to enter his own laboratory of life beside Walden Pond was to teach himself to *see*. "It is something to be able to paint a particular picture," he wrote, "or to carve a statue, and so to make a few objects beautiful; but it is far more glorious to carve and paint the very atmosphere . . . through which we look." At Walden Pond, he immersed himself in the energetic landscape of life and the night sky. He cherished the minutiae of nature yet every day he took time out to find his place and path *within* nature, in all of its vastness.

Near the end of each day when your life gets filled to the brim with details, how can you find a way to pause for a few moments to rekindle your hope and renew your perspective?

---

*I*n my dream, the angel shrugged & said, "If we fail this time, it will be a failure of imagination" & then she placed the world gently in the palm of my hand.
—BRIAN ANDREAS, "Imagining World"

17

Die Young as Late as Possible

Byron wrote, "Years steal fire from the mind as vigor from the limbs." He was right only in the sense that it *is* common to see energy wane, memory decay, and muscles wither away with the passing years. But those losses are in no way predestined.

Barring chronic illness or disease, it's likely that if there's any theft of your energy, it's because you stopped renewing it; if there's any loss of muscle mass, it's because you stopped using your muscles; and if there's any disappearance of your mental powers, it's the result of conventional expectations of senescence.

One belief about growing older is that the mind steadily, irrevocably deteriorates, until you end up stuck in an inevitable web of confusion, frailty, and despair. This belief powerfully affects our thinking, resulting in hundreds of small but insidious habits and choices that conform to our view of an aging person, not a young person, which can shape the second half-century of your life in a self-fulfilling prophecy. After many years of research on this subject, the British anthropologist Ashley Montagu concluded that aging is to a large degree optional, advising, "The goal in life is to die young . . . as late as possible."

Scientists have discovered that with a broad range of active intellectual interests and a vigorous lifestyle, your body, mind, and spirit can keep unlocking hidden capacities and there's a great chance that we can be as sharp—or *sharper*—at age 70, 80, and even 90 as we were at 20. We are designed to last a remarkable 120 years; most of us die in late middle age, around age 75.

Genius Is Childhood Recaptured

Every moment of our lives we are either growing or dying—and it's largely a choice, not fate. Throughout its life cycle, every one of the body's trillions of cells is driven to grow and improve its ability to use more of its innate yet untapped capacity. Research biologist Albert Szent-Gyoergyi, who was twice awarded the Nobel Prize, called this *syntropy*, which he defined as the "innate drive in living matter to perfect itself." It turns conventional thinking upside down.

As living cells—or as people—there is no staying the same. If we aim for some middle ground or status quo, it's an illusion— beneath the surface what's actually happening is we're dying, not growing. And the goal of a lifetime is continued growth, not adulthood. As René Dubos put it, "Genius is childhood recaptured." For this to happen, studies show that we must recapture—or prevent the loss of—such child-like traits as the ability to learn, to love, to laugh about small things, to leap, to wonder, and to explore. It's time to rescue ourselves from our grown-up ways before it's too late.

The African American baseball star Leroy "Satchel" Paige once asked, "How old would you be if you didn't know how old you were?" What would your answer be? If you could remember everything except the exact year you were born, how old would you say you feel right now?

Whenever brain cells are activated—by new sights, sounds, conversations, creative pursuits, or problem-solving, for example—they instantaneously begin to change. They produce far more electrochemical energy, form new connections, remodel nerve endings, improve receptor networks, and revitalize brain function. You become more capable, smarter, and more vibrantly involved with life. The key is to find simple, regular ways to challenge your brain and senses to expand their performance and slow or prevent aging.

If we reject restrictive mindsets, we have a greater chance of replacing years of decline with years of growth and purpose. Because of this, play is a worthy pursuit for its own sake and can serve as creative stimulus for our most significant work.

Apply Your Senses as If This Is Your Last Day

When actively developed and applied, the senses serve as doors and windows to our world. They give life richness and coherence. Underused, they press us into ever-narrowing corridors of emptiness and frustration.

It is highly desirable for each of us to keep using and extending our senses throughout our lives. In many cases, the richer your sensory experiences, the slower you will age. Here are several keys:

- *Increase your sensory awareness.* When was the last time a magnificent sunset filled you with awe? How often have you felt deeply moved by a piece of music, a delicious meal, a compassionate—or passionate—embrace, the laughter of children, the sight and smell of fresh flowers? Whatever soothes or sparks your senses gives distinct signals to your heart and mind.

  To stimulate a greater involvement of the senses, ask yourself questions about what you're experiencing: What, precisely, does this feel like—on my fingertips, on the skin of my arm? How, exactly, is this sound, scent, touch, or taste new or different than anything I've experienced before? How has the lighting changed the image I see before me?

  In this spirit, you might become more keenly observant of the people, places, and objects that enter and leave your awareness. Notice different shapes, textures, colors, scents, shadowing, movement, and any other distinguishing features of each experience.

- *Keep glancing at nature.* Studies indicate that taking a few moments to view a beautiful nature scene can reduce anxiety, boost creativity, increase effectiveness in completing tasks, provide an emotional lift, and make it easier to relax. When was the last time you spent time doing any of the following, or anything like them: gazing at fish swimming in an aquarium; looking out your window at nearby trees or flowers; watching clouds form and swirl against the sky; enjoying the antics of birds or squirrels in a stand of trees; or looking at photographs or paintings of nature? Even brief exposures to such natural scenes can also serve as an antidote to mental fatigue.

- *Become the most curious person you know.* Do everything you can to see again with eyes undimmed by prior patterns. Magnify your curiosity. Soak in more of the richness of each experience, suspend your preconceived notions, and start with a clean slate whenever you explore something new.

Have Fun as If You Never Have to Grow Up

Life without laughter would not be worth living. If someone were to ask you, "How much pure fun have you and your loved ones had lately?" what would your answer be? It's worth thinking about. To what extent have you kept alive your best sense of playfulness and humor—the kind of silliness and exuberance that children excel at? Consider the following practical suggestions:

- *Do some things just "for the fun of it."* In his book *The Laws,* Plato said the model of true playfulness was what he saw in the need of all young creatures to *leap.* To leap you must use the ground as a springboard and know how to land resiliently. True play has everything to do with awe or exuberance, and nothing to do with an aggressive drive to win. Healthy, rejuvenating play is usually best when it's independent of a particular goal. When you stop focusing on time and achievement and do things—leaping, for example—just for the fun of it, you open yourself to precisely the kind of play that has led to broadened horizons, fresh perspectives, unexpected joy, sudden discoveries, and advanced learning.

Play may be the most important factor in the evolution of social behavior and the mental and spiritual life of humanity.

- *Post nuggets of wisdom and playful phrases on your refrigerator.* In many American homes, the refrigerator serves as a bulletin board of wit and focus. Amid phone messages, shopping lists, postcards, and reminder notes there can often be found uproarious cartoons and simple maxims for a meaningful life. My grandmother Cooper's refrigerator had a small postcard on the side which read, "God admires those who work, but he treasures those who also play and sing." Growing up, our Frigidaire displayed my mom's humorous image of a talking peanut saying, "The hurrier I go, the nuttier I get!" It prompted knowing smiles from all of us through the years and a renewed commitment to lend a hand with daily chores. Another old saying taped to the freezer door kept capturing my attention over the years: "Fear less, hope more. Eat less, chew more. Whine less, breathe more. Hate less, love more. And many more good things will be yours." What's posted on your refrigerator for one and all to see?

- *Ease off on the guilt of not getting everything done.* Overstuffed schedules are counterproductive. Frustrations spill over into our attitude. We hurry, overcommit, tire out, forget, fall behind, apologize, and then start the whole process again. Try breaking the loop. Let go of something every day. Start with guilt. Do what matters whenever you can. Ease off a bit on the other things.

- *Spice up your evenings with humor.* In one form or another, humor pokes its head into most chapters of this book, and for good reason. It pays to stay on the lookout for more of the ridiculous, incongruous events that go on around you all the time. Dig deeper for funny moments by pausing from time to time to ask "What if . . . ?" questions, creating limericks, and enjoying puns—which, at their best, push you into looking at familiar things in different ways, escaping from one pattern of thought into another.

How about bedtime stories (or at least some hopeful, positive, and humorous thoughts before falling asleep)? What were your favorites as a child? Do you know the favorites of your young relatives today? If you have young children or grandchildren, you might also try creating short stories about the funniest things you see or hear, and use them to spice up family discussions at the end of the day and on weekends.

- *Know what makes your loved ones laugh the hardest—and make it a point to keep doing these things.* It was Nietzsche, a man who wished he had more fun than he had, who said, "We should consider every day lost in which we have not danced at least once." I see dancing as a metaphor for pure fun. If we don't grab it, it's gone.

- *Start a humor library.* Think about all the things that make you laugh out loud. Whether it's cartoons, letters from friends, posters, biographies, old or new comedy movies, joke encyclopedias, games, or humorous stories (in books or on audiotapes for listening while you work or drive), it's a good idea to expand your collection. Pay attention to whatever humor tickles your funny bone and make it a point to keep it close by.

Dear Aunt Debbie,
I had a great birthday party. Thank you for the pretty skirt
from the Gap. It fell right off me.
   Love, Shanna

(Copy on the refrigerator of a thank you note sent by seven-year-old Shanna Cooper)

18

Keep Glancing Ahead

Everyone loves a winner. The lure of success or fame draws millions of us like moths to a flame. Popularity and celebrity are widely coveted, even idolized.

Beneath the surface, however, this emphasis on winning at all costs and seeking the limelight overshadows—and, at times, conceals altogether—a simple but indispensable human calling: to keep doing the unpopular to make the world a better place. According to George Eliot, "Courage is being willing to fight for a cause even when sure of losing. Look deeply at life and you will find that there are many victories worse than defeat."

One of the proudest memories I have of my father is of the time he lost the most important election of his life. He had devoted many years to helping disadvantaged people receive quality health care. He served on the hospital ship, USS HOPE. He donated time, equipment, and resources to health professionals in many different countries. He campaigned for reforms. And then, nearly twenty years ago, he was nominated for an elected office in a regional professional association. He believed he could use that position of influence to bring greater attention to healthcare needs in parts of the world typically overlooked by American organizations. Yet on the eve of the election, members of the opposition contacted him.

"We'll support you if you stop bringing up these ideas about spending time and money helping people far away," they said. "It's a lost cause, anyway. It won't make enough of a difference in the health of those poor people. There are lots of other issues to focus on. We want your assurance that you won't rock the boat. If you agree to that, we'll support your election." My father rejected the offer and argued his case. He then spent much of the night on the phone trying to rally support.

He lost. By a single vote. Not once, however, did he give any sign that he regretted the loss. When I asked how he felt, he summed it up by saying: "Lost causes are sometimes the only ones worth fighting for. From each defeat, you try to build forward."

The verdict of the moment is not always the verdict of time, as the opening chapters in this section suggest. Certain unpopular or overlooked issues or principles are worth staking our livelihood and honor on—and, in rare circumstances, our very lives.

When Lewis Morris of New York tried to logically gauge the chances of victory for America in a revolutionary war against Great Britain, he realized it appeared to be a lost cause. He supported it anyway. When he was about to sign the Declaration of Independence, his own brother heatedly advised him against it, warning that he would surely lose his lands and the small fortune he had struggled so hard to earn. "Damn the consequences," Lewis replied. "It is the right thing to do. Give me the pen."

Many causes that have appeared to be futile have continued to live in the hearts of people and ultimately prevailed. That's why dedicating at least a small part of your time to championing a few good lost causes serves not only as a needle on your inner compass but also as a lightning rod to keep awakening hidden capacity. Thomas Paine wrote, "That which we obtain too easily, we esteem too lightly. It is dearness only which gives everything its value." Due to their apparent insignificance or implausibility, lost causes may be very different from the big dreams or great goals. Yet, over the course of a lifetime, our support of lost causes can matter just as much to a life well lived.

"It Made a Difference to That One"

Above my desk are two pictures of an uncle I was named after but never knew. He was my father's only sibling. One photo is from a 1943 newspaper article showing Robert Cooper at sixteen helping young boys learn to use a jigsaw in a crafts class at the YMCA. He is smiling as he looks at the children around him. The other photo shows him on a ladder at the Y helping to remove the scaffolding from a statue of Abraham Lincoln that he and a group at the Y had crafted out of iron and plaster. The most remarkable feature of this photo is the light in his eyes. I believe it symbolized one of my uncle's big dreams and a lost cause all rolled into one: Trying to make a difference to kids few other people cared much about or thought could amount to anything great in life.

My grandfather didn't see it that way. Being the first of seven children to go to college and then earn a master's degree, he was very proud that my father had graduated from the university and was serving as an officer in the Army Air Corps. My grandfather grew increasingly impatient—at times angry—with his younger son who loved to help out at the Y instead of studying. The two of them would argue about it. My grandfather was a powerful man with a commanding voice. "Why don't you stop wasting so much of your time there!" he admonished my uncle. "When are you going to *do* something with your life?"

Which in the end was what my uncle did. He rejected my grandfather's rationale and rebelled. He kept giving his time and energy to the "lost kids," as he called them, at the Y. And then at 17 he joined the Army and gave his life not long after storming the beaches on Okinawa. From then on, my grandfather knew that through the YMCA and on the battleground, his younger son had sacrificed his future for our future.

Among my grandfather's greatest regrets was that he had tried so hard to force his youngest son to conform to his own expectations. When I was growing up, I never heard my grandfather criticize big dreams or lost causes. Instead, he embraced them. There were many times when local contractors would offer to provide skilled workers, but, instead, my grandfather would take me with him and we would drive to downtown Detroit to offer a day's work with good pay (and all the lunch you could eat) to people who were out of work. He encouraged me to find my own causes and stick with them. He said, "It doesn't matter how big the need. Small causes count, too. Get involved."

Through the years, one of my favorite examples of the fact that "small things count, too" comes from a village not far from Cambridge University in England. One spring morning, a friend of mine noticed a sign on the road that said, "Toads' Crossing. Please Be Careful." Every March, people in the village have helped toads across the road so they can lay their eggs in a nearby pond.

"Why does it matter?" a college student asked when he walked into a pub for lunch. He was wearing the distinctive tie of a renowned academic fraternity. "Even if lots of toads get run over by cars," he said, "it can't really be worth the effort of trying to save them. Enough will survive to breed."

An old man at the bar overheard the conversation. "Come along," he said, nodding toward the door. My friend and the college student walked outside to the motorway. One by one, the old man lifted toads across the road as cars slowed down to watch and then sped by.

"Why, old man, do you waste your time?" the student said. "Look at all the hundreds of other toads that keep trying to cross the road even when you're not here. They'll get run over. What makes you think what you're doing is making a difference?"

The old man pointed to a small toad he had just set safely across the roadway and said with a knowing smile, "It made a difference to that one."

That was the spirit my uncle had at sixteen when he came home at night, unworried that his homework was unfinished, after helping young people at the YMCA. "With kids like these," he once said to my grandfather, "everything I do makes a difference."

Every Single Week, Stand Up for at Least One Underdog

Imagine yourself years from now at the end of your life. Your children and grandchildren are gathered around you, and one of the youngest ones asks what you did in your life to make the world better. What will you say? Your answer will surely be shaped by lost causes you fought for, or failed to fight for.

We cannot leave this to chance. Each week, can you single out one unheralded or unpopular action to relieve suffering or make things better for generations to come?

Most people say they champion the underdog but they usually follow the top dog; champion some underdogs anyway. When bringing support to a lost cause, all it takes is a dedicated individual or small group. Consider that Wei Jingsheng was once an electrician at the Beijing Zoo, yet he emerged as an eloquent and fearless fighter for individual rights in China during the Democracy Wall Movement of the late 1970s. Although he has spent all but six months of the last twenty years in prison for his views, the spirit of his solitary message in a nation of billions has continued to inspire generations of Chinese democracy advocates from the students at Tiananmen Square to the citizens of Hong Kong. From his solitary confinement cell, he has composed defiant letters to Deng Xiaoping and other Communist leaders, expressing with stunning clarity and boldness his views on economic reform, human rights, Tibet, and other urgent yet taboo subjects. With humor and irony that survive his cruel and debilitating treatment, Wei's letters tell a story of one man's voice of courage in the face of tyranny and inhumanity.

Many people get cynical about those who try to do some good in the world; do some good anyway. Known as "Queen of the Dump," Suzie Valadez drives her old van every morning from El Paso, Texas, with hundreds of sandwiches donated by supermarkets, and boxes of clothing, school supplies such as paper, chalk, pencils, and books, and other donations of food. She crosses the Rio Grande up into the hills above Ciudad Juarez, to the great garbage dump where hundreds of ragged people, ignored by their local government and by other service agencies, forage for food and anything of value that others have thrown away. As the van pulls in, there are cries of welcome. Suzie goes straight to the rickety shack that serves as a school and hands out food and clothes to the children. This gray-haired bundle of energy, now past 70, then takes all that is left and distributes it to the desperate people at the dump. Finally, she goes to the medical building, the third one she has built with donated money and time.

Does this sound beyond your energy, temperament, or means? Most of us will never be a Wei Jingsheng, Suzie Valadez, Nelson Mandela, Gandhi, or even the gentle soul running the local homeless shelter or soup kitchen. We will never be a saint, gold-medal athlete, or president of an organization. But in our own one-of-a-kind way we were each born to make a difference, not just a living.

Perhaps you're already far ahead on this. If not, start anywhere. At schools, reading with children, helping with sports or performing arts. Aiding the homeless. Rescuing animals. Working with troubled or rebellious kids. Helping adults who can't read. Aiding refugees, orphans, or immigrants aspiring to a better future. Those hoping to learn a trade or a language. Battered women. The hungry. Making stuffed hearts for children in the hospital or those whose relatives have died. Hospices.

Boys and Girls Clubs. YMCAs and YWCAs. Boy Scouts or Girl Scouts. Soup kitchens. Nursing homes. Volunteer firefighting. Planting trees or flowers in parks. Guarding street crossings or playgrounds. Walking children safely home after school or women to their cars after work. Big Brothers or Big Sisters. Giving a piece of your time, energy, and heart to lost souls in need of a hot meal, a sip of cool water, a moment of faith or hope, a warm coat for winter.

Consider Mary Jo Copeland, whose ministry called "Sharing and Caring Hands" serves a thousand meals a week in Minneapolis. Every day, Mary Jo herself washes the feet of the homeless, then sends them off with new socks and shoes. "Look after your feet," she tells them. "They must carry you a long way in this world."

Think about how different the direct action of working on a lost cause feels compared to many of today's electronic jobs where you rarely, if ever, see your efforts touch real human lives. This is a cardinal reason for joining lost causes: so you can look back one day and know, "I helped somebody. I made a real difference, even if I was the only person who knew." When you can, bring your children with you. Get them involved early on with lost causes. In Studs Terkel's words, "It shows something I did on earth." If you watch closely, every once in a while you'll see how lost causes can transform themselves into big dreams and great goals of a lifetime.

There is a call within every one of us, a call to do something, however unpopular or unnoticed, to make the world a better place. From time to time, how can you step deeper into life's difficulties and forgotten possibilities, and take it personally?

Nearly everyone takes the limits of his own vision for the limits of the world. A few do not. Join them.
—ARTHUR SCHOPENHAUER

19

Know How to
Get Gone

There's a real difference between slowing down and letting go. Slowing down is fine. It's necessary, often imperative. Yet from time to time throughout every day, the brain and senses must do less than just shift gears—they must stop pushing altogether. If these essential breakaways are not planned, they will occur randomly, causing the space-outs that wreak so much havoc in work and personal relationships. Chances are, you already have lots of experience with such random mental fade-outs and microsleeps-while-standing-up: they're not only dangerous if you're operating heavy equipment, other people believe you are ignoring them or that you just don't care . . . because your eyes are open but, as anyone can plainly see, you're not really in there.

We have dedicated our lives to doing, and inexplicably, we're falling farther behind. Many of us feel there's nothing we can't do—except, of course, doing nothing. Could ten well-chosen minutes of delightful nondoing be more valuable than ten minutes of pushing hard at your job or daily tasks or in traffic or at the gym? Yes. If not, the pushing itself can do us in. As cardiologist Robert Eliot puts it, "Often the first indication of heart disease is sudden death."

One reason is that we've become obsessed with speed. We make lots of plans we can't execute and create packed schedules that can't be followed. We end up feeling inadequate and guilty. Fragmented and overloaded. With all of today's timesaving high-technology gadgets, we've ended up with no free time. The best advice, say researchers, is to go for walks and grow a garden. Do exercises that shouldn't be rushed and include loved ones. But digging a garden as a duty or going for a walk to avoid feeling guilty doesn't give much benefit to someone who can no longer fathom the word "slow."

Getting Really Good at Doing Nothing, Guilt-Free

Years ago, I attended a research seminar at the University of Minnesota as part of a group of 150 doctoral degree candidates who were conducting studies at major universities. The professor began the program by saying, "Some of you in this room don't know how to *lime*—and it's time you learned."

He explained that, years before, while setting up educational programs in the Caribbean, he and his colleagues had worked on a number of islands, including Trinidad. The professors had been amazed when many of the local workers showed up each morning full of energy, listened to the day's assignments and expectations, and then went off to complete them with enthusiasm. That was remarkable, but what really got to him was seeing these same people *after* work.

While the professors were sitting in lounge chairs on the beach, by about 7 in the evening here came the local people with their families. They would dance on the beach and play and sing and tell stories, laughing and enjoying themselves far into the night. Every night. This went on for several weeks and finally the professors thought to themselves, "This can't be normal. No one can have this much energy and fun day after day. It might be some rare form of hyperactivity. Or drug addiction. We should study them." Which they did.

It turned out that this was not some rare disease. These were healthy men and women with lots of energy and a very strong sense of light-heartedness and fun. They were following a tradition on these islands that originated nearly three hundred years before, when the inhabitants had first seen a ship arrive at their shores with Europeans aboard who were alive and well. The other ships had brought dead or dying Europeans, sickened by scurvy. The last ships, however, had limes on board. The voyagers had eaten the citrus fruit during the voyage to prevent scurvy. They arrived looking fully alive. Hence, "liming."

Many Caribbean people had grown up believing that if they gave everything they had to their work, they were entitled at the end of the day and on weekends to spend time with their family and friends "liming." Liming means doing nothing, or anything healthy that you love to do, guilt-free. These men and women could turn off the work mindset in an instant at the end of the day. That's the difference between slowing down and getting gone. How can we ever hope to grasp the deeper possibilities of life, and lead invigorated or meaningful days, if we're all dashing around nonstop like water bugs on the surface of a swirling river?

Practice Vanishing

Few of us are really good at disappearing by plan. Okay, we may space out in front of the television or doze off unexpectedly, but we're poorly equipped to say, "I'm out of here" as we dive into the deep end of doing nothing and savor every moment of it.

Here's one place to give this a try: Stand beside a big pile of unopened mail. Decide to get some breathing space instead of opening any of it. Feel the tension tug inside your gut to go ahead and at least flip through it? You are feeling one of the most powerful pulls of all—the *doing* instinct.

Next, spend some time watching a cat. Cats know almost everything there is about lounging and doing nothing. Emulate what you see. Sink way into the easy chair. No sudden moves. Stretch before you jump up. Notice small things a cat would see that you never noticed before.

How about napping? Here's a principle to test: If you've got too much to do, take a nap—even just for ten minutes. Turns out it can be one of the best ways to revitalize the body and mind to meet upcoming demands with less effort and more ease. Think of it as digging an escape tunnel. When you resurface you have a fresh outlook. Churchill, Kennedy, Edison, and da Vinci all took short daily naps. Feel guilty about disappearing for a few minutes? They didn't. Although your superego may admonish you to keep your nose to the grindstone so that a ten-minute snooze doesn't compromise your eventual fame, that's nonsense.

Which brings us to vacations. For many people the number of days each year spent on holiday—relaxing, having fun, letting go, changing routine, going new places—are dwindling. We are filling this time instead with rushing faster and working longer. However, new research shows that frequent getaways are vital for mind, body, heart, and health. In a long-term study of heart disease among middle-aged men, those who took the most frequent vacations—even if only a few days at a time—during a five year period had a lower risk of dying from any cause, including heart disease, over the next nine years. This was true at every income level, and among the healthy as well as the not-so-healthy.

Step Away: Plan It, Say It, Do It

Whenever friends or loved ones kindly remind us to relax—to take a deep breath, have some fun, or unwind for a day—we almost always protest. Doing nothing takes time away from our goals, we reason. First we have to catch up, *then* we'll relax. That's another illusion: None of us is ever going to catch up no matter how hard we try.

Consider what you personally need to get gone—and how often and for how long each day you might benefit from a disappearing act. Looking at the past year, when was the last time you truly "got away from it all"? When's the next getaway scheduled?

Now, back to today. How well can you just vanish—even briefly? As I have learned the hard way—and with considerable laughter from friends and family members—you cannot *effort* your way into doing nothing. You have to stop trying, and then it happens. I have found it very valuable—and, in my case, obligatory—to practice variations on the six parts of what I call the "Getting Gone Minute":

1. *Let go of time.* Take off your watch and look at it. Decide when you want to return from getting gone. Trust your subconscious to nudge you when time is up. Now turn your watch face down. Release your focus about what's just happened or what's coming up later. With a bit of practice, this letting go process gets easier.

2. *Switch off the outside world.* What would happen if, heaven forbid, you were in a coma for a year? What if you then awakened with a full recovery of your former vibrant state of health? A year later, looking back, what would you have lost for having been in a coma and missed a full year's worth of information? Answer: Zero. Zip. Nothing important in the long run. When you consider your long-term well-being, switching off incoming information from time to time has no negative effect. Beyond the mind-numbing problems of rushing is the daily glut of nonessential information.

Consider how everything you see, hear, smell, taste, and touch throughout the day bombards your mind with stimulation. Too much nonessential news may be hazardous to your health, say researchers. Much of the information bombarding us from our televisions, radios, and the Internet lacks redeeming value, dulls our sensibilities, and leaves us bloated with trivia yet intellectually, emotionally, and spiritually deprived.

That's why in this step you choose to be your own information switchboard. You hit the "off" button. You escape newspapers, newsmagazines, television, phones, pagers, and computers.

3. *Come up for air.* As you let go of the outside world, settle into the most comfortable position. Listen to your breathing. Feel your heart beating. Slow down. Tune in. Shed tension. Bypass worry. Remember who you are.

4. *Think of something funny.* There are strong scientific reasons why people who are quick to laugh—especially at themselves—are generally healthier, more energetic, and better able to bounce back from stressful situations. In order to laugh at yourself, you have to forgive yourself for not being perfect. Humorous thoughts and, in particular, mirthful laughter work their wonders by initially arousing and distracting the mind, and then leaving us feeling more relaxed.

5. *Imagine being at your favorite hideout, doing nothing at all.*
It's your call: Sitting in the hollow of a great old tree in the park.
Reclining beside a hidden pond. Napping in a quiet cabin in the
woods. Soaking up the late-day sun on a lounge chair at the beach.
Snuggling by the fire at a ski hut in the mountains. Whatever setting and type of non-doing gives you renewed energy. Imagine
being there and sinking into the experience of letting go. For example, let's say your favorite hideout is a beautiful lake. Close
your eyes and imagine that you're relaxing at that lake in a very
comfortable small boat. You're about to embark on a short journey. The water lilies are in bloom, the sky is blue, the air is clear,
and the temperature is perfect. Pull up anchor and let the boat
drift. Even if the water feels a little choppy at first, know that it
will smooth out soon. That's the mental imagery that makes it
possible to truly get away from it all, even in moments.

6. *Get the Big Picture.* As you prepare to return to your daily
routine, take a few seconds to acknowledge why getting gone really matters. Unlike other resources, your energy and perspective
cannot be bought or sold, stocked up or saved. All you can do is
keep replenishing them, and remembering why it matters to not
only slow down here and there but to step away and let go of time
and worry. Only then does life return to proper focus and, with it,
the possibilities for renewed meaning and moments of joy.

*Y*ou can't have everything.
Where would you put it?

—MARK TWAIN

FOURTH KEYSTONE

NERVE

20

Test Your Spirit in the Laboratory

In the fourteenth century, Chaucer said, "With life so short, why is the craft of living so long to learn?"

No matter how many times the pundits hail human progress, much of everyday experience still remains difficult and even mystifying. We have more but we worry more. We earn more but demand more. We face immense uncertainty and complexity. We are challenged at almost every turn. There is no end in sight. Yet, by design, we have the capacity and responsibility to learn and grow from every one of the obstacles, inducements, incitements, provocations, and stimuli—I call them *catalysts*—that life sends our way.

Catalysts are a special kind of gift: they challenge us to reach deeper, look farther, search harder, and discover more ways to make every moment count. During times of change, we must summon increased confidence. From our stumbles and mistakes come unexpected lessons. Each setback or failure yields a measure of ingenuity or wisdom, enriching our lives in ways that our successes alone never can.

All of Life Is a Laboratory

An interviewer visiting Thomas Edison at his laboratory asked, "What are the rules you want me to observe while I am here?"

"Hell! There aren't rules around here!" replied Edison. "In this laboratory, we're trying to accomplish something."

I remember being in a systems physiology lab at the Max Planck Institute in Germany, talking with scientists doing research on cellular production of adenosine triphosphate—ATP—the energy of life. I'll never forget the feeling of excitement in that lab. These men and women were venturing from the edges of the known into the unknown.

The institute's director explained to me that the scientists came from more than a dozen countries. Charged with designing and conducting research that no other scientific institution anywhere in the world was doing, they were constantly faced with the unexpected. All experiments were difficult and at the edges of the impossible. Many failed. But there were also moments of awe and wonder, amazing surprises, stunning shifts in perspective, and very tangible measures of progress. This is precisely how new knowledge is often gained.

Like independent and inspired scientists, we too are called to keep experimenting. We are meant to use every catalyst we can—by choice or by chance—to stir things up and see what may be found in venturing from the edges of the known into the unknown.

Unbidden challenges—the occurrences we instinctively try so hard to avoid—are life's golden opportunities to *live* our values and test the limits of our ingenuity. Defining moments reveal who we are and keep offering us important glimpses into what we may yet become.

Face What's in Front of You

I was hiking early one morning with my grandfather Cooper on a bluff near the headwaters of the Mississippi River. I was nine and hardly more than half his height. After I ate breakfast and he drank his cup of coffee, we went to the edge of the woods. We had gone inwards from the edge of the woods along a narrow trail through heavy brush to the overlook above the water. It was very difficult for him to walk but I never heard him complain. Below us, the secluded river glistened in the dawn as the sun cast a wave of light across the valley. The air smelled of pine needles and wildflowers.

A streak of sand and gravel went nearly straight down a hundred feet to the river, like a summertime toboggan run. "Go ahead," my grandfather said. I had gone down this way before. It was tricky but I was smiling as I slid on my heels past patches of sharp rocks. I was almost at the water's edge when, feeling very confident, I tried to jump over a large rock. I landed off balance and fell forward. My arm got snagged by a large thorn bush and my legs slid into the icy river. Suddenly I was filled with panic, thrashing in the water as I struggled to free my arm from the thorns. I finally managed to drag myself back up on shore. My shirt was torn and my boots were drenched. My arm was bloodied, and I was crying.

"I don't like climbing!" I shouted. "I want to go back."

But I knew my grandfather couldn't climb down to help me, and we hadn't brought a rope. The only way out for me was going to be by climbing back up the slope. The air was still and I could hear my heart pounding in my ears. I heard my grandfather's voice from the overlook.

"Robert, there's nothing to be afraid of. Just some old rocks, a few thorns, and cold water."

"But I'm bleeding!"

"You'll be all right."

"I don't want to climb anymore!"

"Put everything else out of your mind. Face what's in front of you."

"What do you mean?"

"You didn't plan to fall but you did. I didn't plan for the drunk driver to hit my car and break my back. But life's like that sometimes. It's one big experiment. Now it's your chance to do something with what you've been given."

"But how?"

"By being stronger than you thought you had to be even a few minutes ago. By trying something new. Just focus on your next step. Come upward toward me. Show me how you can climb."

I gritted my teeth and brushed off my tears. I set my feet and eyed a path upward. I took one step after another. As I reached the overlook, my shivering legs and scratched arms were forgotten.

Stepping Forward to Face Whatever Life Brings

Chances are, you discovered long ago that in many difficult circumstances, the only way out is through. In facing a loss, for example, we must come to terms with it in order to move on. When dealing with a mistake or setback, we learn that making excuses or blaming others ultimately doesn't work. Backing away from challenges often ends up blunting learning and blocking us from discovering new ways to make a difference, however small, in what happens next for ourselves and others.

Courage is a vital ingredient, of course. As Anaïs Nin put it, "Life shrinks or expands in proportion to one's courage." Beyond courage, however, to advance upward it takes a clear sense of perspective: How does *this* experience compare to what I have experienced in the past and to what other people have experienced? This section is about nerve, which I define as "an approach to life characterized by courage, fortitude, and spirit."

My grandfather would ask, "From how far back can a human being come and still make a difference?" How many things can a person lose—such as freedom, physical or mental faculties, health, resources, or opportunities—and still astound us with what he or she is capable of enduring or accomplishing? "Look at a man in the midst of doubt and danger, and you will learn in his hour of adversity what he really is," said the Roman philosopher Lucretius. "It is then that true utterances are wrung from the recesses of the heart. The mask is torn off; the reality remains."

Through the years and across miles of travel, one of my experiences, in particular, continues to shape my view of the unseen possibilities for courage and perspective in facing whatever life brings.

It was years ago and I was standing on a mountain in Tibet. The view and atmosphere elicited in me a profound sense of wonder, a heightened curiosity about the meanings of our existence—the mysteries of who we are, of what we live for, and what we may yet achieve. I gazed at the worlds beyond, across the horizons of my imagination, looking out as if, for that string of moments on the rooftop of the world, nothing was hidden from me.

What I could not have known then, on that day years ago, was that I was about to experience something that would change forever my view of human capacity. Just before reaching the summit, my Tibetan guide asked, "Are you ready?" Ready for what? I wondered as I nodded breathlessly. For the rarefied view? For a feeling of accomplishment in the climb? Yes, I would be ready.

But I was not ready. Not for what came.

Along with my Tibetan guide, an elder was journeying with us that day. He looked very old when I first saw him; I found out later he was fifty-nine. His skin was creased and wrinkled, a weathered brown. His shining eyes were a sharp blue-black, the whites crisscrossed with blood vessels, giving him a weary, or perhaps strained, look. But this was not borne out in the way he walked and climbed—with a quiet confidence and considerable stamina, despite a slight limp on his left side. He wore old mountain boots and a dark blue heavy canvas coat over grey work trousers and a red sweater that was frayed at the collar. The knuckles on his hands were variously enlarged—some looked to have been broken, others gnarled with age or arthritis—and he carried a long ironwood walking staff that the guide told me he had years ago dethorned, smoothed, and oiled by hand until it gleamed.

I was in Tibet completing a research project. When at last we reached the summit's overlook, the guide stood with me beside the elder. Together we gazed across the ancient valleys below. It was a wondrous, breath-taking sight. The sun was warm on our faces. Despite the clear sky, snowflakes were beginning to fall. I turned into the breeze and noticed the source: a cluster of white clouds drifting toward us from the east.

"There." The elder was pointing.

"What is it?" I asked.

"There. The mound."

Not far from the foot of the mountain, several thousand feet below, I could see what appeared to be an open field. As the elder stared at it, his arms began to shake. I looked at him, confused now, noticing that tears had started to run down his cheeks. I glanced over at my Tibetan guide. He, too, was red-eyed, visibly moved by something I could not yet comprehend.

"All of my family," the elder said so softly I almost couldn't hear him, "was buried there . . . before they took the bodies away."*

"What do you mean?" I thought there might have been a climbing accident of some kind, recalling our ascent and my apprehension that a gust of wind or misstep could send us plummeting down the mountain face.

"Do you know what this gesture means?" the elder asked me, bringing his hands together, palm to palm, fingers pointing skyward, in front of his chest.

I nodded. Throughout Tibet and the Himalayas, it was a sign of respect, of greeting, and of prayer.

"In 1959," he went on, "the Chinese Army took over Tibet." He motioned toward the end of the river valley and beyond. "The Red Army came and destroyed our homes, libraries, and temples, and raped many of our women, and forbade us from prayer. For more than a thousand years, for the most part we have been a peaceful people. We had a small army but they were no match for the Red Guard. No countries came to our aid. It was a dark time for Tibet, and still is for those who survived . . ." He wiped tears from his eyes and continued.

"There was a day, years ago, when I was walking along that road"—he pointed to a narrow route that appeared as a slender thread across the valley floor. "I came upon an old friend, and, on

---

* To honor a promise I made to people in Tibet and in an effort to help protect the surviving Tibetans from further persecution at the hands of the occupying Chinese Army, I have altered dates, numbers, times, human and geographic features, and several other elements in this composite story.

instinct, out of respect"—he touched his weathered palms to-gether in front of his chest—"I greeted him in the traditional way and said *Tashi deley*, which means 'I honor the greatness in you,' and we stopped to talk for a while."

"A Chinese army officer saw me do this, and he said, 'Arrest this man. He is praying and spreading religion. He has defied the law. We will make an example out of him.' For years I had spoken out against the way our people were being treated; but I had not attacked anyone or taken up arms. However, there was much un-rest in the valley and I believe the Chinese soldiers were watching me, afraid of a rebellion.

"The next day the Red Guard gathered together my surviving relatives—my wife, brother and sister, mother, father, grand-mother, uncle, aunt, and the family's children. At gunpoint, they ordered some of the villagers to watch and made us dig a hole." He motioned to the mound of earth. "The officers yelled that rules must be obeyed, no matter what. No one must think or feel any-thing the Chinese-appointed group leaders do not tell them to think or feel. Then they told of my crime: They said I defied the ban on prayer and religion and was an enemy of the government and people, and announced my punishment while soldiers held my arms."

For a few moments, the elder was unable to speak. The wind shifted. It seemed a long time before he went on: "They ignored my protests. Maybe they had planned this for a long time. To this day, I do not know. I told them again that my prayer was given on instinct, given out of respect for my friend, and I was not promot-ing religion. It was not an act of defiance or rebellion against the government rulers. I pleaded with them to punish *me*, to make me alone suffer, and no one else. They said, 'Don't worry, you will suf-fer plenty.' Then they ignored me and forced me to watch."

He drew a long breath and exhaled very slowly, gathering him-self. I found myself in the grip of such intense feelings that it seemed I was actually standing there, many years before, beside him as he faced a terrible, pivotal moment in this life. What happened next, I wondered, and how did he respond? What would *I* have done?

"The officers were laughing," he said quietly, "as Red Guards soaked strips of cotton in gasoline and stuffed these down the throats of my wife and relatives and set the cotton on fire and threw them into the hole. The soldiers buried them alive, burning. And the children, the little ones, their cries, their eyes . . ."

He stopped, standing rigid, his hands shaking uncontrollably.

I felt my heart pounding in my chest. I imagined this happening to my family. The snow was easing up and I watched the blue wind cross the beams of mountain light, in the quiet anguish of a man's life, a man I now knew was the sole survivor of his family, a leader singled out in an atmosphere of fear and repression. This was a man whose crime had been to bring his hands together in prayer to honor the greatness in another human being.

Slowly, the elder dried the wetness from his cheeks. His hands were bare and I watched snow fall on them and it didn't melt right away but seemed to rest there, clinging to the old knuckles. The light illuminated his features, worn by weather and life and sun, yet still glowing with intensity. He looked into my face; no, he looked through my eyes, as if into my soul. I know no words to describe it, the look he gave.

"Tell me," his voice grew stronger, "about your life—and about America."

I was incredulous. "My life? America?" I felt a surge of dismay, then anger. "How can you do that?"

"Do what?"

"Tell someone about a loss so devastating and then, just like that, let it go?"

He tilted his head and stared at me with a curious look on his face. "Let it go? I can never let it go. They took away from me everything. Except two things, two things no one can take away: First, what I value and believe—what I *feel*, beneath everything else, is true in my heart, even when my mind can't prove or explain it. And second, short of killing me, they could not take away how I express *who I am* on the path of my destiny. These are the things that make me real and give me hope, no matter what difficulties come."

"But how—" I began.

"Robert," he interrupted me, "it was the most terrible thing. The hardest thing in my life, beyond anything I ever could have imagined. But I wanted you to know about it. Without knowing this, you do not know me. The deep me, the real me. Think of this: Could you trust me simply because someone, like the Red Guard officer, commanded you to? No. But now, if you choose to, you can begin to know me and trust me. Now I am not just a name. I have a heart and a voice and a life story. I am not just some stranger who climbed a mountain with you."

"As for your other question," he added, "the one about how could I tell you of such a devastating experience and then turn my attention away from it? It's because of you, you are alive. You are here, now. My family is dead. All things die. Sooner or later. When they were murdered, at the most desperate moment of my life, I knew I had to choose: To strike out at the soldiers and die, too, or to make a much more difficult choice. Would my spirit be strong enough to carry such a tragedy? It was my soul, or perhaps my shattered heart, that decided for me: I must try to keep living on behalf of every loved one I had lost. Now it would be left to me alone to do whatever I could to touch the world in memory of them. Each day, I tell myself that. I have work left to do."

The elder saw my confusion.

"You must understand, Robert, that this is not something only of the mind's making. It is from the heart." He touched his chest.

There's an old Tibetan saying: "Out before me the path rises, the path I was born to take . . ." By design, life goes upward. What I learned half way around the world has nothing to do with traveling far away. It is within reach of us all, with taking a single step from our own door.

In each of the defining moments across a lifetime, we are tested: How well do we call forth our spirit and marshal inner reserves? Can we face the change, loss, or pain without collapsing or running away? In the midst of it all, can we still search for every line of hope, however slim, going forward? According to Elie Wiesel, Holocaust survivor, Nobel laureate, and supporter of the Tibetan people, "We must understand that there can be no life without risk—and when your spirit is strong, everything else is secondary, even the risks."

Every journey has difficult stretches where the path suddenly grows steeper and part of you wants to turn away or turn back. This is life's laboratory. As the clergyman Henry Ward Beecher reminded us more than a hundred years ago, "We are always in the forge, or on the anvil; by trials God is shaping us for higher things."

It is heartening to realize that although we may crave comfort and routine, we nourish the soul's growth primarily through what is hard. As Darwin saw it, it's not the strongest of the species that survives, nor the most intelligent, but those who are most responsive to change. How often do you pause to re-set your perspective by remembering someone who has lost almost everything and still lived a meaningful life?

Whenever I begin to lose my way in the challenges of the day or the difficulties of life, I pause to remember an old man standing beside me on a mountain in Tibet.

With all your science can you tell me how it is, and when it is, that light comes into the soul?

—THOREAU

21

Make Adversity
Your Ally

When reaching the most difficult passage of a climb—known as the crux—those who are afraid of falling hold back. "Looks too difficult," they rationalize. "Better stop here. Why chance it?"

But that's not what exceptional climbers do. They are vigilant about safety yet see each ascent as a new chance to learn, with their missteps serving as the best possible teachers. They face every crux with a mix of excitement and toughness. They know that making adversity their ally and overcoming built-in resistance are keys to advancement. Theirs is a counterintuitive view: When they fall, they are falling forward in life, not actually downward. This is because each time you learn something new from a fall, it increases your ability to climb different and higher routes tomorrow.

Beyond the preceding chapter's message of marshalling the nerve to face life's greatest challenges is the question of taking the next step: developing skills to get better at crossing the various cruxes of life, transforming stress and adversity into an ally instead of an enemy.

Every time we are brought face to face with moments of risk, fear, or uncertainty, we are given the chance to learn from them as a way to unearth hidden capacity. Such experiences determine our biographies as surely as all the moments of thoughtfulness and carefully planned daily routine.

Once when I was hiking with my grandfather Cooper in one of the last virgin forests of Minnesota, we stood together looking up at an immense cedar tree that had been estimated to be 1,200 years old. Its trunk rose upward like a sculpted spiral, with powerful twists and gnarly turns. I wondered out loud why it wasn't perfectly straight. My grandfather said great trees grow strongest when exposed to powerful winds from time to time. So do humans, he added. In one way or another, adversity arrives in every life unbidden. What we do with it can make all the difference.

Hardiness Is Developed, Not Found

People who are mentally, physically, and emotionally hardy are better able to grow from the harsh tests of life. Such individuals seldom feel victimized by circumstances and tend to learn more from challenges and stay healthier along the way.

To increase hardiness, you must first learn to avoid linearity. All living things exist in oscillating cycles. Darkness follows light, spring follows winter. In people, periods of recovery must follow episodes of stress. Researchers call this the stress-recovery cycle. When you sit for hours or rush without pause or think nonstop, such linearity steadily weakens your adaptability. The greater the pressure, the more difficult it is to oscillate. That's why certain practices can help condition you to master stress-recovery cycles and make the most of adversity.

For example, every half hour or so throughout the day, keep pulling back by taking a Strategic Pause or Essential Break (Chapter 9). Here are several additional ways to begin increasing your physical, emotional, and mental resilience:

- *Balance your stress-recovery cycles.* This is where you focus on establishing a healthy balance between the times you push hard and the times you let go and rejuvenate your energies. If you mapped out a typical 24-hour day, how many hours would you spend:

Pushing Hard	*Hours*	*Recovering Well*	*Hours*
Working hard, concentrating intensely:	____	Thinking informally and creatively:	____
Resting tensely or poorly:	____	Sleeping deeply and well:	____
Dealing with interruptions/emergencies:	____	Enjoying healthy meals and snacks:	____
Complaining:	____	Laughing:	____
Must-do errands/chauffeuring for others:	____	Vital and fun time with loved ones:	____
Doing added/extra/unexpected work:	____	Taking effective breaks and pauses:	____
Intensive exercise time:	____	Enjoyable, relaxed, fun activities:	____
Focus on immediate/short-term details:	____	Focus on the big picture or long view:	____
Subtotal of hours:	____	*Subtotal of hours:*	____

How did the total 24 hours add up? Ideally, more than half of the hours are for recovering well and less than half are for pushing hard. If not, how can you gain better balance?

- *Use change-of-pace exercise to build resilience.* One of the best ways to increase the capacity to handle adversity may be to expose yourself to increased positive physical stress intermittently through aerobic exercise. Researchers have found that low levels of a brain hormone called norepinephrine are associated with feelings of helplessness and a low tolerance for adversity. Aerobic exercise stimulates a more optimal amount of norepinephrine. Aerobic exercise is steady, rhythmic physical activity that increases your ability to deliver maximum amounts of oxygenated blood throughout the body and brain to make energy. Aerobic activities include walking, jogging, cycling, swimming, skating, and rowing. Regular aerobic exercise strengthens your ability to recover rapidly from high-stress situations and enables you to respond more energetically and appropriately to challenges.

  Before beginning any fitness program, check with your physician regarding your readiness. Once you're involved with a regular aerobics routine, consider adding some variety—and further resilience boosting—with easy speed-ups and slow-downs. Once you can exercise at a comfortable, moderate pace, add some intervals where you change the pace to go faster, then slower. The goal is to develop increased recovery ability. Follow your body's signals—you should never feel pain when exercising. If you're a walker, warm up, walk moderately for five minutes or longer, then walk more briskly for a few minutes, then slowly for a while. If you're a runner, run fast—and maybe occasionally sprint—and then jog for a while or walk slowly. A similar pattern can be used for other aerobic activities.

- *Stay tall.* During difficult moments and tough times, make a conscious effort to control your posture and stay relaxed yet upright; don't let it collapse even slightly. As noted in Chapter 15, whenever you react to stressful situations with a slouching posture you can magnify feelings of helplessness and panic.

- *Toughen and tone your abdomen.* The foundation of all strength in the body is in the abdominal muscles, and to have the ability to make the most of adversity you must literally have the stomach for it. From the abdominal muscles comes the ability to exert and resist force. A weak abdominal area can be linked to lower back pain and problems with posture, movement, and breathing. Along with the Transpyramid Breathing Exercise (see Chapter 15) for toning the lower abdominal muscles, one of the best ways to strengthen the middle and upper abdomen is with modified crunches or curl-ups, not sit-ups or leg-lifts. Here's how to do them:

  Lie on your back on a padded or carpeted surface, with your knees bent and your feet flat on the floor. Cross your arms on your chest or clasp your hands *lightly* behind your head. With your middle and lower back flat on the floor, slowly raise your head and shoulders off the ground about 30 degrees. Keep your lower abdomen flat (do not let your lower back arch and stomach stick out during the upward movement). Pause for a second at the top of the motion and then slowly lower yourself to the original position. Begin with only a few repetitions and, as long as there is no serious discomfort or pain, over a period of weeks work your way up to 50 slow repetitions every other day.

- *Stay flexible.* First, in attitude. The older we get, the more rigid we tend to become—mentally, emotionally, and physically. You can't let that happen. Devote at least a few minutes a day to some gentle yet purposeful stretches for your neck, shoulders, back, hips, wrists, fingers, and other key areas of the body. Sit a bit less. Bend and dance a little more. Keep loosening up.

- *Increase your ability to effectively manage intense emotions— in yourself and others.* Studies of people subjected to some of the most severe forms of adversity—concentration camp survivors, battle veterans, and survivors of prisoner-of-war camps during the Vietnam War—show that those who handled the adversity best from a health perspective possessed the most effective coping strategies:

  - They did not surrender or give up their spirit.

  - They maintained a sense of inner control: No matter how bad things were, they could control their outlook and thoughts.

  - They attributed some important meaning to their suffering and pain.

  - They focused on whatever was positive throughout each day ("I got food today").

  - They maintained a strong sense of purpose and vowed to make it through their ordeal.

Similar qualities can be highly beneficial in meeting the demands of daily life and work. The following section describes several practical ways to develop and apply such qualities.

Make Adversity Your Ally

For bringing out more of the best in yourself and others in stressful situations, consider the following three-part approach:

- **Calmness** Under Pressure
- **Analysis** of Evidence and Alternatives
- **Action** to Be Taken

PART ONE: Calmness Under Pressure

Adversity comes in all shapes and sizes. How we respond to the irritations of everyday life—such as delays, moments of anger, interruptions, disappointments, feelings of rejection or betrayal, broken appointments, the inescapable telephone, financial worries, bad weather, traffic jams, and deadlines—is often a far better predictor not only of calm energy but also of psychological and physical health than is our reaction to major life crises.

It's not just the big pressures—final exams, marriage, parenting, divorce, job changes, illnesses or deaths of friends and relatives—that overload us with stress; it's the lives of quiet desperation that millions lead. Which small frustrations are most annoying? That varies from one individual to another, but daily hassles—and the way we respond to them—shouldn't be ignored. There's a long-term penalty, too: When mishandled, the chronic, unavoidable "small stresses" of everyday life may accelerate aging.

It is common to react to adversity in ways that accelerate or exacerbate a loss of control. More than fifteen years ago, I began some pioneering research on a practical strategy I called the *instant calming sequence,* or ICS for short. It received praise from a number of scientists and performance psychologists. Over the years I have made further revisions as I explored its effectiveness and application. I encourage you to put the ICS to the test, starting today. It can head off tension and needless over-reactions to adversity. With practice, you can use it anywhere, anytime, in five "chunked" steps that can be triggered by the brain in a split second. Those steps, which I'll describe in some detail, are as follows:

1. Continue breathing.
2. Lighten your eyes.
3. Release tension.
4. Notice uniqueness.
5. Shift your view of time.

One of the most effective ways to master pressure-filled situations is to learn to catch the first stimulus or signal of tension or distress and then trigger an immediate control response. Chemical and hormonal changes in the brain and body can tighten muscles and unleash negative emotions so quickly that it's much more difficult and time-consuming to reverse negative reactions once they've occurred.

Applying ICS is a way to instantly stop the negative effects of stress and stay in better control of your thoughts, feelings, and actions whenever you're facing adversity. It promotes inner calmness—of thought, emotions, and body—whenever peak stress situations occur. It helps you take a higher vantage point and avoid anguishing over life's frustrations and unexpected challenges. It provides a buffer against worry and guilt while preserving more or your best physical and mental capabilities in the present moment.

Because an ICS is performed while you are fully alert, with eyes open, the technique may be used unobtrusively in a wide range of circumstances. The ICS is successful whether you're standing, sitting, or moving. You can call upon this response in the first moments of facing adversity, whenever you don't want frustrations or distractions clouding your thinking, lowering your mood, or interfering with your actions. No matter what pressures you face—major "out in the open" crises and performance challenges or quiet, nagging self-doubts that worsen each time something or someone reminds you of past mistakes or present weaknesses—the ICS is a direct and simple skill you can start using right away.

ICS Step 1: Continue Breathing

The ease and rhythm of our breathing, and the oxygen we consume, must also serve as a natural stimulus to the inner breathing of the 100 trillion cells in your body that enable you to produce biological energy, and in particular calm energy. When we are tense and tired, our breathing tends to become shallow and intermittent. Each time stress levels rise, we tend to halt our breathing—if only for a few seconds. This creates a ripple effect of tension and anxiety. Because oxygen is vital to life, the body and brain are extremely sensitive to even very small reductions in its availability. When we unknowingly halt our breathing during the first moments of each stressful situation, it propels us toward feelings of anxiety, panic, anger, frustration, faulty reactions, and a general loss of control.

Notice when pressures rise and consciously keep your breathing going without interruption, smooth and steady.

ICS Step 2: Lighten Your Eyes

The muscles of the face not only react to our mood, they help *set it*. When the face or jaw are tense, within moments we feel increasingly tense throughout the body. Easing off on the

intensity in your eyes and, at the same time, maintaining a neu-
tral, or better yet, a slightly positive facial expression can make a
big difference during stressful situations.

One reason for the speed and power of this response is that
positive reactions in the facial muscles increase blood flow to the
brain and transmit nerve impulses from the face and eyes to the
limbic system, where your immediate reactions are guided. Lightening the eyes and smiling even slightly changes neurochemistry
toward favorable emotions and more constructive actions. These
changes can be powerful and swift.

ICS Step 3: Release Tension

A common self-victimizing response to frequent and sudden
rises in everyday pressure is slouching, which not only restricts
breathing and reduces blood flow and oxygen to the brain and
senses but also adds needless muscle tension, slows reaction time,
and intensifies feelings of dread and helplessness.

There are two parts to this ICS step: balancing your posture
and releasing all excess tension. With balanced posture you have
an exhilarating sense of no effort in action, moving buoyantly and
comfortably. I discussed posture at length in Chapter 15. During
an ICS, the key is to keep your posture buoyant and "up"; don't let
it become tense or collapse even slightly.

Next, perform a split-second tension check by scanning all of
your muscles in one fast sweep of your mind—from your scalp, jaw,
tongue, and face to your fingertips and toes—to locate unnecessary
tension. At the same time, you flash a mental "wave of relaxation"
through your body—as if you're standing under a waterfall that
sweeps away all unnecessary tension. Your mind remains fully alert,
your senses engaged, and your body calm.

ICS Step 4: Notice Uniqueness

The fastest way to get trapped in old patterns (overreacting, lashing out at others, feeling victimized) is to instantly identify a new challenge or problem as if it were *just like,* or even worse than, a previous stressful event. Example: *Not again,* you think. Or, *He's or she's always doing that!* You can head off this natural tendency by taking a split second to sidestep old mindsets and reaction patterns and sustain calm energy and heightened mental clarity. In this ICS step, you *notice uniqueness,* that is, you take a conscious moment to identify the *unique* features of this situation or challenge, pinpointing some of the ways it's *different* from anything you've dealt with before.

In this simple and direct way, you bypass the brain's innate, lightning-fast tendency to categorize people and situations by snap judgments and magnified negative presumptions.

ICS Step 5: Shift Your View of Time

This ICS step takes molehills appearing as mountains and turns them back into molehills again. Your view of time plays a key role here. First, *acknowledge reality.*

Far too many of us get tangled up bemoaning every challenge we face. "Not *another* problem! Why does this *always* happen to me?" Or "Well, that blows my day! It's just been one disaster after another." Or "Please—not now! I need more (time, money, energy, rest, experience, . . .) to prepare for this." Or "Oh *no!* Why couldn't I be somewhere—*anywhere*—else right now?"

By wishing the situation weren't happening, regretting you didn't have more time to prepare, wanting to be somewhere else, or anguishing over life's unfairness, you set off a biochemical avalanche of victimizing thoughts and feelings. You actually *help* yourself lose control and get loaded up with anxiety and frustration. When mishandled, a single stressful moment can disrupt an entire day. ICS breaks that pattern. Practice this key thought: *What's happening is real and I'm finding the best possible way to deal with it right now.*

Face Each Challenge with Calm Energy

In large part, what you do with your mind and emotions in the initial moment of a challenge determines the outcome. In the first instant of a crisis, for example, the nervous system reacts—and can choose a panic-paralysis or positive-action response.

If you look back at times in your life when you reacted poorly to situations, it's usually obvious that, had you remained calmer and thought more clearly during the first moments of the crisis (big or small), you could have chosen a better response. That's the key to the ICS—learning to insert that calm energy and clear-mindedness *in precisely the right place* at the very *beginning* of each high-pressure challenge or situation.

This is the place to choose to learn instead of repeating old reactionary habits; to pause for a moment, to listen with an open mind instead of blindly responding; to resolve conflict rather than creating it; to apply your personal golden rule or spiritual philosophy in place of anxiety or anger; to be skilled enough to protect yourself without harming other people; and to think clear, honest thoughts instead of distorted ones.

The idea in this step is to develop powerful mental "radar" that instantly scans each new situation, drawing out all your options for most effectively dealing with it. If you find it especially difficult to keep from overreacting to daily hassles, don't get discouraged. Like millions of us, you've probably had years of practice reacting unproductively.

One final note on this mental control step of the ICS: A number of psychologists and motivational speakers suggest that all you really need is the right mental self-talk to master stressful situations. That's a myth. I am all for positive thinking, but by itself it just isn't enough. In fact, it's all but impossible to think truly positive thoughts when you've halted your breathing, frowned, collapsed your posture, tensed your muscles, and opened the floodgates to negative emotions—all about as fast as you can blink your eye. Try it and you'll see what I mean.

How do you learn to use the ICS? You rehearse it in slow motion, gradually increasing the speed. And you choose to use it every day. Notice I didn't say *try* or *hope*. Choose means bringing the skill to life right now.

First, imagine a stressful situation or moment of adversity. Vividly imagine—*in extra-slow motion*—that this particular tension-producing or pressure-filled situation is just beginning to happen. Stall the stress signal right there. Now picture yourself effortlessly, successfully going through the ICS: (1) continue breathing, (2) lighten your eyes, (3) release tension, (4) notice uniqueness, and (5) shift your view of time.

Now repeat the process, a little faster. Remember, the ICS is a natural, flowing sequence. You unleash it; you don't force it. Practice it a number of times a day, using different stress cues, increasing the vividness of the mental images and the speed of your ICS response. If at first you have difficulty with any of the steps, practice them one at a time until they become comfortable. If you get partway into the ICS and feel yourself starting to lose control, back the sequence up and slow things down. Be absolutely certain that you freeze the image of the stress cue at the first instant— don't let the stressful image keep rolling to the point at which you become tense or anxious.

You are training to automatically slip the ICS into the situation right behind the first signal of stress or tension. This can make all the difference in the world in the outcome. When rehearsing for especially intense situations, you might try lightening the image of the pressure cue (by seeing yourself move farther away from it in your mind or by dulling the vividness of the scene) until you are at ease with using the ICS to handle it.

Be patient with yourself, especially during the first weeks. The really tough stress challenges often require quite a bit of rehearsing before you can handle them with relative ease. Remember, most of us have had years of practice strengthening the bad habits the ICS can replace. If you try an ICS for a difficult challenge and happen to get impatient and revert to an old counterproductive response, take some time later that day to sit down in a quiet place, relax, and replay the beginning of the scene in slow motion in your mind, clearly seeing the ICS succeeding this time. Each time you use it, the sequence will flow more easily and become more automatic.

By using the ICS, with senses alert, breathing steady, posture relaxed yet upright, emotions level, and your mind clear and looking for solutions, you are far better prepared for Part Two of the overall process for bringing out your best in stressful situations. Let's move on to that.

PART TWO: Analysis of Evidence and Alternatives

Here are several questions to consider:

- *Is there proof that I have absolutely no control over what happens next?* Only in rare situations is there a total loss of control. Instead of letting a sense of helplessness sweep over you, in nearly every situation you always have at least some degree of control. Preserving some sense of control helps you make the most of any adversity.

■ *To what degree will this adversity affect other areas of my life or work?* In handling adversity, it really pays to do whatever you can to localize the bad event or limit your perception of its transference to other areas of your life or work. A misunderstanding with another person, or a difficult conversation, is just that, and not automatically a sign that you are a bad person, your career is going down in flames, or your life in falling apart.

Those who don't cope well with adversity tend to argue that any bad event will cause another and another. This is rarely true and can seriously undermine your sense of optimism across the board, rippling from one situation to your life or work in general. The key is to immediately separate your assumptions from the facts. Most adversities *could* reach other areas of your life but they usually don't have to.

■ *How long must this adversity last?* There are often reasons to *imagine* how adversity might last for a long time but there usually isn't much evidence that it *has* to.

Once you have a clearer sense of what actually happened and what your alternatives are, you are ready for Part Three, Action to Be Taken. Let's move on to that.

PART THREE: A̲ction to Be Taken

As Aeschylus observed, "Great spirits meet calamity greatly." When facing adversity, taking action mobilizes positive energy and focus. It limits distractions and negative reactions while raising your ingenuity and vantage point. I have found several action-oriented questions to be very useful:

- *What can I do, however small, to gain some control over this situation and what happens next?* What can you do to better the situation right now, to step forward and do whatever it takes to resolve things in a meaningful way? Such acts of accountability and growth are important here, but be careful not to let self-responsibility turn into a heavy dose of self-blame. It's easy to get trapped feeling helpless or victimized. It's also important to note that avoidance doesn't work either. Those who handle adversity well are not the ones who deflect bad events, blame everyone else but themselves, and learn nothing. In truth, those who make the most of adversity increase their sense of ownership, or accountability. They acknowledge their part of the responsibility and link it to some important element of purpose or learning: "I'll use this adversity to learn how to better manage a personal weakness or bring out more of my strengths." These stress-hardy individuals accept their responsibility in cleaning up the mess and moving forward rather than finger-pointing or blaming or waiting for someone else to take action. We almost always have some small degree of control. Which actions can you take now?

- *What can I do to limit the reach of this adversity into other areas of my life and limit how long it endures?* What additional information do you need so you can take exactly the right actions to contain this? It's good to gather missing facts right away so you can avoid destructive and false assumptions.

When considering action, make certain that the timing is right. Some setbacks and tragedies naturally leave us stunned and grieving. In other difficult situations, we find ourselves with nothing specific we can do right away to move things forward. In these cases, consider the value of using *positive distractions* to help raise your vantage point, help stifle catastrophizing and negative assumptions, and positively change your physiology. (Spacing out in front of the television is usually not a positive distraction; it's simply numbing.) Here are some positive distractions to help this happen:

- *Light activity or exercise.* As noted in Chapter 9, this helps flood the brain with endorphins that raise mood and provide increased resiliency against negative stress. As little as five to ten minutes of light physical activity—a walk outside may be best, or climbing a few flights of stairs, or even pacing back and forth in front of a window—can help shift your physiology toward increased toughness and positive control. Researchers have found that going for walks helps people step back from irritations and detach themselves from feelings of anger or frustration, increasing their empathy for seeing things from other people's viewpoints. Cardiologists have suggested that exercise appears to burn up excess stress chemicals by using them for energy expressed outwardly rather than harming the body internally.
- *Music, light, food, or fluids.* Any of these, or all, may help. Experiment to find what works best for you in renewing your energy and stamina.
- *Talk it through.* For some people, taking with others about facing a difficult situation is a productive pattern of coping with stress and adversity.
- *Re-set your perspective.* Remember your purpose for working or living. Think of what matters most to you, and why you're making the efforts you are, even when adversity

sometimes gets in the way for a while. Nietzsche once observed, "A person with a strong enough *why* can bear almost any *how*." You might also imagine yourself gazing at the stars or standing on the beach at sunrise, or gazing upward from the foot of a huge mountain. When I think back to my travels through Tibet's mountain ranges, it quickly helps to put my "big" current problems right back into proper perspective. You might also recall the person you have known in your life who has lost or suffered the most and still made a positive difference in the lives of others.

- *Write it down.* The act of writing about an experience has been shown to release negative emotions and create heightened ability in dealing with adversity. Here's where you can use your day book or journal as an aid. Research indicates that those who write about traumatic events for 20 minutes a day for four consecutive days have significantly more robust immune systems and report less distress than the people who did no writing.

- *Help someone else.* Empathy has immense—and often immediate—power to help us cope with our own adversity. Go spend a brief time helping someone whose problems are bigger than yours. Spend an evening helping homeless families, or mentally challenged children, or nursing home residents. By doing good for them you are also helping regain your own perspective on moving forward in your own life.

Build Forward

From time to time, life knocks us all down. How fast you get back up, how far ahead you can look, and what you learn during tough times determine how much of your untapped capacity gets revealed.

After Candace Lightner lost her child to a drunk driver, she grieved her tragic loss and then used it as a catalyst for creating a very constructive course of action that has saved countless children and benefited millions of other lives. She started MADD, Mothers Against Drunk Drivers, and helped lobby for legislation that has significantly improved the laws against drunk driving and the vast suffering it has created in every corner of the country.

In one way or another, we all have the opportunity to make adversity our ally and grow stronger from it. Instead of backing away from life's difficult situations, we can learn better ways to meet them and unlock hidden reserves of inner strength and commitment. Looking back years later, we are likely to say, "This was what brought out more of the best in me." As Hemingway put it in *A Farewell to Arms*, "The world breaks every one of us and afterward many are stronger at the broken places."

*A*dversity calls forth the soul's courage
to bear unflinchingly whatever Heaven sends.

—EURIPIDES

22

Bury Your Crystal Ball

John Le Carré, the spy novelist, penned a great line. He said, "A desk is a dangerous place from which to view the world." Whenever we gaze down at our experiences through narrow mindsets or fixed perspectives, it's all too easy to make snap judgments and sweeping presumptions. We think we're applying our inherent smarts or saving time but usually we're doing neither. Few things shut down initiative or relationships faster than assuming we know what's going on. Without asking, we generalize. We categorize. We make one-sided conclusions. Instead of learning, we defend our positions and act all-knowing.

We are not.

It's time to stop the guessing game that ultimately makes our lives miserable. By habit—and, to a degree, by hardwiring of the brain—we are primed to make assumptions about almost everything, especially other people's motives and intentions. Often we assume that others somehow instinctively "know" exactly what we think and, therefore, we don't have to say what we mean, need, or want. Such assumptions create countless misunderstandings that waste time, damage relationships, produce a whole distracting drama that is rarely ever true. They also create persistent stumbling blocks to unlocking human potential.

The truth about other people and life is rarely what we initially assume it to be. If you look back across your life, you may have already realized that your most meaningful relationships and experiences arise when you dig in for what's real instead of settling for what's easy.

According to researchers, one of the fastest, most powerful ways to stimulate creative intelligence and new learning is to first—for a minute or more—focus on the uniqueness in each person and challenge. Doing so bypasses the brain's innate tendency to make *this* person, or *this* challenge, just like another from the past.

Nearly all of us—especially when we're feeling rushed or behind—use our intuition to guess why others appear to be doing or feeling what they are doing or feeling. But this kind of intuition is off-kilter and even dangerous. Over 90 percent of the time, we are wrong. In presuming to know the intentions and motives of others, we trap ourselves.

Observe Yourself from Above

Observation improves with regular practice and a bit of altitude. In many situations, we're so close to what's going on that we can't see the forest for the trees. We don't even realize that we're using a crystal ball or trying to make sense of the world through a magnifying glass.

During the summer when I was eight, I was staying a few days with my grandparents. As he often did, my grandfather Cooper had hired some workers who were newly arrived immigrants, in this case escapees from the terrors in Hungary. Together, we were going to spend the day clearing brush from a hillside near one of the local parks. At the park board's request, my grandfather had volunteered to see that it was accomplished. The men spoke no English.

Because I was grandfather's "official helper," the men kept asking me things. I couldn't understand or answer. When we were taking a break in my grandparents' yard, the workers began repeating themselves more loudly and making forceful gestures, bringing their clenched hands to their faces. It felt as though I was surrounded by shouting giants making fists. Finally, the whole situation overwhelmed me and I covered my ears and looked away.

When my grandfather walked over, he peered into my eyes and then motioned for the workers to step back. He lifted my chin up and then pointed to a nearby oak. "Robert, what if you were up in the branches of that tree watching what was just happening here? What would you have seen?"

"I would've seen yelling men waving their fists."

"And what else?"

"A boy who can't understand them."

"Why?"

"I don't know their words."

"Do people talk just with words? They also talk with their eyes and hands. If you were up in the tree looking down at yourself, what were you doing with your eyes and hands?"

"I looked away and covered my ears."

"What else could you have done?"

"I could have tried harder."

"Or tried *differently*," my grandfather said. "Let me show you what I mean."

He turned and used some simple gestures instead of words as he tried to communicate with the men. First, he raised his palms and gave an inquisitive look: What do you need? The workers said something in Hungarian. A tilt of grandfather's head indicated: I'm not sure what you mean. A louder voice replied but my grandfather stayed very calm and very curious. I watched him slow down his gestures when the tension of the men rose higher. He was confident he could sort this out. He pointed to things: A shovel. A pair of gloves. The door to the porch and bathroom of the small duplex where my grandparents lived. A seedling in a burlap bag at the edge of the driveway. The workers shook their heads, no. An empty pitcher of water on the picnic table. Yes, they nodded, gesturing as if they were drinking water from a glass.

My grandfather smiled and went over to turn on the garden hose, showing the men how to do it, and then filling the pitcher with cold water. "All they wanted was more water to drink," my grandfather said to me as we sat with the men at the picnic table. "The next time you think you're stuck, go back up into that tree and look down at what's happening. You can notice things you might miss down here on the ground."

Don't Assume; Ask and Observe

When trying to understand someone or something in life, it's essential to begin with as few assumptions as possible, to hesitate when presuming to know anything by guesswork about others. Instead, we must ask and observe. One way to keep yourself from making assumptions is to pause when you're about to use guesswork and, instead, to ask questions. Listen intently and communicate with care until you are as clear as possible about what you and others feel about the situation at hand and what you each will commit to doing. Ask for what you want. Encourage others to do the same.

Whenever we experience vague or mixed messages, the brain is primed to instinctively assume the worst. We may presume, for example, that others are selfish and manipulative—and begin to treat them or talk about them that way—even if this isn't true. The best antidote I know is clarity. Avoid settling for murky motives or dangling commitments. Talk to individuals about personal matters "off stage." Ask for their view. Admit what you're uncertain about or need to know. Perceive and demystify. Observe and learn. Such efforts at clarity save time and promote trust.

There is evidence that the number one practical competency of a successful life is empathy. This is the ability to sense what another person feels and to imagine, even for a few moments, "What if I were you?" What if I had your background, experiences, education, responsibilities, difficulties, and dreams—what would it be like? How many of us stop often enough to wonder such things these days? When someone turns away from you in a conversation or meeting, do you tend to automatically assume the action was directed at you, and react accordingly? Unfortunately, when we try to guess another person's motives or intentions, almost always we are wrong.

To understand, we first need to ask and observe. Begin observations by saying, "From my point of view . . ." It's vital to own your feelings and views as your own. "Maybe my intuition's off, but I'm sensing that you're under lots of pressure today . . ." Or "I could be wrong, but I'm sensing that you're quite excited about X but not Y . . ." Once you own your impressions as your own and ask a sincere question, let the other person react: yes, no, or with something specific. This is a respectful way to learn more about someone or engage in a meaningful conversation. It also creates an opportunity for each individual to express distinctive, and perhaps surprising, feelings and opinions.

It is through simple, practical actions such as these that we are again reminded to relate to others one-to-one, and to invite them to learn who we truly are instead of who they may assume we are. Watch what happens.

*W*hen *learning about life and people,*
make no more assumptions than are absolutely necessary.
Ask and observe.
—WILLIAM OF OCCAM, QUODILBETA, C. 1324

23

Develop the Skin of a Rhino and the Soul of an Angel

As a physician and humanitarian, Albert Schweitzer's credo was "reverence for life." Those who worked beside him in his hospital in Lambaréné, Africa, saw him struggle to make this the guiding principle of all that he did. It earned him the Nobel Peace Prize. His credo called for both courage and sensitivity of the highest order, and meant the avoidance of inflicting unnecessary suffering on any living being and the alleviation of suffering with all the medical and human means at his disposal. Through the years, his work touched many people.

Once he was asked, "What does it take to create a life worth leading?" Schweitzer thought about it and answered, "The skin of a rhino and soul of an angel." What a rare yet essential combination that is directly at odds with a society that, in pervasive ways, entices us to smile and schmooze. Hint and pretend. Lie and look away. Feign loyalty and then seize what we want or backstab for our own gain. Such theatrics are a psychic jail so common that most of us don't see that we're in it.

Develop the Skin of a Rhino

A thin skin leads to heightened troubles in life. The thinner the dermis, the less able we are to talk straight or handle self-doubt or criticism from others.

In the opening section of this book, we explored the value of standing out from the crowd and distinguishing yourself through values. In this chapter, let's take that principle a step further, examining why it's necessary to have a thick enough skin to meet the barbs and arrows of life while having the courage to say what you mean and mean what you say, even when others don't like it. As Walt Whitman observed, "Have you learned lessons only of those who admired you, and were tender with you, and stood aside for you? Have you not learned great lessons from those who braced themselves against you, and disputed the passage with you?" In this regard here are some insights that I have found useful:

- *Don't take things personally; someone's always going to be mad at you and that's okay.* What other people convey—in what they think, feel, say, and do—is rarely about you; instead, it's almost always about them. No two individuals ever see the world, or react to life, in the same way. If you take things too personally, you're destined for needless suffering at the hands of those who believe they can feel good only when their words or actions make someone else feel bad. There's no point in hitching your self-esteem to the fickle whims of others. Cut the cord. Practice standing a bit apart and on your own two feet. Know your own heart and keep your own word. Don't gossip about others. Don't waste time trying to please them, either. Let your life speak.

- *Design your own template for giving the most effective feedback.* Start from scratch. If you were to teach a young person how to give or receive the most effective feedback, what would the essentials be? When I work with leaders, I encourage them to put it in writing and then reflect on it. Important considerations might include such things as setting the context ("Here's why I believe these comments matter . . ."); choosing a good time and private setting to deliver the feedback; being clear, specific, and caring; emphasizing the other person's strengths and the degree of fit between talents and roles; identifying weaknesses and working together to manage them out of the way; setting next steps for follow-through. Putting pen to paper to create a personal template for feedback prompts each of us to give such important interactions the care they deserve.

Flaw-finding is the most dominant approach to giving feedback or criticism. This helps explain why people experience criticism as a disturbing, negative encounter that feels like a personal attack. Deep down, we each feel one-of-a-kind and need to be recognized for it. We loathe critical remarks from people who know us little, if at all. Yet every day millions of people grin and bear it, enduring critical remarks from others with rank or title but little if any knowledge of who they are, leaving them seething inside yet struggling to smile and say something inane like, "Thank you so much for the feedback." Yet what we really feel is, "How dare you! You have no idea who I am or what

I'm capable of." What we fail to notice when we point out weaknesses in others is that motivation is primarily intrinsic; it must come from within a person. We cannot force it from outside.

When fielding criticism from others, decide if this feedback is based on genuine concern and support for your well-being and advancement. If it is, consider it with care. What are the threads of truth here?

If not, ask yourself, Is this criticism given from a place of jealousy, envy, or politics? If it is, then acknowledge hearing it but don't internalize it. The old axiom, "If the shoe fits, wear it. If not, throw it away . . ." applies here. Few good things ever happen from letting others take unwarranted potshots at your inner confidence.

■ *Talk straighter than you have to.* Society conditions us to approach life more as theatrics than truth-telling. But lying not only stresses people, it also kills them. In building trusting relationships, one of the most important things is putting your money where your mouth is. If you believe in something, do it, don't just say it.

In real dialogue there are twists and turns and surprises. Yet one of the surest pitfalls is the use of happy talk. "Things are fine here," we say. "Nothing to worry about." Or we spread rumors or "troubles talk" in hopes of protecting or preserving the status quo. Looking away from reality, we shade things. We feign ignorance. We defend or deceive. We pretend life's fine, even when it isn't and we're feeling embattled or lost. These are poison, plain and simple. Whatever we're trying to ignore or smooth over—or sabotage—is likely going to get bigger.

The aspect of lying that is most destructive is withholding: keeping back information from someone we believe may be adversely affected by it. Go out of your way to stop hiding things. Adolescents waste lots of time playing this game. But the more we continue with this hide-and-seek in adulthood, the more we become trapped by it, losing time and energy trying to conceal things. Free yourself.

First, get better at revealing the facts as you perceive them. Catch yourself concealing the truth and stop innocent lies and the false presentation of yourself that you may be trying to maintain by withholding. Keep clarifying.

Second, get more honest about your current thoughts and feelings. Yes there are times to be reticent. But observe the truth more closely in yourself, and talk more honestly to others than you might have in the past. This is where you can share more openly, as life happens, without the usual barriers and rehearsals. It elicits greater trust from others. Besides, there's no faking honesty. Either you're honest about your own perception of truth or you're not, even when others may not like it. I remember how Thoreau was ever exploring honesty and Emerson admired him for it, saying, "I ought to go upright and vital, too, and do all I can to speak the straight truth."

■ *Stop trying to "fix" anyone else or "take care of" their struggles—it's not your job.* There are two typical patterns in relationships:

1. *Taking care of others.* The premise here is that the way to build good relationships is to make people feel comfortable and satisfied and avoid disagreements or friction at all costs. This stymies growth by producing an

environment of masks and motion and, even worse, spawning a sense of entitlement and dependency. It inadvertently interferes with individual accountability and often creates a demeaning and angry undertone beneath the exterior pleasantries. All too often such surface coating fuels denial of problems and avoidance of difficult choices and defining moments.

2. *Caring about others.* This approach encourages accountability and growth. It requires honesty and detachment backed by caring *about* others but refusing to become their caretaker. By challenging existing attitudes and behaviors, you stimulate healthy development in others. By being unwilling to sweep difficult issues under the rug, you demonstrate that you are willing to invest the time and energy to tackle tough issues that you could easily have avoided. You give room for each individual to take responsibility for shaping solutions rather than trying to impose your own problem-solving habits on others.

- *Own your impressions and feelings as your own.* "I could be wrong. Here's my view of this . . . What's yours?" "From where I am, here are my feelings and concerns . . . What are yours?"

  It also pays to readily acknowledge others' points, whether you agree with them or not:

  "I can see that you feel very strongly about this."

  "I've never thought about it that way."

  "I hear what you're saying."

- *Choose truth over harmony.* Constructive conflict is a rich, complex experience that stimulates creative thinking, involves our interests and goals, and challenges us to grow. We must raise our children to distrust rigid explanations and ask why or why not. Among our most common mistakes: We tell our children that they must sit still and pretend to be interested even when they're not, that they must get good grades if they're going to be successful in life, and that if they don't have anything nice to say, they should not say anything at all. Nonsense. There are mountains of evidence showing these old rules are not true. Encouraging a more curious and independent spirit in ourselves and those around us is certainly not the way to make life easier, but it's the way to keep each of us looking deeper for what matters most and is most true.

Seeking the truth—or a true way to face and solve a difficult situation—almost always matters more than preserving harmony. In the long run, this effort toward honesty saves time and energy and livens up everyday life. It helps clarify and streamline efforts.

By the way, when I refer to truth I don't mean *the* truth, I mean *your* truth. We all see the world differently. When you search for truth in yourself and others and get ready to express yourself, don't confront, convey. In nearly every situation, avoidance is not good and confrontation is not necessary. The most important thing is to be yourself and be heard. On occasion, we must take risks with our voice and views, even when we're certain to anger others. Time these moments with care. That's because we must also know how to balance speaking up with exceptional listening skills, practicing constraint and calmness in certain volatile situations to avoid being seen as merely a nuisance.

- *Ban gossip, beginning with you.* Who among us doesn't complain about gossip? But then why do nearly all of us contribute to it from time to time? When you hear yourself or others talking about individuals who are not present, pay careful attention. If not, you're almost always headed for trouble. Be ready to end your own involvement with gossip by saying, "I'd like to not talk about anyone who's not here. I'm concerned we're making faulty assumptions. If we have a concern about another person's motives or intentions, I want to ask him directly before we talk about it."

Go out of your way to be decent and fair and insist that others act accordingly in your presence. Remember that second- and third-hand impressions have little value but vast potential for harm. Do not tell or laugh at any hurtful joke—racial, ethnic, religious, age, ability, or gender-related—or any other practice that demeans another human being. To say afterwards, "Just kidding," doesn't abate the hurt. It is only through daily acts of moral courage that we can counter such attitudes and behaviors.

Develop the Soul of an Angel

Throughout history, the great prophets and saints in virtually every culture have spoken of angels. They are sought for encouragement or advice during difficult times. They are drawn to laughter and beauty and are summoned to shield us from harm. People who claim to have seen angels are rare, yet angels inspire some of our noblest aspirations. They are bright lights in our world, often likened to invisible friends watching over us but rarely interfering or intervening. They transcend the usual physical limitations of our everyday existence.

We speak of angel investors as those who are first to see, and courageously fund, the promise of a new idea or venture. When describing people who go out of their way to protect others, we call them guardian angels or angels in the workplace. Mother Teresa was called both a living saint and an angel of mercy. She professed to being neither, yet touched the world in much the way that an angel might. New research indicates that many of the individuals who make the greatest difference in the world combine the paradoxical qualities of personal humility and unwavering resolve to do what is right; personal accountability when times are hard and a great willingness to credit others when things go well. When Dr. Schweitzer talked of developing the "soul of an angel," I believe he meant it in unsentimental and very practical terms. Consider the following:

- *Angels don't worry about you, they believe in you.* According to legend, angels don't get trapped in the worries that plague our world. Instead, they remind us why we're here and help us sense our own hidden possibilities. Even the smallest effort to apply some aspect of the soul of an angel can lift us out of our everyday limitations. In what ways do you help others sense their own possibilities?

- *Angels don't try to fix everything or take away life's lessons.* Angels are believed to possess amazing detachment. They wait patiently nearby, observing the lessons being learned. They aren't interested in giving us an easy way out. They watch over our learning—or resistance to learning—and only rarely interfere or intervene. They quietly guard the space around us so that we can better focus on making learning happen. They may plant a thoughtful question or kind reminder. From time to time, they inspire us to shift our gaze or give us a needed nudge in a new direction. When we stop trying to make everything all right for others and, instead, can stand back a step and encourage their own growth, we may have found another small thread of the soul of an angel.

- *No matter what their size, angels are large in spirit.* As the legends have it, many angels are young at heart yet wise. They are unabashed about letting us see what we need to grow. They know when to choose being kind over being correct, and when to remain detached from our own necessary, and sometimes difficult, learning.

- *Angels take the high road.* Like the best mentors and teachers, angels are unwilling to leave anyone behind. They encourage both planned and spontaneous acts of goodness and generosity.

One of the ways you might make this concept practical is by pausing during interactions to consider how you aid others: Do you have the soul of an angel in helping to bring out the best in them? If not, why not? Maybe we've been assuming that the soul of an angel is out of our reach. Maybe we're wrong. Perhaps it is right here, and has been all along, and we've been too busy or distracted to see it.

You might keep a page in your day book with two headings: "Angelic things I have done" and "Angels I have encountered."

Schweitzer came to believe that from moment to moment we can choose a different way of living: we can choose to be more angelic. As he worked hard to prove by example in his own life, some of the things that are said of angels may one day be said about you.

. . . he allowed himself to be swayed by his conviction
that human beings are not born once and for all
on the day their mothers give birth to them,
but that life obliges them over and over again
to give birth to themselves.

—GABRIEL GARCÍA MÁRQUEZ,
Love in the Time of Cholera

24

Keep Challenging Your Edges

It's an ancient truth that those who risk the least usually live the least. At times, risk is daunting and even dangerous. It many cases, however, it is also necessary. Without first-hand knowledge of hardship, prosperity is forever hollow. Only through direct experience of loss and sadness can love and joy become rich and meaningful. In many aspects of life, the biggest risk is not to risk at all.

Discretionary, or optional, risks may be relatively small, such as having an important but uncomfortable conversation with someone close to you, raising your hand to speak up in a public forum, or testing a new way of working or exercising. Or they may be something big, such as changing jobs, following your heart after facing a major setback, standing without blinking in the midst of the pain and discomfort of a struggling relationship while trying to learn from it, visiting a distant and unknown land, or starting toward a new summit.

Climb a Different Mountain: Your Own

A story I know goes like this: Early one autumn, a group of well-equipped and experienced Western climbers prepared to ascend an old mountain in Tibet. Poring over their maps and memorizing an old, well-used route up the slope, they were leaving nothing to chance. An hour earlier, they had watched a trio of others—an elder, a young man, and a young woman—set off for the peak, climbing with different techniques up differing routes. "Amateurs, obviously," thought the leader of the Western climbers.

The Western climbers ascended with exacting technical skill—just the way they had climbed other inclines. By the book. No room for divergence here. The younger ones mimicked the older ones, following their lead and copying their moves. Consistency of style was the mark of greatness, maintained the technical experts.

However, the higher the climbers went, the less the mapped route seemed to work. The mountain was unlike any other; it seemed to be alive, ever-changing. Handholds gave way. Grips melted. Solid-looking rocks crumbled. Rope anchors failed. Ice axes proved to be of little aid. Footholds vanished. Despite competitive experience, a proven map, and expensive technical gear, the climbers grew tense and anxious. Cursing filled the air. It took them until dusk to reach the summit. Exhausted and fuming, they pitched camp.

It was then that members of the expedition noticed the elder sitting beside a small fire not far away. He was sharing stories and laughter with his climbing partners, the young man and his sister. They appeared rested and relaxed, preparing themselves to retire to their bivouacs for the night. It had taken them just over four hours to reach the summit. They had spent the afternoon taking in the view from various overlooks, reflecting on what each of them had learned during the ascent.

"It's as if you climbed a different mountain!" exclaimed the guide in charge of the second group. He was incredulous that these three—with outdated gear and no fame—made it look so easy.

The elder gazed at him with curiosity and then smiled. "You are right."

"What?" snapped the guide.

"We climbed a different mountain," said the elder, who had found his own route up the rock face. "A mountain is big or small not because of its height in the sky but because of what each person brings to the climb."

He was right. The old route is not always the best or fastest. Conditions change. Memorizing an approach or carrying an old map may prove to be of little help.

A Leap Sideways and Beyond

I recall Kierkegaard's story of the lone journeyer who arrived in a village in the hill country only to find the road ahead was blocked by a mountain. Tired and dismayed, he sat down and waited for the mountain to move. Years later, he was sitting in the same place, old and decrepit, still waiting. The essence of Kierkegaard's message is that providence doesn't move mountains. It is we who must *climb* them or find a route around them. If we are waiting for the mountain to move or approaching it the same old way as everyone else, then we're lost, whether we realize it or not.

From time to time we must summon something more: a willingness to challenge our edges, as climbers call them—the boundaries of our past skill and confidence. When you challenge your edges, you reach deeper, see farther, and unlock added ingenuity in preparing yourself for what happens next. Tiny steps, one after another and all in a line, may not get us very far. There are times when we must choose what Nietzsche called "a leap sideways and beyond." If not, the brain is primed to react in ever-narrowing old ways, suspending curiosity and growth.

Years ago, I lost almost everything I owned in a fire. Among the things that survived were two of the keepsakes I treasured. The first was a small piece of porcelain artwork from my mother with an inscription that said in Spanish, *La necesidad enseña más que la universidad:* Necessity teaches more than the university. A small book also survived the fire. It was a gift from my grandfather Cooper, a story written in 1921 by Peter Kyne called *The Go-Getter.* It describes a soldier who lost an arm and part of a leg in the First World War yet used those losses as the impetus to care more, do more, and create more than he ever would have done before. From time to time, I pull out that little book to remind myself to keep taking new risks because life is so short.

Not long ago I had the opportunity to talk with Jim Stockdale. Vice-Admiral Stockdale won the Congressional Medal of Honor and twenty-six military combat decorations. I was introduced to him by his son, a school principal in Pennsylvania.

Admiral Stockdale was a fighter pilot aboard an aircraft carrier. On his second combat tour, he was shot down over North Vietnam. As senior naval prisoner of war, he was tortured fifteen times, put in leg irons for two years, and placed in solitary confinement for four years. His writings since then have all focused on how individuals can rise with spirit and dignity to face adversity.

He talked with me about all the years of his training prior to being shot down. He knew everything, all the facts about survival.

He knew which survival knife to strap to his pilot's vest. What radio to take, what boots to wear, what food to bring. And then his plane went down and his leg was broken and he was captured. They took it all away from him. The vest, knife, boots, food, radio. Everything.

Except one thing. It was not what he had on his survival vest, it was what was *inside* him that made the difference. His inner capacity. His practiced skill in taking risks. Deep within him, he had awakened the spirit of looking forward, upward, outward, and onward.

Here are several considerations for deepening or expanding such qualities in yourself:

- *Get better at listening to your own drummer.* You and I were born originals yet we live in a world that seems bent on doing everything it can to make us copies of someone else from Main Street, Hollywood, or Wall Street. Ultimately it won't work. As Thoreau observed, "If a man does not keep pace with his companions, perhaps it is because he hears a different drummer. Let him step to the music which he hears, however measured or far away."

- *Make unreasonable requests of yourself.* Abraham Maslow observed that many of us "tend to evade personal growth because this . . . can bring a kind of fear, of awe . . . And so we find another kind of resistance, a denying of our best side, of our talents, of our finest impulses, of our highest potentialities, of our creativeness." Therefore, make it a point to keep stirring things up. Alter routines. Break some old habits. Turn over a new leaf. Cultivate the spirit of looking forward, upward, outward, and onward.

For much of our lives we repeat old habits and reactions. Parts of our daily routine have been repeated thousands of times. They are imbedded and ingrained. This leaves us rigidly conditioned to think and behave only in a certain way. But isn't this your personality? Perhaps some part of it once was. Now it's fossilized. The challenge is to increase your awareness enough that, whenever you're primed to launch into an old reaction, instead you can pause and deliberately change the pattern. Think differently. Care more. Try something new. Grow more, learn more. In what situation or part of your life could you apply this right now?

- *Remember how much fun it was to discover things when you were a kid.* Whatever happened to your most adventurous spirit? The one you had at shining moments as a child. Think about it. Kids aren't bashful about getting their hands dirty. They eat toothpaste. They color anywhere they want, way outside the lines. They turn their bicycles into rocket ships. They make mistakes. They fall off the wall after climbing most of the way up. They laugh out loud and don't care who's listening. They think wild thoughts. They take things apart just to see how they work, for the sheer fun of it and the pleasure of finding out more about how the world ticks. All these things are part of what Richard Feynman referred to as "the kick in the discovery." Since the beginning of time they have incited growth in people. At their best, kids take lots of risks and have bundles of fun, starting with the impossible, which is usually where adults stop altogether.

- *Push past current habits, hobbies, and hopes.* Start anywhere. Pick something you now do, dabble at, or dream about. Zero in on the edges of it. How can you build on it, reinvent it, or enjoy it more? Can you skip it altogether? Investigate. Shed some light on why you're holding so tight to one view or one way of coming at it. Ask, What else—however small—might I try right now to deepen or expand my insights, skills, or fun in pursuing this habit, hobby, or hope? Then do it. See what happens.

- *Say no to the drug of gradualness.* It was Martin Luther King, Jr., who spoke out strongly against making slow changes. Either we risk or we don't, he said. Either we change or we don't. There is no acceptable middle ground because it lulls us into complacency. Lasting changes rarely occur when we ease our way into the future. They come when we leap. The leaps themselves can be small or large. Once we take action, we see things differently and for many of us there's no going back.

- *When you find a back door that's open, close it.* One of the common barriers to change is having an easy way out, or what I call a back door. When a child can work one parent against the other to get his way, that's having a back door. Why change behavior when you don't actually have to? When you can dabble on the rim of a new risk but never have to commit or take responsibility or be accountable, it's like putting your toe in the pool and calling it swimming. When you challenge your edges, by all means go ahead and get good instruction where you must—but take the plunge. When the back door is open, true learning rarely happens. So close it.

- *Use the rocking chair image.* Whenever he would notice that I was balking at taking some relatively small risk, my grandfather

Cooper used to say, "Robert, imagine you are 95 years old and sitting in a rocking chair looking back across your life. How would you want others to remember you: for ignoring or accepting what's in front of you right now, today?" Do you have the guts to keep challenging your edges? The courage and attitude of others is constantly being influenced by the example of those around them. That would be by you and me. The buck stops with us.

John F. Kennedy loved to tell the story of little boys in Ireland who would throw their favorite hat over the fence just so they'd have to climb over to chase it. We need to get better at throwing our hats over the fence of life and chasing after them.

The way to your dreams can only be found
with one foot in eternity and the other on shaky ground.
　　　　　—RICK TARQUINIO, "One Foot in Eternity"

25

Care as If Everything Depends on Your Caring

My grandfather Cooper attended more funerals than most people do. In a lakeside town less than an hour's drive from Minneapolis, he served as a minister between 1910 and 1920. It was during this time, he said to me, that one funeral stood out from all the rest.

The death of Thomas VanCarlton was announced in every local newspaper within a hundred mile radius. My grandfather officiated. And no one came.

VanCarlton had become wealthy; he was a towering and dapper figure; everyone in town knew him, as did many of the well-to-do in Minneapolis, St. Paul, and Duluth. He held impressive positions on the board of the local bank and for several years he had been a member of the congregation at my grandfather's church. Yet my grandfather knew almost nothing about him.

VanCarlton owned extensive properties. He was a painstaking organizer. He had even planned his own funeral in advance, drafting the announcement for the papers, selecting his gravesite and choosing an immense carved-walnut casket and ornate marble headstone. He prepaid for a hundred years of having fresh flowers placed at his grave every week by the cemetery caretaker. It turned out that no one else would have placed those flowers, because through the years VanCarlton had alienated every one of his relatives, associates, employees, and neighbors.

When I was a boy, this story puzzled me. "If Mr. VanCarlton was well-known and successful, grandfather, why didn't anyone come to his funeral?"

"He pretended he cared about others, but he didn't. He cared only about himself. Because of that, no one cared enough to pay tribute to his life when he was dead."

At the funeral service, my grandfather read the obligatory words to an empty room. The funeral director and hearse driver sat alone in the adjoining family room. No one walked through the doorway with a ribbon of mourning. No one shared memories of this man's life, signed the empty guest register, lit a memorial candle, or sang a hymn of blessing. No one grieved or wept for Thomas VanCarlton.

My grandfather paid some young men out of his own pocket to serve as pallbearers. At the cemetery, the hearse driver had been standing not far away, watching the ceremony draw to a close. The casket had been lowered into the grave and the earth was shoveled in. My grandfather turned to leave. As he walked back toward the cemetery entrance, he looked back to see the man at the hearse reach into his driver's window and pull out one of the flowers from the perfunctory funeral bouquet on the front seat.

The hearse driver walked slowly over to VanCarlton's grave. He held the flower in the air for a moment, saying something my grandfather could not hear, and then gently placed the bright bloom at the base of the headstone and walked away.

My grandfather said this man taught him a great lesson. This man who drove the funeral hearse to the cemetery almost every day found it unimaginable that no one had come to the funeral. He decided that he should care as if everything depended on his caring and no one else's. He was willing to care more than he had to. As Abraham Heschel put it, "We may not all be equally guilty of not caring, but we're all equally responsible for working to create a decent and just world."

What Comes from the Heart Goes to the Heart

According to the fourteenth-century scholar Rumi, the ultimate goal in life is not a grand monument or an eloquent epitaph but to live on in the hearts of those still alive. To accomplish this, our reverence for life and for the lives of others needs to be appropriately out of whack.

Martin Luther King, Jr., said, "We are caught in an inescapable network of mutuality, tied to a single garment of destiny." Every human being is a thread in this garment of destiny. Yet in many neighborhoods and workplaces it has become every person for himself or herself. Caring takes a back seat to getting more and pushing harder, no matter what the cost.

It's not enough to merely speak out against such behaviors; we must also counter them by example. My parents' and grandparents' attitude toward life was that it involves obligations of sincere concern and compassionate action for those less fortunate than we are. In countless ways, they demonstrated this to me.

When in doubt, we must care more, not less. "What comes from the heart goes to the heart," Samuel Coleridge wrote. Care more than you have to; it matters from one human being to another. Be slower to judge. Be quicker to look deeper to sense the goodness in others. Engage in what Wordsworth called "small, nameless, unremembered acts of kindness and love." Live so that when children think of compassion, courage, and caring, they think of you.

I have found the following considerations to be valuable:

■ *Look deeper than usual to affirm that the spark of Life can shine even in the most unpromising people and places.* Over the past decade, one of my points of reference has been Hikari Oe, the most popular classical composer of our day who was born with a medical deformity so severe that his parents had to fight to keep him alive. He arrived in life with a herniated brain: in essence with two heads. The doctors recommended letting him die. If his parents elected for him to have the risky operation to correct his condition, he would surely be profoundly disfigured and developmentally disabled: an outcast according to customs that still prevailed in Japan. Against everyone's advice, the parents elected to proceed with the operation. They named their little boy Hikari, which means "light."

He lived, but he was severely disfigured and developmentally disabled. Now in his thirties, he has an IQ of 65, but an amazing thing happened when he was five: Hikari demonstrated an ability to compose music like a young Mozart or Chopin.

He has been a beacon of inspiration. He has miraculous musical gifts, including a phenomenal memory and the ability to compose chamber works that have broken sales records and delighted untold numbers of people around the world. His father, Kenzaburo Oe, whose boundless love for his son has led to writing many essays and novels about his experiences, was awarded the Nobel Prize for Literature in 1994.

The Supreme Court Justice Oliver Wendell Holmes, Jr., said, "Most of us go to our graves with our music still inside us, unplayed." For Hikari Oe that could have been literally true. We all benefit because his parents acted as if everything depended on their caring, and they chose to take the chance to give him a life instead of letting him die.

■ *Care for what you treasure and give away the rest.* I remember a small piece of wisdom from a story my grandmother Downing once told me about the final days of an aunt I never knew. When my mother's sister, Helen Downing, was eight years old, she came down with measles. Before long, the measles turned into spinal meningitis. This little girl had brought a glow to people's hearts wherever she went. There was an outpouring of sympathy for Helen and her parents—my grandparents.

The neighbors knew that Helen loved dolls and they sent her more of them, dozens more. Although she played with them for a few days, she soon stopped playing with them altogether. Not many days before Helen died at the Mayo Clinic, my grandmother noticed that her youngest daughter snuggled only a single doll, one of her own that was marred and ragged from the years she had carried it and kept it beside her.

My grandmother pointed to the other beautiful dolls piled along the side of the bed and said, "What's the matter, don't you like them?"

Helen looked up and said, "Momma, I don't know how to love that many dolls. Can we please give them away to other children who can love them?"

■ *Remember your mortality.* Philosophers have long said that it is only when we face our own death that we become truly alive. When your grandparents, parents, or others dear to you have died, do you take your children and friends to the cemetery? Such visits don't have to be sad or melancholy.

Go on a bright and sunny day with a gentle breeze in the air. Recall stories of your family—especially those that bring both tears and smiles. Such times can be filled with remembrance and tribute—to the gifts and imperfections and, above all, the love of these people from the past whose lives have touched your own. It is here that we may glimpse some of their legacy and a bit more of our own destiny.

■ *Care more than you have to.* "What you can do in response to the ocean of suffering may seem insignificant," said Gandhi, "but it is very important that you do it." Consider the following wish expressed by a schoolteacher:

> Let's say a prayer and accept responsibility for those children who like to be tickled and eat Popsicles before supper and can never find their shoes; but let's also commit to praying and advocating for those children who can't bound down the street in a new pair of sneakers, who never get dessert, are not spoiled by anyone, go to bed hungry, who don't have any rooms to clean up, whose pictures aren't on anybody's dressers or refrigerators, who will grab the hand of anyone kind enough to offer it, who cry themselves to sleep, and whose monsters are real.

What more can we do—you and I—to see that no child is left behind?

■ *When making decisions, ask ethical caring questions:*

> If someone did this to you, would you think it was fair?
>
> Would you be comfortable if this were to appear on the front page of your hometown newspaper?
>
> Would you like your parents to see you do this?

- *Keep taking actions confirming that you care.* Gandhi said, "You must *be* the change you wish to see in the world." When you care, show it. Edward Abbey warned, "Sentiment without action is the ruin of the soul." Don't just tell others that you care more than the minimum daily requirement—demonstrate it . . . again and again.

  Most lasting changes are brought about not by intellectual musings but by small yet bold gestures that keep confirming that you care. Rosa Parks refusing to give up her seat on the bus. That lone dissident student facing a line of tanks in Tiananmen Square. The first bricks in the Berlin Wall coming down. A hand reaching out to help someone struggling with a bag of groceries or a heavy door. A driver waving you through a four-way stop even though it was his turn to go. A child stepping forward to hand a cookie or soda to a homeless person on the street. Only by clear, committed actions, however small, can we overcome feelings of cynicism and indifference.

- *Use the lanterns of your life to help light your way.* We can all draw upon examples to remind ourselves of what happens when caring is made visible:

  - *How would you describe the most exceptional mentor or teacher who helped shape what you have become?* These are people who gave a piece of their life to you. Perhaps they saw a possibility in you and held you to it. What was it like to spend time with this mentor or teacher? If they could be with you today, what would you say to them? How could you repay them? If asked, they would probably say, "Pass it on." In that spirit of caring, look back at the past month of your life: Exactly how many minutes of your own time have you been this kind of mentor or teacher to others? The most common answer I hear is "None."

- *If tomorrow you lost the person you love most, how would your life and work change?* Woven into our everyday experiences are poignant and powerful reminders that life is fragile and fleeting. Over the past several generations my family has experienced the deaths of children, and the loss of other family members to diseases, wars, and other tragedies. I have learned how easy it is to take others for granted, even those we love. How convenient to say, "I'll be there for you later"; "I'll make it up to you later"; or "I'll show you how much I love you, later." Yet in a heartbeat, later can get taken away.

  My own life has brought another kind of experience: I got part of my family back at the very last moment. Seven and a half years ago, when my wife, Leslie, was pregnant with our youngest child, Shanna, she came down with a rare illness that suddenly threatened her own life and that of the little girl that was several months old inside her. Fifty years ago not one mother or child survived this ailment. But because this happened seven and a half years ago, Leslie and Shanna survived. Every morning since then I pause to look in their eyes and this is what I feel inside: "I am receiving one more gift: I have you in my life for another day."

- *If you had $20 million and not more than five years left to live, what would you stop doing and start doing?* Over the past decade, I have made it a point at least once every month to take out a blank piece of paper. Across the top I write two things: first, some imaginary amount of money—$20 million, for example—and second, five years to live. The premise is that no matter what I do, I will not live one day past five years from today, and I also have more money than I could imagine, so money's not an issue. If those things were true, then looking at my life the past month and looking ahead to next month, what would I stop doing and what would I start doing? For many years I have tried to live as if this were true. As a result, I have stopped doing a number of things I was efficient at doing but would choose not to do under these circumstances. And I've started doing things that matter much more to me and to my loved ones. It reminds me how much I gain every time I care more than I have to about people and life.

At the end of Dante's *Comedy,* he shares a hard-won vision that "the scattered leaves of all the universe" are gathered inward and drawn together by the invisible force of the "love which moves the sun and the other stars." Each of us can discover new ways to make such caring more visible in our lives.

On the surface, I am an average person,
but to my heart I am not an average person.
To my heart, I am a great moment.
The challenge I face is how to dedicate everything I have
*   inside me*
to fulfilling this moment.

—ABRAHAM HESCHEL, 1965

26

Raise a Banner Where a Banner Never Flew

"Take the trail to where it ends, and then go on from there," my grandfather Cooper would say to me when we hiked together on the hillsides or in the woods. At first, I doubted him. Where there was no trail, every step was an act of faith in crossing from the known to the unknown. One way or another we must come to see that the next frontier is not only in front of us, it's also inside us. "That's what your ancestors did, Robert," my grandfather said. "They found the courage inside to cross an unknown sea and shape an unseen future, and what they dreamed and did still touches our lives today."

Each of us is born with a unique potential that defines a destiny. We are given the chance to do what no one has ever done before and to leave our own distinctive mark on the world before we die. Few of us ever glimpse this hidden, one-of-a-kind capability or consciously choose to shape it.

What Will Be Your Unique Imprint on the World?

When I was a boy I spent time after school playing baseball during warm weather. One day during practice I quit early. "I just don't really like it," I said to my grandfather Cooper after I walked from the schoolyard to his house before heading home.

I can still see the expression in his eyes as he wondered to himself whether he should force me to go back and keep practicing. I had obviously had my fill of playing catch and running the bases. Of course, he could give me a lecture on the importance of practice, practice, practice. But would that inspire me or make me more defensive than he sensed I already was?

He motioned for me to follow him into the small, dusty storage building along the driveway to my grandparents' house. He stepped into the shadows and reached up to a high shelf, retrieving what I saw was a dusty baseball glove.

It looked odd—small, thick-fingered, and darkened with age. The only time I had ever seen a glove like that was in sepia photographs in baseball history books. It was the kind of glove you'd expect to find in the Hall of Fame next to a picture of baseball founder Abner Doubleday—not tucked on a shelf in a darkened storage building.

With his handkerchief, my grandfather gently cleaned off the glove and handed it to me. I gazed at the leathery relic and stepped back to the brightness of the doorway so I could examine it. I turned the glove this way and that in my hand as my grandfather explained that it had belonged to his younger brother, Will. As a young man growing up in the 1890s and early 1900s, Will had been an enthusiast of the newly created game of baseball.

I was puzzled. Knowing that my grandfather had an innate dislike for "quitters," I braced for the expected lecture on the value of perseverance and tenacity. Instead, he said nothing and simply watched me holding his brother's glove.

"Try it on," he said.

I slid my hand inside. My fingers were too small to fit snugly. Will, after all, had probably been twice my age when he wore this glove. Even though it was a loose fit, I could feel the deep and distinct impression of a young man's hand in the leather.

"It doesn't fit me," I said.

"That's because with any baseball glove, you have to shape it to fit your own hand," my grandfather said.

He explained that Will's coach had instructed him with great care on how to break in the glove, and he had followed the instructions to the letter. He had soaked it in leather oil, then worked it by hand, leaving it wrapped tightly around a baseball at night beside his pillow. Through innumerable practices and games, the finger pads and pocket of the glove had taken on the exact shape of his fingers and palm.

"You are touching Will's hand," my grandfather said. "This game was one of his greatest loves. In our small town, he taught young children how to play. When Will died, I kept his glove. When I slide my hand inside, I can still feel the shape of his hand, a memory of the trace he left on me and on everyone around him. Robert, I am wondering: What will be your unique imprint on the world?"

Inside the glove, my fingers tingled. For a few moments it was as if Will's hand, the hand that had created these indentations, was alive here, even in memory, after all these years.

Just then, it was more than an old leather baseball glove. It was the mark, or very essence, of another person's life, across time and space.

"Robert, you know you don't have to keep playing baseball," said my grandfather. "There are many other pursuits in your life that you already seem to love more than this game. You must keep learning what you're most drawn to do—and then follow these things with energy and commitment. But before you say goodbye to baseball, I want you to carefully remember the shape of Will's hand. Whenever you do something, you have the chance, like Will did, to leave it better in some way and to leave a mark on its memory."

With the afternoon light shining through the doorway, my grandfather turned and walked away from the storage building, leaving me with the old baseball glove of his younger brother who died long ago.

We are each given the chance to leave a unique imprint on the world. What will be yours?

Become a Relentless Architect of the Untapped Possibilities of Human Beings

As the years go by, I find myself paying less and less attention to what people say or think or wish. Instead, I notice what they do, what I feel from them, and what they are working to become.

Aristotle said, "Time does not exist except for change." The origin of the word *change* is the Old English cambium, which means "to become." In other words, time does not exist except for becoming something new. What, exactly, are you choosing to become? Day after day, each of the body's trillions of cells is measurably changed, influenced by your choices or failure to choose. Similarly, throughout your lifetime virtually every aspect of your brain is open to development but only if, by your attitude and actions, *you* are open to development.

But what do we teach our children in school? Essentially the same things we were taught: That one and one is two, and that Athens is the capital of Greece. When do we teach them what we had to struggle so hard to recognize about ourselves: that they are unique and possess enormous capacity, most of it hidden? In the millions of years on earth there has never been another person exactly like them—or you or me. And never will be again. If the schools won't teach this to our children, then we must. Once we realize what's at stake, it becomes evident that the highest reward from school or work is not what we get for it but what we become by it.

Your Path Has a Purpose Beyond Where It Leads

In my hands is a small leather pocket folio my grandfather Downing carried through medical school, residency, and the early years of his surgical practice. There are indentations along the edges from all the times he held it in his left hand as he jotted on the notepaper with his right. Inside are some of the messages he wrote. Neat, clear lines. Just the way he messages to me about what he believed mattered the most. Every pen stroke was deliberate, in his distinctive hand. There are few possessions that I have from him and this small, frayed folio is the one I treasure most of all—the touch of a simple piece of leather shaped over time by his hand. In its own small way it reminds me of his mark on the world. He was here.

All these years later I still remember. Whenever I write a note or hear someone tell me about a second chance at life or when I pass a farm and send a silent prayer for good weather and healthy crops or when I stand gazing, just as he did, at schoolchildren on the bus or playground, imagining how their hidden brilliance, if realized, might one day change the world.

Part of what I learned from him was to pick myself back up right away when I fell hard and came up bruised or bleeding. "Nothing that won't heal," he used to say with the quiet assurance of a surgeon who made it his mission to study the outer reaches of what was possible in healing. And when I would seem to be ignoring my conscience, he would say, "Why do you imagine that God gave us strong shoulders? To accept the weight of life's challenges or simply to hang your shirt on?"

There are times when I get real quiet, the way he did, and try to gauge the clarity of my perceptions or scope of my imagination or the depth of my spirit or resolve. In every one of these ways, and many more, I carry my grandfather Downing inside me. Just as I do my grandfather Cooper, and my parents and mentors.

I never know where any of these lanterns in my life will reappear as if out of nowhere. Late at night when I've been away in my work and return home and glance up at the stars. When I'm hugging my children or caught somewhere in traffic or facing a difficult moment or searching my soul.

All these years later I still remember. I have written notes my whole life. I still prefer a hand-written message to one typed at a keyboard and sent by electronic mail. And if I pause in my writing and close my eyes what I feel is my grandfather's touch, extending through my hands, extending through his.

"Your path has a purpose beyond where it leads," he said to me. We are each weaving an imprint on the world in ways that extend far beyond the horizon of our comprehension. Every thought, feeling, dream, and action that you and I bring to life is woven in some secret yet measured way into the fabric of human destiny.

- *Give yourself daily assignments.* When I would stop by my grandfather Cooper's house after school, he would ask if I had homework. If I said no, he would say, "Then why don't you go ahead and assign yourself some?" There's no point in waiting for anyone else to tell you what to do when you have a chance to move ahead on the path by yourself. As my grandfather reminded me, the rungs on the ladder of life are not meant for stopping or clinging to; they are meant to support you just long enough to reach higher. What you or I deserve is based on what we give, on what we struggle to learn and sweat to accomplish. Grumbling and bystanding amount to nothing in the end. When you're inclined to grumble, try giving yourself a daily assignment instead.

- *Keep charging what remains of your life with utmost awareness.* If you were to write your life story and then read it aloud, how would you feel? If you could change anything as you write the story forward, what would it be?

  It was Hillel the Elder who said two thousand years ago: "If not now, when? If not you, then who?" It is an apt call to action for every one of us. As Harvard biologist Richard Lewontin observes, "No two humans . . . who have ever lived or ever will live are likely to be identical even for a handful of commonest molecular polymorphisms." Keep reminding yourself of your own uniqueness and, with it, your special responsibility to use it wisely.

  There's no escaping the fact that each of us is constantly being erased, our cells dying. Every single day we are being remade, molecule by molecule, some parts of our body more swiftly, such as the skin and senses, others more slowly, like the heart and brain. With each renewal, we are given another brief opportunity to shape the person we are becoming and the difference we are making or failing to make on the world, not only in brain and body but also in heart and spirit. Walter Benjamin, the German philosopher who died while fleeing the Nazis, once described this as "the constant attempt to charge what remains of a lifetime with the utmost awareness." It can be done.

■ *Keep asking, What does it mean to be a successful human being?* Life is too short, people say. And it's true. Life is too short for theatrics, for face time, for jumping through hoops, for excuses, for blaming, for trying too hard to please others, or for chasing society's illusion of distant riches or fame. But most of all, life is too short because we die. When you're awake late at night, pause to wonder what matters most in life and assess the difference you are making in the world around you

My great-grandfather, William Downing, used to share a small statement of ageless wisdom about the paradox of life: "A person should always wear clothes that have two pockets," he said. "In one of the pockets, keep a note that says, 'I am nothing but dust and ashes.' In the other pocket, keep a note that says, 'For me, the world was created.'"

■ *Write a one-page message for the coffee table or kitchen counter.* Imagine that you have to write a note today, the most important note of your life. It can be a single line or fill a whole page but not a word beyond that. If you knew that you would then go home and place this note on the coffee table or kitchen counter for future generations to read, and you would never be seen again, what would you write down?

I have undertaken this exercise on a number of occasions through the years. I write something different each time. It is hard work. Sometimes it startles me. It always rivets my attention and brings a sharpened focus to my mind and heart. With pen in hand, I am distilling something of my life's meaning and message. It puts me face to face with the gaps between the words I want to write and the message I am already sending by my own example. When Abraham Lincoln was asked how long it took him to write the single page of the Gettysburg Address, he replied, "All my life."

- *Close the distance between the work you do and the difference it makes in the world.* One of life's central challenges is to keep closing the gap between where we are and where we most want to be. This includes the connection between the work you do and knowing in your heart the actual difference your efforts are making in the world. On average, we spend 60 percent of our waking adult lives working. However, none of us feel compelled to give the best of our discretionary effort when it's only for a paycheck. We need something more.

To begin with, do you know the hearts, faces, and stories of those who benefit from the efforts you make? If not, how can you learn what your contribution does to help people in their own work or their own lives. Learn these real-life stories; jot down some notes. They are the single most vital catalyst for prompting us to keep giving more of our untapped capacity to our daily efforts.

- *Keep calling upon the best in yourself.* In 1966, my grandfather Downing was dying of pancreatic cancer. I was fifteen years old. As a surgeon, he knew without a doubt that his disease was lethal. He faced what was before him without complaining. Nearing the end of his life, he grew very weak. At times, the nurses had to hold him up at the bedsides of the patients he still faithfully visited on his rounds at the hospital.

One day the phone rang. It was the emergency room director of a hospital in a nearby city. There had been an accident and one of the victims—a child—was still alive, being rushed in for emergency surgery. There was no other surgeon available who was skilled enough to perform the operation and able to reach the hospital in time. Would my grandfather come right away?

"Isn't there any other surgeon who can perform the operation?" he asked. "No," came the reply. "Only you."

My grandmother happened to be standing beside my grandfather when he answered, yes, he would come. He didn't know if he could help, but he would come. He could not *not* come.

My grandmother drove him. When he arrived at the emergency room, he stepped from the car slowly and was helped down the corridor on my grandmother's arm. He scrubbed for surgery and when he walked into the operating room, the surgical team—four nurses and three other physicians—gasped when they saw him, so gaunt and emaciated by the cancer that had left him at scarcely a hundred pounds. It was obvious that he was struggling even to stand.

But his eyes were glowing with determination, they said. And something more.

My grandfather Downing taught me that before surgery he would pause outside the operating room and offer up this silent prayer: "Understanding the mysteries of life is beyond me. Understanding the ultimate powers of healing is beyond me. But at this moment, with every ounce of my energy and spirit, I am here. Call upon the best in me."

Those who were with him that day said an amazing thing happened. At the edge of the operating table, trembling and with sweat—or perhaps tears—soaking through his surgical mask, he took a deep breath and gathered himself. From that moment on, during the surgery his hands did not shake even a single time. The child lived. Not long afterward, my grandfather died. Nearly a thousand people attended his funeral service. Another thousand visited the funeral home and cemetery. As a surgeon, he had saved many lives. But it was more than that. In hundreds of small and very quiet ways, he had touched many more lives than he had saved.

"Call upon the best in me" is a prayer to give all we have to the challenge before us. None of us can give more. With practice, we will never be satisfied giving less.

No matter who you are, no matter how hard your life has been, no matter what challenges you are facing right now, every moment you have within your reach what my grandfather knew we all have—the opportunity to shape what you are becoming. Perhaps, as I do, you might pause when entering life's difficult challenges and repeat a small prayer that ends with the words I learned from my grandfather:

> . . . At this moment, with every ounce of my energy and spirit, I am here. Call upon the best in me.

- *You have been brought into life for a time such as this.* In the Old Testament, when Mordecai spoke to Queen Esther and advised her that she had to save the Jews, he said, "You have been brought into life for a time such as this." That was a phrase I heard often when I was growing up. We have each been given life for a reason. Of all the moments in history, this is the one—right now—that is filled with the greatest promise.

This is your time. This is your chance.

In my family it is a tradition that each New Year's eve, someone will say a few words about what we have learned from the past or hope for the future. Last year, on the eve of the millennium, I awakened early. Far in the distance I saw the first hint of dawn's arrival as a faint glow arose across the horizon. I sat quietly and alone, alive to the weight of the memories of my life and the dreams in my heart for the world yet to come. I wrote a short poem that captured something of the hope I have for my children, and all children. Just before midnight, surrounded by family and friends, I read the words aloud, ending with the following challenge for us all:

. . . To lead by example,
Love as if you will live forever,
Work as if you have no need for money,
Dream as if no one can say no,
Have fun as if you never have to grow up,
Sing as if no one else is listening,
Care as if everything depends on your caring,
And raise a banner where a banner never flew.

ACKNOWLEDGMENTS

As for me, I know of nothing else but miracles.

—WHITMAN

Every book is a miracle after it is completed. The writing process, especially in this case, spanned a number of years and involved an intensive soul-searching that drew together many eyes and hearts. I was moved to write this book as an independent thinker in search of the hidden possibilities of what it means to be most human and alive.

Whatever the shortcomings of this effort, they are mine alone; whatever value may be here owes much to the generous contributions of others.

First and foremost, I thank God and the Powers of Light and Love. As my parents and grandparents taught me, we all warm ourselves by fires we did not build and drink from wells we did not dig.

With all of my energy and spirit, I thank my immediate family: Leslie, my wife, who gave me the greatest gift of all: her love and the opportunity to share our lives. And my children, Chris, Chelsea, and Shanna, you are the stars in my sky. Loving you is the wisest thing I ever do.

I am filled with gratitude for my father, Hugh, my mother, Margaret, and my grandparents, Hugh and Nora Cooper and Wendell and Marion Downing, for all you have loved, lost, learned, and lived. In many and varied ways, your presence in my life has strengthened me. Every day I endeavor to live the questions and responsibilities you passed on to me.

In my writing, I have drawn from many years of notes in which I gathered my thoughts and ideas, reactions to meaningful conversations, reflections after reading or mentoring, and explorations of compelling questions about life and work. To the best of my ability, I have tried to provide credit and sources for the statements and ideas I have drawn from others.

"Those who love wisdom," wrote Heraclitus, "must be inquirers into many things indeed." In all phases of writing, I have relied on a wide and warm circle of friends who encouraged me, broadened or deepened my view, and kept my feet on the ground. These individuals include:

My colleague and friend, Jerry de Jaager. Your keen eye and creative insights made this book far more than it otherwise would have been.

My literary agent, Stephanie Tade. I am blessed by your enduring friendship and exceptional talents.

John Mahaney, executive editor at Crown Business Books. Thank you, John, for your wisdom and guidance in bringing this work to fruition. I also deeply appreciate the efforts made on my behalf by many others at Crown Publishers.

My sister, Mary, her husband, Pedro, and children: Andie, Becky, and Tricia. My brother, David, his wife, Nanette, and their children: Nate and Anna Marie. Thank you for the many years of love and bright memories.

Larry Taylor, president of Pinkerton Security, across time and miles, my best friend.

Deborah J. Kiley, director of Executive Development at Arthur Andersen. Thank you for a decade of close friendship and collaboration in developing a new caliber of leaders.

My research partners, especially Esther Orioli. Beyond our longtime friendship, you are a beacon of dedication in encouraging organizational change that grows and lasts.

My colleagues in the Lessons in Leadership Distinguished Speaker Series, including: Ken Blanchard, Stephen Covey, Bob Nelson, Tom Peters, and Martha Rogers. Shine on.

My partners in various ventures: Juliane Ross, Esther Orioli, Ayman Sawaf, Susan Duggan, and George Sidman. I am ever grateful for your friendship.

The team at Q-Metrics and Essi Systems: Esther Orioli, Karla Carmony, Karen Trocki, Myron Binder, Dina Ishibashi, and Brenda Aguilar. It has been an honor to work with you.

Larry and Bunny Holman, founders of Wyncom, for your spirit of partnership and inspiration. To the many exceptional individuals at Wyncom and Rhyno Productions, including (alphabetically): Melissa Adkins, Linda Allin, Mary Allison, Lionel Aucoin, Judy Bishop, Paula Boycott, Joe Brumley, Rita Cambron, B.J. and Karen Cobuluis, Tony Condi, Keith Elkins, Melissa Fightmaster, Shirley Gilbert, Julie Gudlewski, Sheila Hardaway, Bob Heiple, Matt Henson, Deloris Hill, Connie Holman, Lee Katz, Frank Lovejoy, Sam Lynch, George Mears, Karen Miller, Tom Neitzel, Justin Rains, Robin Roth, Paul Sanders, Robin Smith, Debbie Taylor, Nettie Van Alstine, Leigh Ann Wagner, Chad Walker, Carol Wallace, Jim Whitaker, Retta Wilhite, and Jacob Zimmer. To one and all, I value our partnership: past, present, and future.

Special friends:

Nancy Badore, founding director of the Executive Development Center at Ford Motor Company.

Susan Duggan, founder and CEO of the Silicon Valley World Internet Center.

John Horton, founder and CEO of the Leadership Center and the Leadership Forum.

Gayle Holmes, John Ramberg, and Jan Logan, of MenTTium.

Jim Erison, founder and director of the Masters Forum, and his colleague, Tom Miller.

Howard and Lynda Schultz, founders and directors of the Triangle Learning Consortium (TLC).

Lodi Gyari, executive director of the International Campaign for Tibet.

Heidi Ream, founder and director of Executive Exchange.

Alan Horton, co-founder of The Learning Corporation.

The deans of the many business schools that have sponsored my leadership seminars.

The Arthur Andersen partners who have participated in the Masters Program. Special thanks to the mentoring partners: Bob Allgyer, Jeff Bergeron, Deb DeHaas, Jeff Dobbs, Tom Fischer, Gary Holdren, Jim Kackley, Larry Katzen, Dave Kay, Paul Laughlin, Helen Lemmon, and Steve Polacek.

The Leigh Bureau, including Danny Stern, Phyllis Bockus, Larry Leson, Karen Liodice, Tom Neilssen, Anne Pace, Ron Szymanski, Les Tuerk, and Robin Wolfson.

And (alphabetically): Julie Anixter, Sven Atterhed, Sam Baughey, Harold Bloomfield, Dan Brandenburg, Elly Rose Cooper, Kenneth Cooper, Bruce Cryer, Antonio Damasio, Jan Dehesh, Wen and Joyce Downing, Brian Doty, Alan Fox, Josh Freedman, Hans-Gerd Füchtenkort, Karen Hansen, Ruth and Norman Hapgood, Chuck Harstad, Mary Hershberger, Michael Hoppé, Mary "Bunny" Huller, Carol Kelsey, Rushworth Kidder, Peter Koestenbaum, Jim Loehr, Susan Marshall, Agnew and Peg Meek, George and Karen McCown, Michael Patton, Barry Posner, Michelle Post, Karl Pribram, Nido Qubein, Michael Ray, Doug Richard, Charlotte Roberts, Carl Rogers, Suanne Sandage, Dawn Sorenson, Jim Stockdale, Lynn Taylor, Teresa Tomlin, Rowan Sawaf, Nan Summers, Sirah Vettese, Kristine Walker, Bob and Tina Webster, Jim White, Jeff Willet, and Kathryn Young.

NOTES

page xvi. He would have: See, for example, A. Winter and R. Winter. *Build Your Brain Power* (New York: St. Martin's Press, 1996); E. Jaques and K. Cason. *Human Capability: A Study of Individual Potential and Its Application* (Alexandria, VA: Cason Hall & Co., 1994); R.J. Sternberg. *Successful Intelligence* (New York: Simon & Schuster, 1996); and D.N. Perkins. *Outsmarting IQ: The Emerging Science of Learnable Intelligence* (New York: Free Press, 1995).

page xvi. "All of life . . .": W. James. *Talks to Teachers* (New York: Norton, 1958); E. Hardwick. *The Selected Letters of William James* (Boston: Godine, 1960); and L. Simon. *Genuine Reality: A Life of William James* (New York: Harcourt Brace, 1998).

page xvii. "There is no . . .": N. Mandela. *Long Walk to Freedom* (New York: Little, Brown, 1994).

Chapter 1

page 5. "I was sitting . . .": D. Brinkley. *Rosa Parks* (New York: Penguin, 2000).

page 60. Edison remembers: V. Goertzel and M.G. Goertzel. *Cradles of Eminence* (Boston: Little, Brown, 1962).

page 6. He left us: See, for example, N. Baldwin. *Edison: Inventing the Century* (New York: Hyperion, 1995); and V. Goertzel and M.G. Goertzel. *Cradles of Eminence* (Boston: Little, Brown, 1962).

page 6. When no one: A.S. Berg. *Lindbergh* (New York: Berkley Books, 1999); and C.A. Lindbergh. *Autobiography of Values* (New York: Simon & Schuster, 1992).

page 7. It is through: J. Pfeffer and R.I. Sutton. *The Knowing-Doing Gap* (Boston: Harvard Business School Press, 2000).

page 9. When we live: See, for example, E. Aronson. " Self-Justification." In *The Social Animal* (San Francisco: W.H. Freeman, 1972); R.B. Cialdini. "Commitment and Consistency." In *Influence*. 2nd ed. (Glenview, IL: Scott, Foresman, 1988); and J. Pfeffer and R.I. Sutton. *The Knowing-Doing Gap* (Boston: Harvard Business School Press, 2000).

page 10. Although studies: See, for example, E. Jaques. *Executive Leadership* (Arlington, VA: Cason Hall, 1991) and E. Jaques. *The Form of Time* (New York: Crane Russak, 1982).

Chapter 2

page 13. Yet Richard: I have drawn on two primary sources: "Richard Branson" In C. Handy and E. Handy. *The New Alchemists* (London: Hutchinson, 1999); and R. Branson. *Losing My Virginity* (New York: Times Business Books, 1998).

page 13. According to: V. Goertzel and M.G. Goertzel. *Cradles of Eminence* (Boston: Little, Brown, 1962).

page 13. She works: G. Buchenholz. "Something Had to Be Done." In *Courage Is Contagious*. Ed. J. Kasich (New York: Doubleday, 1999) pp. 185–194.

page 14. Each year: A. Coffman and B. "The Happy Helpers." In *Courage Is Contagious*. Ed. J. Kasich (New York: Doubleday, 1999) pp. 33–43.

page 15. There are: G. Claxton. *Wise Up: The Challenge of Lifelong Learning* (New York: Bloomsbury, 1999).

page 16. Known as: M.D. Gershon. *The Second Brain* (New York: Harper-Collins, 1999).

page 16. Scientists who: M.D. Gershon. *The Second Brain* (New York: HarperCollins, 1999); and S. Blakeslee. "Complex and Hidden Brain in Gut Makes Stomachaches and Butterflies." *New York Times* (January 23, 1996).

page 16. Comprised of: See, for example, J. Armour and J. Ardell (Eds.). *Neurocardiology* (New York: Oxford University Press, 1994); and D. Childre and H. Martin. *The HeartMath Solution* (New York: HarperCollins, 1999); Institute of HeartMath; 800-450-9111; www.heartmath.org.

page 16. It has powerful: See, for example, D. Childre and B. Cryer. *From Chaos to Coherence* (Boston: Butterworth Heinnemann, 1999); J.A. Armour. "Anatomy and Function of the Intrathoracic Neurons Regulating the Heart." In *Reflex Control of the Circulation*. Ed. I.H. Zucker and J.P. Gilmore (Boca Raton, FL: CRC Press, 1991); M. Cantin and J. Genest. "The Heart as an Endocrine Gland." *Clinical and Investigative Medicine*, 9, 4 (1986) pp. 319–327.

page 16. The electrical: See, for example, D. Childre and B. Cryer. *From Chaos to Coherence* (Boston: Butterworth Heinnemann, 1999); J.A. Armour. "Anatomy and Function of the Intrathoracic Neurons Regulating the Heart." In *Reflex Control of the Circulation*. Ed. I.H. Zucker and J.P. Gilmore (Boca Raton, FL: CRC Press, 1991); M. Cantin and J. Genest. "The Heart as an Endocrine Gland." *Clinical and Investigative Medicine*, 9, 4 (1986) pp. 319–327.

page 21. Recent studies: See, for example, K.H. Pribram and D. Rozman. "Early Childhood Development and Learning: What New Research About the Brain and Heart Tell Us." (San Francisco: White House Conference on Human Development and Learning, 1997) and K.H. Pribram (Ed.). *Brain and Values* (Mahwah, NJ: Erlbaum, 1998).

page 17. With every: J. Armour. "Neurocardiology: Anatomy and Functional Principles." In *HeartMath: A New Biobehavioral Intervention for Creasing Coherence in the Human System*. Ed. R. McCraty, D. Rozman, and D. Childre (Amsterdam: Harwood Academic, 1999).

page 17. This creates: See, for example, P. Langhorst, G. Schultz, and M. Lambertz. "Oscillating Neuronal Network of the 'Common Brain System.'" In *Mechanisms of Blood Pressure Waves*. Ed. K. Miyakawa (Tokyo: Japan Scientific Societies Press, 1984) pp. 257–275.

page 17. One such: G. Telegdy. "The Action of ANP, BNP, and Related Peptides on Motivated Behavior." *Reviews in the Neurosciences*, 5, 4 (1994) pp. 309–315; see also, C.A. Pert. *The Molecules of Emotion* (New York: Scribner, 1997).

page 17. If we don't: See, for example, Epictetus *The Art of Living* (San Francisco: HarperSanFrancisco, 1995) and M. Aurelisu. *Meditations* (New York: Knopf, 1992).

page 17. The brain in: See, for example, L. Song, G. Schwartz, and L. Russek. "Heart-Focused Attention and Heart-Brain Synchronization: Energetic and Physiological Mechanisms." *Alternative Therapies in Health and Medicine*, 4, 5 (1998) pp. 44–62.

page 17. In fact, it: See, for example, L. Song, G. Schwartz, and L. Russek. "Heart-Focused Attention and Heart-Brain Synchronization: Energetic and Physiological Mechanisms." *Alternative Therapies in Health and Medicine*, 4, 5 (1998) pp. 44–62.

page 18. The electrical: R. McCraty, M. Atkinson, and W.A. Tiller. "The Effects of Emotions on Short-Term Heart Rate Variability Using Power Spectrum Analysis." *American Journal of Cardiology*, 76 (1995) pp. 1089–1093; and see, for example, L. Song, G. Schwartz, and L. Russek. "Heart-Focused Attention and Heart-Brain Synchronization: Energetic and Physiological Mechanisms." *Alternative Therapies in Health and Medicine*, 4, 5 (1998) pp. 44–62.

page 18. Every single: R. McCraty, M. Atkinson, and W.A. Tiller. "New Electrophysiological Correlates Associated with Intentional Heart Focus." *Subtle Energies*, 4, 3 (1995) pp. 251–268; see also, J.J. Lynch. *The Language of the Heart* (New York: Basic Books, 1985).

page 18. After an extensive: Battery of studies on success at work; for details, contact Jodi Taylor, vice president, Center for Creative Leadership, Colorado Springs, April 1998.

page 18. The RAS connects: R. Carter. *Mapping the Mind* (Berkeley: University of California Press, 1998); J. Fincher. *The Brain: Mystery of Matter and Mind* (Washington, DC: U.S. News & World Report Books, 1992); and K.H. Pribram. *Brain and Perception* (Hillsdale, NJ: Erlbaum, 1991).

page 18. Although human: N. Nicholson. "How Hard-Wired Is Human Behavior?" *Harvard Business Review* (July/August 1998) pp. 134–147 and N. Nicholson. *Executive Instinct* (New York: Crown Business Books, 2000).

page 21. The limbic: R. Carter. *Mapping the Mind* (Berkeley: University of California Press, 1998); J. Fincher. *The Brain: Mystery of Matter and Mind* (Washington, DC: U.S. News & World Report Books, 1992); and K.H. Pribram. *Brain and Perception* (Hillsdale, NJ: Erlbaum, 1991).

page 21. There is evidence: L. Machado. *The Brain of the Brain* (Cidade do Cérebro, Brazil, 1990) pp. 56–57.

page 22. We have to: A.R. Damasio. *The Feeling of What Happens* (New York: Harcourt Brace, 1999).

page 22. Yet without: For an overview, see, A.R. Damasio. *Descartes' Error: Emotion, Reason, and the Human Brain* (New York: Grosset/Putnam, 1995) and A.R. Damasio. *The Feeling of What Happens* (New York: Harcourt Brace, 1999).

page 24. That kind: See, for example, J.P. Kotter. *Leading Change* (Boston: Harvard Business School Press, 1996).

Chapter 3

page 29. An intense: See, for example, A. Kohn. *No Contest: The Case Against Competition*. Rev. ed. (Boston: Houghton Mifflin, 1992); J.F. Moore. *The Death of Competition* (New York: HarperBusiness, 1996); and R.J. Sternberg. *Successful Intelligence* (New York: Simon & Schuster, 1996).

page 29. Competition inhibits: J. Pfeffer and R.I. Sutton. "When Internal Competition Turns Friends into Enemies." In *The Knowing-Doing Gap* (Boston: Harvard Business School Press, 2000).

page 29. Even thinking: K. France. "Competitive vs. Non-Competitive Thinking During Exercise: Effects on Norepinephrine Levels." Paper presented at the Annual Meeting of the American Psychological Association (August 1984).

page 29. Performance improves: K. France. "Competitive vs. Non-Competitive Thinking During Exercise: Effects on Norepinephrine Levels." Paper presented at the Annual Meeting of the American Psychological Association (August 1984).

page 30. Deming found: W.E. Deming. *Out of the Crisis* (Cambridge, MA: Massachusetts Institute of Technology Center for Advanced Engineering Study, 1986) p. 102.

page 30. Recent studies: J.O. Whitney. *The Economics of Trust* (New York: McGraw-Hill, 1996).

page 30. That's why so: R.H. Frank and P.J. Cook. *The Winner-Take-All Society* (New York: Penguin, 1995) pp. 19–20.

page 31. The degree: A. Kohn. *No Contest: The Case Against Competition*. Rev. ed. (Boston: Houghton Mifflin, 1992).

page 31. They are: J. Pfeffer and R.I. Sutton. "When Internal Competition Turns Friends into Enemies." In *The Knowing-Doing Gap* (Boston: Harvard Business School Press, 2000).

page 31. In fact, according: A. Kohn. *No Contest: The Case Against Competition*. Rev. ed. (Boston: Houghton Mifflin, 1992).

page 31. Star-performing: My sources for this include extensive research at Q-Metrics and Essi Systems in San Francisco, and findings from Selection Research International and People Management International. See also, R.E. Kelley. *Be a Star at Work* (New York: Times Books, 1997).

page 32. To excel demands: G. Claxton. *Wise Up: The Challenge of Lifelong Learning* (New York: Bloomsbury, 1999).

page 33. When Grace: J.M. Fenster. "Amazing Grace." *Inventions & Technology* (fall, 1998) pp. 24–31.

page 35. Some people: L. Armstrong with S. Jenkins. *It's Not About the Bike: My Journey Back to Life* (New York: Putnam, 2000).

Chapter 4

page 41. In one: B.Z. Posner and W.H. Schmidt. "Values Congruence and Difference between the Interplay of Personal and Organizational Value Systems." *Journal of Business Ethics*, 12, 2 (1992) pp. 171–177.

page 42. A friend: Conversation with Nan Summers, May 7, 2000. Used with permission.

Chapter 5

page 45. When Daniel: See, I.E. Scarborough. "Lincoln and the Power of Principle." *Chicago Tribune* (1993).

page 46. The soldiers of: See, for example, W.C. Davis. *Lincoln's Men: How President Lincoln Became Father to an Army and a Nation* (New York: Free Press, 1999).

page 48. (FedEX founder . . .): J.C. Wetherbe. *The World on Time* (Santa Monica, CA: Knowledge Exchange, 1996).

page 49. A single: See, for example, S.S. Hendler. *The Oxygen Breakthrough* (New York: Pocket Books, 1989).

page 49. Neuroscientists have: See, for example, S.H. Elgin. *Success with the Gentle Art of Verbal Self-Defense* (New York: Prentice Hall, 1989).

page 51. It is: T. Cleary (Trans.). *Further Teachings of Lao Tzu: Understanding the Mysteries* (Boston: Shambhala, 1991).

Chapter 6

page 52. Since 1959: For more information and a summary of human rights reports, contact: The International Campaign for Tibet, 1825 K Street, N.W., Washington, DC 20006; ict@peacenet.org or www.savetibet.org.

page 55. The terror: The Tibet Press Watch (International Campaign for Tibet,1825 K Street, N.W., Washington, DC 20006; ict@peacenet .org or www.savetibet.org.

page 56. One of: Survey by Robert Half International, 1994. See, J.M. Kouzes and B.Z. Posner. *Encouraging the Heart* (San Francisco: Jossey-Bass, 1999).

page 57. Instead, learn: R. Farson. *Management of the Absurd* (New York: Touchstone, 1997).

page 57. Margaret Mead: M. Mead. "Meade's Maxim." In *1,001 Logical Laws* J. Peers (Compilation) (1979) p. 155.

page 58. Throughout our: R. Josselson. *The Space Between Us: Exploring the Dimensions of Human Relationships* (San Francisco: Jossey-Bass, 1992).

Chapter 7

page 68. We have: See, J.E. Loehr. *Stress for Success* (New York: Times Books, 1998); R.E. Kelley. *How to Be a Star at Work* (New York: Times Books, 1997); and J. Loehr and T. Schwartz. "The Making of a Corporate Athlete." *Harvard Business Review* (January 2001) pp. 120–128.

page 69. In the longer: See, for example, E.L. Rossi. *The Twenty Minute Break* (New York: Tarcher/Putnam, 1991).

page 69. The alternative: R.E. Thayer. "Factor Analytic and Reliability Studies on the Activation-Deactivation Adjective Check List." *Psychological Reports,* 42 (1978) pp. 747–756.

page 70. It is essential: R.E. Thayer, P.J. Takahashi, and J.A. Pauli. "Multidimensional Arousal States, Diurnal Rhythms, Cognitive and Social Processes, and Extraversion." *Personality and Individual Differences,* 9 (1988) pp. 15–24 and R.E. Thayer. *The Biopsychology of Mood and Arousal* (New York: Oxford University Press, 1989).

page 70. The highest: M. Csikszentmihalyi. *Flow: The Psychology of Optimal Experience* (New York: HarperCollins, 1991) and M. Csikszentmihalyi. *The Evolving Self* (New York: HarperCollins, 1993).

page 70. With high: M. Csikszentmihalyi. *Finding Flow* (New York: Basic Books, 1997) p. 21; R.E. Thayer, P.J. Takahashi, and J.A. Pauli. "Multidimensional Arousal States, Diurnal Rhythms, Cognitive and Social Processes, and Extraversion." *Personality and Individual Differences,* 9 (1988) pp. 15–24; and R.E. Thayer. *The Biopsychology of Mood and Arousal* (New York: Oxford University Press, 1989).

page 72. An intriguing: For introductory reading, see E.L. Rossi. *The Twenty Minute Break* (New York: Tarcher/Putnam, 1991); L. Lamberg. *Bodyrhythms: Chronobiology and Peak Performance* (New York: Morrow, 1998); and M. Smolensky and L. Lamberg. *The Body Clock Guide to Better Health* (New York: Henry Holt, 2000).

page 73. Although many: See E.L. Rossi. *The Twenty Minute Break* (New York: Tarcher/Putnam, 1991); R.E. Janaro et al. "A Technical Note on Increasing Productivity Through Effective Rest Break Scheduling." *Industrial Management,* 30, 1 (January/February 1988) pp. 29–33; J. Penc. "Motivational Stimulation and System of Work Improvement." *Studia-Socjologiczne,* 3, 102 (1986) pp. 179–197; S.E. Bechtold and D.L. Sumners. "Optimal Work-Rest Scheduling with Exponential Work-Rate Decay." *Management Science,* 34 (April 1988) pp. 547–552; G.P. Krueger. "Human Performance in Continuous/Sustained Operations and the Demands of Extended Work/Rest Schedules: An Annotated Bibliography." *Psychological Documents,* 15, 2 (December 1985) pp. 27–28; R.E. Janaro and S.E. Bechtold. "A Study of the Reduction of Fatigue Impact on Productivity through Optimal Rest Break Scheduling." *Human Factors,* 27, 4 (August 1985) pp. 459–466.

page 73. Introducing short: E. Grandjean. *Fitting the Task.* 4th ed. (New York: Taylor & Francis, 1988).

page 73. By one: See, for example, R.K. Cooper. *The Performance Edge* (Boston: Houghton Mifflin, 1991).

page 73. But if: See E.L. Rossi. *The Twenty Minute Break* (New York: Tarcher/Putnam, 1991); L. Lamberg. *Bodyrhythms: Chronobiology and Peak Performance* (New York: Morrow, 1998); R.E. Thayer, P.J. Takahashi, and J.A. Pauli. "Multidimensional Arousal States, Diurnal Rhythms, Cognitive and Social Processes, and Extraversion." *Personality and Individual Differences,* 9 (1988) pp. 15–24 and R.E. Thayer. *The Biopsychology of Mood and Arousal* (New York: Oxford University Press, 1989); Thayer; G.G. Globus et al. "Ultradian Rhythms in Human Performance." *Perceptual and Motor Skills,* 33 (1971) pp. 1171–1174; J. Gertz and P. Lavie. "Biological Rhythms in Arousal Indicies." *Psychophysiology,* 20 (1983) pp. 690–695; W. Orr et al. "Ultradian Rhythms in Extended Performance." *Aerospace Medicine,* 45 (1974) pp. 995–1000.

page 73. What we're: J.E. Loehr. *Stress for Success* (New York: Times Books, 1998); R.E. Kelley. *How to Be a Star at Work* (New York: Times Books, 1997); J. Loehr and T. Schwartz. "The Making of a Corporate Athlete." *Harvard Business Review* (January 2001) pp. 120–128; and M. Csikszentmihalyi. *Creativity* (New York: HarperCollins, 1996).

page 74. According to: W.C. Dement. Foreword to L. Lamberg, *Bodyrhythms: Chronobiology and Peak Performance* (New York: Morrow, 1998).

page 74. When we: D. Norfolk. *Executive Stress* (New York: Warner, 1986); E. Grandjean. *Fitting the Task.* 4th ed. (New York: Taylor & Francis, 1988); and K.S. Peterson. "Why Is Everyone So Short-Tempered?" *USA Today* (July 18, 2000) pp. A1–2.

page 74. Essential breaks: For further details, see R.K. Cooper. *High Energy Living* (Emmaus, PA: Rodale Books, 2000).

page 74. Conversely, whenever: S.S. Hendler. *The Oxygen Breakthrough* (New York: Pocket Books, 1989) and R. Fried. *The Breath Connection* (New York: Plenum, 1991).

page 74. Without a: J. Stellman and M.S. Henifin. *Office Work* (New York: Fawcett, 1989) p. 28.

page 75. In studies: R. Kaplan. "The Role of Nature in the Context of the Workplace." *Landscape and Urban Planning*, 26 (1993) pp. 193–201; R.S. Ulrich. "Natural versus Urban Scenes: Some Physiological Effects." *Environment and Behavior*, 13, 5 (1981) pp. 523–556; R.S. Ulrich. "View Through a Window May Influence Recovery From Surgery." *Science*, 224, 4647 (1984) pp. 420–421.

page 75. People with: *Mental Medicine Update*, 2, 2 (fall, 1993).

page 75. More than: J.W. Hyman. *The Light Book* (Los Angeles: Tarcher, 1990); D. Ackerman. *A Natural History of the Senses* (New York: Random House, 1990).

page 75. Because of: D. Sobel and R. Ornstein. *Healthy Pleasures* (Reading, MA: Addison-Wesley, 1989).

page 75. This process: A. Zajonc. *Catching the Light* (New York: Bantam, 1993).

page 75. Many people: I. McIntyre et al. *Life Sciences*, 45 (1990) pp. 327–332 and *Brain/Mind Bulletin* (January 1990) p. 7.

page 75. For those: See, for example, E. Grandjean. *Fitting the Task*. 4th ed. (New York: Taylor & Francis, 1988).

page 76. Poor posture: R. Cailliet and L. Gross. *The Rejuvenation Strategy* (New York: Doubleday, 1987) p. 52.

page 76. Every time you: M. Moore-Ede. *The Twenty-Four Hour Society* (Reading, MA: Addison-Wesley, 1993) pp. 55–56.

page 76. You get an: J. Duncan. In *Prevention's Health Guidebook 1994* (Emmaus, PA: Rodale Books, 1994) p. 3.

page 77. Water may: E. Darden. *A Day-by-Day 10-Step Program* (Dallas: Taylor Publishing, 1992) p. 43 and E. Darden. *A Flat Stomach ASAP* (New York: Pocket Books, 1998).

page 77. Too much: See, for example, A.M. Nezer et al. "Sense of Humor as a Moderator of the Relation Between Stressful Events and Psychological Distress: A Prospective Analysis." *Journal of Personality and Social Psychology*, 54 (1988) pp. 5220–5225.

page 79. Whenever you: L.E. Lamb. *The Weighting Game* (New York: Lyle Stuart, 1988) pp. 95–96.

page 79. Eating smaller: E.L. Rossi. *The Twenty Minute Break* (New York: Tarcher/Putnam, 1991) pp. 122–123.

page 79. Research suggests: D.A. Jenkins et al. "Nibbling versus Gorging: Metabolic Advantages of Increased Meal Frequency." *New England Journal of Medicine*, 321, 4 (October 5, 1989) pp. 929–934; P.J. Jones, C.A. Leitch, and R.A. Pederson. "Meal-Frequency Effects on Plasma

Hormone Concentrations and Cholesterol Synthesis in Humans." *American Journal of Clinical Nutrition*, 57, 6 (1993) pp. 868–874.

page 79. This matters: J.J. Wurtman. *Managing Your Mind and Mood through Food* (New York: HarperCollins, 1987) and A. Drewnowski. Report to the American Heart Association Scientific Sessions. *USA Today* (November 11, 1989).

page 79. What you: See, for example, D.G. Amen. *Change Your Brain, Change Your Life* (New York: Times Books, 1998); J.J. Wurtman. *The Serotonin Solution* (New York: Fawcett, 1996); and J.J. Wurtman. *Managing Your Mind and Mood through Food* (New York: HarperCollins, 1987).

page 79. Just a: See, for example, D.G. Amen. *Change Your Brain, Change Your Life* (New York: Times Books, 1998); J.J. Wurtman. *The Serotonin Solution* (New York: Fawcett, 1996); and J.J. Wurtman. *Managing Your Mind and Mood through Food* (New York: HarperCollins, 1987).

page 80. This kind: See, for example, D.G. Amen. *Change Your Brain, Change Your Life* (New York: Times Books, 1998); J.J. Wurtman. *The Serotonin Solution* (New York: Fawcett, 1996); and J.J. Wurtman. *Managing Your Mind and Mood through Food* (New York: HarperCollins, 1987).

page 81. From the: B.A. Stamford and P. Shimer. *Fitness Without Exercise* (New York: Warner, 1990).

page 81. With four: For further details, see R.K. Cooper. *High Energy Living* (Emmaus, PA: Rodale Books, 2000).

page 81. Where possible: P. Hauri and S. Linde. *No More Sleepless Nights* (New York: Wiley, 1993).

page 82. The body: C.H. Czeisler et al. "Bright Light Induction of Strong (Type O) Resetting of the Human Circadian Pacemaker." *Science*, 244 (June 16, 1989) pp. 1328–1333 and C.H. Czeisler et al. "Human Sleep: Its Duration and Organization Depend on Its Circadian Phase." *Science*, 210 (December 12, 1980).

page 82. For many: For introductory reading, see E.L. Rossi. *The Twenty Minute Break* (New York: Tarcher/Putnam, 1991); L. Lamberg. *Bodyrhythms: Chronobiology and Peak Performance* (New York: Morrow, 1998); and M. Smolensky and L. Lamberg. *The Body Clock Guide to Better Health* (New York: Henry Holt, 2000).

page 82. However, even: See, for example, R.E. Thayer et al. "Mood and Behavior Following Moderate Exercise: A Test of Self-Regulation Theory." *Personality and Individual Differences*, 14 (1993) pp. 97–104.

page 83. As little: See, for example, M. Moore-Ede. *The Twenty-Four Hour Society* (Reading, MA: Addison-Wesley, 1993) pp. 55–56 and R.E.

Thayer. *The Origin of Everyday Moods* (New York: Oxford University Press, 1997).

page 83. More than: D.G. Schlundt et al. "The Role of Breakfast in the Treatment of Obesity." *American Journal of Clinical Nutrition,* 55 (1992) pp. 645–651; *Obesity & Health,* 6, 12 (November/December 1992) p. 103; D.L. Hager. "Why Breakfast Is Important." *Weight Control Digest,* 3, 1 (January/February 1993) pp. 225–226.

page 83. When this: V. Zak, C. Carlin, and P.D. Vash. *Fat-to-Muscle Diet* (New York: Berkley, 1988) p. 30.

page 83. A breakfast: E.L. Rossi. *The Twenty Minute Break* (New York: Tarcher/Putnam, 1991); L. Lamberg. *Bodyrhythms: Chronobiology and Peak Performance* (New York: Morrow, 1998); and M. Smolensky and L. Lamberg. *The Body Clock Guide to Better Health* (New York: Henry Holt, 2000).

page 83. In fact: See R.E. Thayer et al. "Mood and Behavior Following Moderate Exercise: A Test of Self-Regulation Theory." *Personality and Individual Differences,* 14 (1993) pp. 97–104; Thayer and D.A. Jenkins et al. "Slow Release Dietary Carbohydrate Improves Second Meal Tolerance." *American Journal of Clinical Nutrition,* 35 (1982) pp. 1339–1346.

Chapter 8

page 86. Yet, when: J. Katz. "The Stuff of Tears." *The University of Chicago Magazine,* 92, 3 (February 2000) pp. 17–22.

page 86. Consider the: See J. Kasich. *Courage Is Contagious.* (New York: Doubleday, 1999) pp. 231–239.

page 87. His name: S. Perkins. Interview by J. deJaager, October 10, 2000. Used with permission.

page 88. Recent studies: M.D. Smye. *Is It Too Late to Run Away and Join the Circus?* (New York: McGraw-Hill, 1998).

page 88. This new: M.S. Albion. *Making a Life, Making a Living* (New York: Warner Books, 2000).

page 89. Research on: See, for example, R.S. Sternberg. *Successful Intelligence* (New York: Simon & Schuster, 1996); D. Clifton and P. Nelson. *Soar with Your Strengths* (New York: Delacorte, 1992); M. Buckingham and C. Coffman. *First, Break All the Rules* (New York: Simon & Schuster, 1999); and M. Buckingham and D.O. Clifton. *Now Discover Your Strengths* (New York: Free Press, 2001).

page 89. It can: M.C. Diamond. *Enriching Heredity* (New York: Free Press, 1988).

page 89. Art Tatum: J. Lester. *Too Marvelous for Words: The Life and Genius of Art Tatum* (New York: Oxford University Press, 1994); and G.C. Ward and K. Burns. *Jazz* (New York: Knopf, 2000) pp. 204.

page 90. At one: C. Correa. "Piano Legends." (New York: Jazz Video, 1986).

page 90. To sample: "Art Tatum: Jazz Archives Masterpieces 16" (Paris: EPM, 1996): On CD.

page 92. You'll know: R.E. Thayer. *The Biopsychology of Mood and Arousal* (New York: Oxford University Press, 1989) and R.E. Thayer. *The Origin of Everyday Moods* (New York: Oxford University Press, 1997).

page 92. Otherwise, these: See, for example, W. Tiller, R. McCraty, and M. Atkinson. "Toward Cardiac Coherence." *Alternative Therapies* (1996).

page 92. It turns: D.G. Myers. *The Pursuit of Happiness* (New York: Morrow, 1992).

page 92. Research also: D. Childre and B. Cryer. *From Chaos to Coherence.* Rev. ed. (Wobrun, MA: Butterworth-Heinemann, 2000).

page 93. My favorite: Levenger: Circa Notebook. www.levenger.com; 800-544-0880.

page 93. John F. Kennedy: M.T. Kennedy (Ed.). *Make Gentle the Life of This World: The Vision of Robert F. Kennedy* (New York: Harcourt Brace, 1999).

page 93. Studies also: See, for example, M.E. Francis and J.W. Pennebaker. "Talking and Writing as Illness Prevention." *Medicine, Exercise, Nutrition, and Health,* 1, 1 (January/February 1992) pp. 27–33 and J.W. Pennebaker. *Opening Up* (New York: Morrow, 1990).

page 93. Richard Branson: R. Branson. In *The New Alchemists.* Ed. C. Handy (London: Random House, 1999).

Chapter 9

page 95. When he: C.M. Schultz. Microsoft Encarta, 2000; "*Peanuts* Creator Charles M. Schultz Dead at 77." Reuters (February 13, 2000); G. Suanders. "Charles Schultz: Strip Mind." *New York Times Magazine* (January 7, 2001) pp. 52–53 and P. Aurandt. *Destiny* (New York: Morrow, 1983).

page 97. In most: Survey data from 50,000 people since 1970 by People Management. Results reported in A.F. Miller, Jr. *Why You Can't Be Anything You Want to Be* (New York: Zondervan, 1999).

page 98. Each free: Survey data from 50,000 people since 1970 by People Management. Results reported in A.F. Miller, Jr. *Why You Can't Be Anything You Want to Be* (New York: Zondervan, 1999).

page 98. That's a: See, for example, M. Buckingham and D.O. Clifton. *Now, Discover Your Strength* (New York: Free Press, 2001).

page 98. Four decades: See, for example, M. Buckingham and D.O. Clifton. *Now, Discover Your Strength* (New York: Free Press, 2001) and D. Clifton and P. Nelson. *Soar with Your Strengths* (New York: Delacorte, 1992).

page 99. Consider the: H.H. Hickam, Jr. *Rocket Boys* (New York: Delacorte, 1998).

page 101. Studies indicate: D. Clifton and P. Nelson. *Soar with Your Strengths* (New York: Delacorte, 1992) and survey data from 50,000 people since 1970 by People Management. Results reported in A.F. Miller, Jr. *Why You Can't Be Anything You Want to Be* (New York: Zondervan, 1999).

page 102. There is: See, for example, survey data from 50,000 people since 1970 by People Management. Results reported in A.F. Miller, Jr. *Why You Can't Be Anything You Want to Be* (New York: Zondervan, 1999); N. Nicholson. "How Hard-Wired Is Human Behavior?" *Harvard Business Review* (July/August 1998) pp. 134–147; and N. Nicholson. *Executive Instinct* (New York: Crown Business Books, 2000).

page 103. To get: One of the standardized measures in this field is the Motivated Abilities Pattern (MAP) from People Management International, Ltd. (101 Bell Ct., Nicholasville, KY 40356).

page 105. What will: One helpful measurement instrument is the StrengthsFinder Profile (available at www.strengthsfinder.com). One of the standardized measures in this field is the Motivated Abilities Pattern (MAP) from People Management International, Ltd. (101 Bell Ct., Nicholasville, KY 40356).

page 105. This issue: See, for example, B. Decker. *You've Got to Be Believed to Be Heard* (New York: St. Martin's Press, 1991).

page 106. As one: See, for example, R.S. Sternberg. *Successful Intelligence* (New York: Simon & Schuster, 1996); D. Clifton and P. Nelson. *Soar with Your Strengths* (New York: Delacorte, 1992); M. Buckingham and C. Coffman. *First, Break All the Rules* (New York: Simon & Schuster, 1999); and M. Buckingham and D.O. Clifton. *Now Discover Your Strengths* (New York: Free Press, 2001).

Chapter 10

page 113. When we: R.B. Cialdini. *Influence: The Psychology of Persuasion* (New York: Quill, 1993).

page 113. Promise clearly: J. Collins. "Level 5 Leadership." *Harvard Business Review* (January 2001) pp. 67–76.

page 113. Taking even: R. Cialdini. *The Psychology of Influence* (New York: Prentice Hall, 1993).

page 114. Over time: J. Collins. "Level 5 Leadership." *Harvard Business Review* (January 2001) pp. 67–76.

page 114. Demonstrate an: See, for example, G. Claxton. *Wise Up: The Challenge of Lifelong Learning* (New York: Bloomsbury, 1999).

page 114. It's rarely: See, for example, G. Claxton. *Wise Up: The Challenge of Lifelong Learning* (New York: Bloomsbury, 1999).

page 116. This is: See, for example, J. Gauld. *Character First* (San Francisco: Institute for Contemporary Studies, 1993).

page 116. I decided: R. Whelan (Ed.). *Self-Reliance: The Wisdom of Ralph Waldo Emerson* (New York: Harmony Books, 1991).

page 116. An understanding: See, for example, A. Schweitzer. *On the Edge of the Primeval Forest* (London: A. and C. Black, 1922) and A. Schweitzer. *Out of My Life and Thought.* A.B. Lemke (Trans.) (New York: Henry Holt, 1990).

Chapter 11

page 118. Everyone just: W.W. Arnold and J.M. Plas. *The Human Touch* (New York: Wiley, 1991).

page 119. Among the: W.W. Arnold and J.M. Plas. *The Human Touch* (New York: Wiley, 1991).

page 119. These and: See, for example, W.W. Arnold and J.M. Plas. *The Human Touch* (New York: Wiley, 1991) and W. Nagler. *The Dirty Half-Dozen: Six Radical Rules to make Relationships Last* (New York: Warner Books, 1991).

page 119. Such small: See, for example, R.E. Thayer et al. "Mood and Behavior Following Moderate Exercise: A Test of Self-Regulation Theory." *Personality and Individual Differences,* 14 (1993) pp. 97–104.

page 120. That means: See, for example, D. Myer. *The Pursuit of Happiness* (New York: Morrow, 1990) and R. Ornstein and D. Sobel. *Healthy Pleasures* (Reading, MA: Addison-Wesley, 1988).

page 120. Yet, he: A.H. Maslow. *Maslow on Management* (New York: Wiley, 1998).

page 121. In your: See W.W. Arnold and J.M. Plas. *The Human Touch* (New York: Wiley, 1991); W. Nagler. *The Dirty Half-Dozen: Six Radical*

Rules to make Relationships Last (New York: Warner Books, 1991); and Nagler and P. McGraw. *Relationship Rescue* (New York: Hyperion, 1999).

Chapter 12

page 126. This is: M. Moore-Ede. *The Twenty-Four Hour Society* (Reading, MA: Addison-Wesley, 1993) pp. 55–56 and R.E. Thayer. *The Origin of Everyday Moods* (New York: Oxford University Press, 1997).

page 126. In many: B. Mackoff. *The Art of Self-Renewal* (Los Angeles: Lowell House, 1992).

page 127. No matter: B. Mackoff. *The Art of Self-Renewal* (Los Angeles: Lowell House, 1992).

page 128. What's missing: E. Imber-Black and J. Roberts. *Rituals for Our Time* (New York: HarperCollins, 1992) and J.R. O'Neil. *The Paradox of Success* (New York: Tarcher/Putnam, 1993).

page 128. Little do: B. Mackoff. *The Art of Self-Renewal* (Los Angeles: Lowell House, 1992).

page 129. Low blood: W. Nagler. *The Dirty Half-Dozen: Six Radical Rules to make Relationships Last* (New York: Warner Books, 1991) pp. 47–48.

page 129. Or you: M. Moore-Ede. *The Twenty-Four Hour Society* (Reading, MA: Addison-Wesley, 1993) pp. 55–56.

page 129. For some: B.J. Rolls, I.C. Fedoroff, J.F. Guthrie, and L.J. Laster. "Foods with Different Satiating Effects in Humans." *Appetite,* 15 (1990) pp. 115–120.

page 129. A few: J.M. Davis et al. "Weight Control and Calorie Expenditure: Thermogenic Effects of Pre-Prandial and Post-Prandial Exercise." *Addictive Behaviors,* 14 (1989) pp. 347–351; M. Gleeson. "Effects of Physical Exercise on Metabolic Rate and Dietary Induced Thermogenesis." *British Journal of Nutrition,* 47 (1982) p. 173; and R. Bielinski et al. "Energy Metabolism During the Postexercise Recovery in Man." *American Journal of Clinical Nutrition,* 42 (1985) pp. 69–82.

page 129. Walking after: J.M. Davis et al. "Weight Control and Calorie Expenditure: Thermogenic Effects of Pre-Prandial and Post-Prandial Exercise." *Addictive Behaviors,* 14 (1989) pp. 347–351; M. Gleeson. "Effects of Physical Exercise on Metabolic Rate and Dietary Induced Thermogenesis." *British Journal of Nutrition,* 47 (1982) p. 173; and R. Bielinski et al. "Energy Metabolism During the Postexercise Recovery in Man." *American Journal of Clinical Nutrition,* 42 (1985) pp. 69–82.

page 130. If you: See E.L. Rossi. *The Twenty Minute Break* (New York: Tarcher/Putnam, 1991).

page 130. "If you . . .": See R.K. Cooper. *High Energy Living* (Emmaus, PA: Rodale Books, 2000).

page 131. In one: A. Ziv and O. Gadish. *Journal of Social Psychology,* 129 (1990) pp. 759–768.

page 131. Instead of: E.J. Langer. *Mindfulness* (Reading, MA: Addison-Wesley, 1989) p. 137.

Chapter 13

page 136. Pearse encouraged: For an intriguing view of these times in Ireland, see, M. Llywelyn. *1916: A Novel of the Irish Rebellion* (New York: Forge, 1998).

page 136. He had: P. Pearse. "The Fool." In *The 1916 Poets.* Ed. D. Ryan (Dublin: McGill and Macmillan, 1963).

page 137. Such great: See, for example, J.C. Collins. *Good to Great* (New York: HarperBusiness, 2000) and J.C. Collins and J. Porras. *Built to Last* (New York: HarperBusiness, 1994, 1997).

page 138. In response: M. Teresa. *In the Heart of the World* (Novato, CA: New World Library, 1997).

page 139. For Martin: M.L. King, Jr. *I Have a Dream* (San Francisco: HarperSanFrancisco, 1963, 1993).

page 139. From time: See, for example, D. Allen. *Getting Things Done* (New York: Viking, 2001).

page 142. His mother: W. Wachhort. *The Dream of Spaceflight* (New York: Basic Books, 2000).

page 142. Raised by: A. Koestler. *The Watershed: A Biography of Johannes Kepler* (Lantham, MD: University Press of America, 1960) p. 195.

page 142. "In the . . .": A. Koestler. *The Watershed: A Biography of Johannes Kepler* (Lantham, MD: University Press of America, 1960) p. 195.

page 142. "Kepler was . . .": A. Einstein. *Out of My Later Years* (New York: Philosophical Library, 1950) pp. 224.

page 142. Ralph Mosca: F. Haas, C.S. Goldberg, R.G. Ohye, R.S. Mosca, and E.L. Bove. "Primary Repair of Aortic Arch Obstruction with VSD in Preterm and Low Birth Weight Infants." *American Heart Journal,* 136, 02 (1998).

page 143. At age: A. Rueter. "Anna's Gift." *Ann Arbor News* (August 13, 2000) pp. C1–2.

page 144. As Tom: T. Peters. *The Project 50.* (New York: Knopf, 1999).

Chapter 14

page 148. Instead, we: See, for example, R. Fritz. *The Path of Least Resistance* (New York: Fawcett, 1989).

page 148. Individuals who: See E. Jaques and K. Cason. *Human Capability* (Falls Church, VA: Cason Hall, 1994); E. Jaques. *Time-Span Handbook* (Falls Church, VA: Cason Hall, 1964); and M. Buckingham and C. Coffman. *First, Break All the Rules* (New York: Simon & Schuster, 1999).

Chapter 15

page 154. In the: J. Bradley. *Flags of Our Fathers* (New York: Bantam, 2000).

page 155. It expresses: See R. Cailliet and L. Gross. *The Rejuvenation Strategy* (New York: Doubleday, 1987) p. 52; W. Barlow. *The Alexander Technique* (New York: Bantam, 1978); and T. Hanna. *Somatics* (Reading, MA: Addison-Wesley, 1988).

page 155. It restricts: See, for example, S.S. Hendler. *The Oxygen Breakthrough* (New York: Pocket Books, 1989); R. Fried. *The Breath Connection* (New York: Plenum, 1991); R. Cailliet and L. Gross. *The Rejuvenation Strategy* (New York: Doubleday, 1987) p. 52; and K. Sedlacek. *The Sedlacek Technique: Finding the Calm Within* (New York: McGraw-Hill, 1989).

page 155. It also: J.H. Riskind and C.C. Gotay. "Physical Posture: Could It Have Regulatory or Biofeedback Effects on Motivation and Emotion?" *Motivation and Emotion*, 6, 3 (1982) pp. 273–298.

page 156. We have: W. Barlow. In *Somatics* (spring/summer, 1987) p. 11.

page 157. It's amazing: W. Barlow. *The Alexander Technique* (New York: Bantam, 1978).

page 157. The resulting: See R. Cailliet and L. Gross. *The Rejuvenation Strategy* (New York: Doubleday, 1987) p. 56.

page 157. Feel your: See R. Cailliet and L. Gross. *The Rejuvenation Strategy* (New York: Doubleday, 1987) pp. 64–65.

page 157. For example: See W. Barlow. *The Alexander Technique* (New York: Bantam, 1978) p. 24.

page 157. One of: J.H. Warfel. *The Head, Neck, and Trunk.* 4th ed. (Philadelphia: Lea & Febiger, 1973) p. 46.

page 157. When strengthened: T. Binder. *Position Technic: The Science of Centering* (Boulder, CO: Binder, 1977).

page 159. When that: "Don't Be Slack About Good Posture." *Berkley: University of California, Wellness Letter* (October 1986) p. 6.

page 160. There is: See, J.E. Loehr. *Stress for Success* (New York: Times Books, 1998); J. Loehr and T. Schwartz. "The Making of a Corporate Athlete." *Harvard Business Review* (January 2001) pp. 120–128.

page 160. They flatten: R. Cailliet. *Understand Your Backache* (Philadelphia: F.A. Davis, 1984) pp. 118–121 and E.M. Mensendieck. *Look Better, Feel Better* (New York: Harper & Row, 1954) p. 48.

page 160. Unfortunately, America's: F.I. Katch et al. "Effects of Sit Up Exercise Training on Adipose Tissue Cell Size and Activity." *Research Quarterly for Exercise and Sport,* 55 (1984) pp. 242–247 and N. Clark. "Sit-Ups Don't Melt Ab Flab." *Runner's World* (March 1985) p. 32.

page 160. These exercises: B.J. Sharkey. *Physiology of Exercise* (Champaign, IL: Human Kinetics, 1984) p. 336; R. Cailliet. *Understand Your Backache* (Philadelphia: F.A. Davis, 1984) pp. 122–124; and R. Cailliet and L. Gross. *The Rejuvenation Strategy* (New York: Doubleday, 1987) p. 52.

page 161. Two specific: L. Daniels and C. Worthingham. *Therapeutic Exercise for Body Alignment and Function* (Philadelphia: W.B. Saunders, 1977) p. 77 and M. Yessis. "Kinesiology." *Muscle & Fitness* (February 1985) pp. 18–19 and 142.

page 161. This is: L.E. Lamb. *The Weighting Game* (New York: Lyle Stuart, 1988) p. 201.

page 161. Work up: To learn more about abdominal exercises, see R.K. Cooper. *Health and Fitness Excellence* (Boston: Houghton Mifflin, 1989) and R.K. Cooper. *Low-Fat Living* (Emmaus, PA: Rodale Books, 1996).

page 162. Once formed: A.E. Sola et al. "Incidence of Hypersensitive Areas in Posterior Shoulder Muscles." *American Journal of Physical Medicine,* 34 (1955) pp. 585–590.

page 162. They cause: G.H. Kraft et al. "The Fibrositis Syndrome." *Archives of Physical Medicine and Rehabilitation,* 49 (1968) pp. 155–162.

page 162. In addition: The standard medical text in this field is J.G. Travell, M.D., and D.G. Simons, M.D. *Myofascial Pain and Dysfunction: The Trigger Point Manual* (Baltimore: Williams & Wilkins, Vol. I: 1983; Vol. II: 1992). These highly-technical manuals, complete with several thousand scientific and medical references, are the result of decades of research by the authors, and are strongly endorsed by the author of the foreword to the first volume, Dr. Rene Cailliet, professor and former chairman of the Department of Physical Medicine and Rehabilitation at the University of Southern California School of Medicine.

Chapter 16

page 168. That assumption: P. Romer. *Speech at Reason Weekend* (Scottsdale, AZ, March 22, 1996).

page 168. The only: See, for example, C. Peterson and L.M. Bossio. *Health and Optimism* (New York: Free Press, 1991) and M.E.P. Seligman. *Learned Optimism* (New York: Knopf, 1991).

page 168. From his: V.K. McElheny. *Insisting on the Impossible: The Life of Edwin Land* (New York: Perseus Books, 1998).

Chapter 17

page 172. But those: R. Cutler. "Evolution of Longevity in Primates." *Journal of Human Evolution,* 5 (1976) pp. 169–202 and W.M. Bortz, II. *We Live Too Short and Die Too Long* (New York: Bantam, 1991).

page 172. This belief: See E.J. Langer. *Mindfulness* (Reading, MA: Addison-Wesley, 1989) pp. 95–98.

page 172. After many: A. Montagu. *Growing Young* (New York: McGraw-Hill, 1981).

page 173. Scientists have: S. Kra. *Aging Myths* (New York: McGraw-Hill, 1986); M. Le Poncin. *Brain Fitness* (New York: Fawcett, 1990); M.D. Chafetz. *Smart for Life* (New York: Penguin, 1992); and "Building a Better Brain." *Omni Longevity,* 1, 1 (November 1986) pp. 1–2.

page 173. We are: W.M. Bortz, II. *We Live Too Short and Die Too Long* (New York: Bantam, 1991) p. 47.

page 173. Every moment: G.T. Land. *Grow or Die: The Unifying Principle of Transformation.* Rev. ed. (New York: Wiley, 1986).

page 173. Research biologist: A. Szent-Gyoergyi. "The Drive in Living Matter to Perfect Itself." *The Graduate Faculty Newsletter of Columbia University* (1974).

page 173. For this: See A. Montagu. *Growing Young* (New York: McGraw-Hill, 1981).

page 174. They produce: See M. Le Poncin. *Brain Fitness* (New York: Fawcett, 1990) p. 65 and M.Y. Zhang et al. "The Prevalence of Dementia and Alzheimer's Disease in Shanghai, China: Impact of Age, Gender, and Education." *Annals of Neurology,* 27, 4 (April 1990) pp. 428–437.

page 174. The key: K.W. Schaie. "Late Life Potential and Cohort Differences in Mental Abilities." In *Late Life Potential.* Ed. M. Perlmutter (Washington, DC: Gerontological Society of America, 1990) p. 43.

page 174. If we: See E.J. Langer. *Mindfulness* (Reading, MA: Addison-Wesley, 1989) pp. 112–113.

page 174. It is: M.C. Diamond. *Enriching Heredity: The Impact of Environment on the Anatomy of the Brain* (New York: Free Press, 1988).

page 174. Here are: For a comprehensive review of this subject, see R.K. Cooper. *High Energy Living* (Emmaus, PA: Rodale Books, 2000).

page 175. Whatever soothes: R. Ornstein. *The Evolution of Consciousness* (New York: Prentice-Hall, 1991).

page 175. Studies indicate: See R. Kaplan. "The Role of Nature in the Context of the Workplace." *Landscape and Urban Planning*, 26 (1993) pp. 193–201; R.S. Ulrich. "Natural versus Urban Scenes: Some Physiological Effects." *Environment and Behavior*, 13, 5 (1981) pp. 523–556; R.S. Ulrich. "View Through a Window May Influence Recovery From Surgery." *Science*, 224, 4647 (1984) pp. 420–421.

page 175. Even brief: See *Mental Medicine Update*, 2, 2 (fall, 1993).

page 177. Play may:W.H. Thorpe. *Animal Nature and Human Nature* (New York: Anchor Press, 1974).

page 178. Dig deep: R.R. Provine. *Laughter: A Scientific Investigation* (New York: Viking, 2000).

Chapter 18

page 180. Look deeply: G.S. Haight (Ed.). *Letters of George Eliot* (New Haven: Yale Press, 1955–1978, 6 Vols).

page 181. Certain unpopular: G. Grant and K. Grant. *Lost Causes* (Nashville: Cumberland House Publishing, 1999).

page 181. "It is . . .": J. Powell. *The Triumph of Liberty* (New York: Free Press, 2000).

page 185. Consider that: W. Jingsheng. *The Courage to Stand Alone* (New York: Viking, 1997).

page 185. Known as: "Suzie Valadez, Queen of the Dump." In *Some Do Care: Contemporary Lives of Moral Commitment*. Ed. A. Colby and W. Damon (New York: Free Press, 1992).

page 187. In Studs: S. Terkel. *Working* (New York: Pantheon, 1972) p. 589.

page 187. There is: R. Coles. *The Call of Service* (Boston: Houghton Mifflin, 1993).

Chapter 19

page 189. As cardiologist: R.S. Eliot. *From Stress to Strength* (New York: Bantam, 1994).

page 189. Do exercises: M.R. Della Cava. "The Price of Speed." *USA Today* (August 3, 2000) p. 10D.

page 191. We are: See, for example, J. Gleick. *Faster* (New York: Pantheon, 1999).

page 191. However, new: "Psychosomatic Medicine." In *Berkeley: University of California, Wellness Letter*, 17, 4 (January 2001) p. 8.

page 193. Too much: R. Restak. *The Brain Has a Mind of Its Own* (New York: Harmony, 1991) pp. 60–61.

page 193. Much of: See E.L. Rossi. *The Twenty Minute Break* (New York: Tarcher/Putnam, 1991) pp. 27–28 and Chafetz. *Smart for Life* (New York: Penguin, 1992) pp. 63–65.

page 193. There are: L. Ljungdahl. "Laugh If This Is a Joke." *New England Journal of Medicine*, 261 (1989) p. 558; K.M. Dillon et al. "Positive Emotional States and Enhancement of the Immune System." *International Journal of Psychiatry in Medicine*, 15, 1 (1985–1986) pp. 13–18; P. Eckman et al. "Autonomic Nervous System Activity Distinguishes Among Emotions." *Science*, 221 (1983) pp. 1208–1210; A.L.S. Berk et al. *Clinical Research*, 36 (1988) pp. 121 and 435A and A.L.S. Berk et al. *The Federation of American Societies for Experimental Biology (FASEB) Journal*, 2 (1988) p. A1570.

page 193. Humorous thoughts: H.M. Lefcourt and R.A. Martin. *Humor and Life Stress* (New York: Springer-Verlag, 1986) and A.M. Nezer et al. "Sense of Humor as a Moderator of the Relation Between Stressful Events and Psychological Distress: A Prospective Analysis." *Journal of Personality and Social Psychology*, 54 (1988) pp. 5220–5225.

Chapter 20

page 198. "In this . . .": T.A. Edison. In "Edison in His Laboratory." Ed. M.A. Rosanoff. *Harper's* (September 1932).

page 201. As Anais: A. Nin. *Diary of Anais Nin: 1966–1974 Vol. 6* (New York: Simon & Schuster, 1977).

page 201. Beyond courage: See, for example, A.R. Damasio. *The Feeling of What Happens* (New York: Harcourt Brace, 1999); S. Pinker. *How the Mind Works* (New York: Norton, 1999); and K.H. Pribram. *Brain and Perception* (Hillsdale, NJ: Erlbaum, 1991).

page 201. Through the: Adapted from R.K. Cooper, Prologue to R.K. Cooper and A. Sawaf. *Executive EQ: Emotional Intelligence in Leadership and Organizations* (New York: Grosset/Putnam, 1997).

page 203. "In 1959 . . .": J.K. Knaus. *Orphans of the Cold War: America and the Tibetan Struggle* (New York: Public Affairs, 1999) and M. Craig. *Tears of Blood: A Cry for Tibet* (Washington, DC: Counterpoint, 1999).

page 203. "The Red Army . . .": See, for example, M. Craig. *Tears of Blood: A Cry for Tibet* (Washington, DC: Counterpoint, 1999); P. Gyatso. *Fire Under the Snow: Testimony of a Tibetan Prisoner* (London: Harvill, 1997); P. Gyatso. *The Autobiography of a Tibetan Monk* (Boston: Shambhala, 1997); and B. Kerr. *Sky Burial: An Eyewitness Account of China's Brutal Crackdown in Tibet* (Chicago: The Noble Press, 1993).

page 205. I know: I have no way of knowing whether the officer in charge of this reported tragedy was a Red Guard rogue, or if he and his soldiers were ever disciplined for their alleged actions. By recounting elements of this tragedy as described to me, as well as writing about some of my experiences with the Tibetan people, I am not intending, in any way, to condemn the Chinese people or their vast and rich history or culture; they had no say in their government's illegal invasion of the sovereign nation of Tibet or the attempted genocide and terror-based repressions there. I also want to make it clear that none of the leaders or organizations I work with were in any way connected with my travels in Tibet— which took place years ago and were purely personal journeys. As Nobel laureate Elie Wiesel has said, "What has happened, and is still happening, in Tibet is a crime against all of humanity." My wife and I founded The Legacy Fund to help the Tibetan people, especially children, who still survive in Tibet. All author proceeds from my book *Legacy: A Novel of Seventh Century Tibet and the Lost Pages of History* are donated to this fund which is administered by the Internal Campaign for Tibet (ICT). To learn more, contact the ICT (1825 K St., N.W., Suite 520, Washington, DC 20006, USA; 202-785-1515; Website: www.savetibet.org or www.ict@peacenet.org).

page 207. There's an: R.K. Cooper. *Legacy: A Novel of Seventh Century Tibet and the Lost Pages of History* (published in Germany by Schneekluth Publishers and in Spanish-speaking countries by Salamandra).

page 207. According to: E. Wiesel. *All Rivers Run to the Sea* (New York: Simon & Schuster, 1996) and E. Wiesel. Address at "A Tribute to Tibet." Warner Theatre, Washington, DC (April 28, 1993).

page 207. As Darwin: D. King-Hele. *Erasmus Darwin* (London: Giles de la Mare, 2000).

Chapter 21

page 210. People who: See, for example, P.S. Stoltz. *The Adversity Quotient* (New York: Wiley, 1997); P.G. Stoltz. *The Adversity Quotient at Work* (New York: Morrow, 2000); and S. Maddi and S. Kobasa. *The Hardy Executive: Health Under Stress* (Homewood, IL: Irwin, 1984).

page 210. Such individuals: See J.E. Loehr. *Stress for Success* (New York: Times Books, 1998).

page 210. Researchers call: See J.E. Loehr. *Stress for Success* (New York: Times Books, 1998); R.E. Kelley. *How to Be a Star at Work* (New York: Times Books, 1997); and J. Loehr and T. Schwartz. "The Making of a Corporate Athlete." *Harvard Business Review* (January 2001) pp. 120–128.

page 212. Researchers have: J.M. Weiss et al. "Effects of Chronic Exposure to Stressors on Avoidance-Escape Behavior and on Brain Epinephrine." *Psychosomatic Medicine,* 37 (1975) pp. 522–533.

page 212. Aerobic exercise stimulates: See J.E. Loehr. *Stress for Success* (New York: Times Books, 1998); D. Sinyor et al. "Aerobic Fitness Level and Reactivity to Psychosocial Stress." *Psychosomatic Medicine,* 45 (1983) pp. 205–217 and S. Keller and P. Seraganian. "Physical Fitness Level and Autonomic Reactivity to Psychosocial Stress." *Journal of Psychosomatic Research,* 28, 4 (1984) pp. 279–287.

page 212. Aerobic exercise is: For a more comprehensive review, see, R.K. Cooper. *Health and Fitness Excellence* (Boston: Houghton Mifflin, 1989) and R.K. Cooper. *Low-Fat Living* (Emmaus, PA: Rodale Books, 1996).

page 212. Regular aerobic: R.A. Dienstbier. "Arousal and Physiological Toughness: Implications for Mental and Physical Health." *Psychological Review,* 96, 1 (1989) pp. 84–100; J.E. Loehr. *Stress for Success* (New York: Times Books, 1998); and T.E. Backer. "How Health Promotion Programs Can Enhance Creativity." In *Health and Fitness in the Workplace.* Ed. S.H. Klarreich (New York: Praeger, 1987) pp. 325–337.

page 213. As noted: J.H. Riskind and C.C. Gotay. "Physical Posture: Could It Have Regulatory or Biofeedback Effects on Motivation and Emotion?" *Motivation and Emotion,* 6, 3 (1982) pp. 273–298.

page 213. A weak: See R.K. Cooper. *High Energy Living* (Emmaus, PA: Rodale Books, 2000); R.K. Cooper. *Health and Fitness Excellence* (Boston: Houghton Mifflin, 1989); and R.K. Cooper. *Low-Fat Living* (Emmaus, PA: Rodale Books, 1996).

page 214. Studies of: M.T. Singer. "Vietnam Prisoners of War, Stress and Personality Resiliency." *American Journal of Psychiatry,* 138, 3 (1991) pp. 345–346 and J.E. Dimsdale. "The Coping Behavior of Nazi Concentration Camp Survivors." *American Journal of Psychiatry,* 131, 7 (1974) p. 792.

page 215. How we: R.S. Lazarus. *American Psychologist,* 30 (1975) pp. 553–561; A. DeLongis et al. "Relationship of Daily Hassles, Uplifts, and

Major Life Events to Health Status." *Health Psychology,* 1 (1982) pp. 119–136 and A.D. Kanner et al. "Comparison of Two Modes of Stress Measurement: Daily Hassles and Uplifts Versus Major Life Events." *Journal of Behavioral Medicine,* 4 (1981) pp. 1–39.

page 215. There's a: A. Brodish et al. *Brain Research,* 426 (1987) pp. 37–46.

page 216. It provides: M.R. Ford et al. "Quieting Response Training: Predictors of Long-Term Outcome." *Biofeedback and Self-Regulation,* 8, 3 (1983) pp. 393–408; M.R. Ford et al. "Quieting Response Training: Long-Term Evaluation of a Clinical Biofeedback Practice." *Biofeedback and Self-Regulation,* 8, 2 (1983) pp. 265–278; R.G. Nathan, T.E. Staats, and P.J. Rosch. *The Doctors' Guide to Instant Stress Relief* (New York: G.P. Putnam's Sons, 1987); C.F. Stroebel, M.R. Ford, P. Strong, and B.L. Szarek. "Quieting Response Training: Five-year Evaluation of a Clinical Biofeedback Practice." (Institute for Living, Hartford, CT 06106; 1981); K.H. Pribram. *Holonomic Brain Theory* (Hillsdale, NJ: Erlbaum, 1988); Pribram. Lecture (June 1987); and J.E. Loehr. *Stress for Success* (New York: Times Books, 1998).

page 217. Because oxygen: See S.S. Hendler. *The Oxygen Breakthrough* (New York: Pocket Books, 1989).

page 217. When we: "Breathing Linked to Personality." *Psychology Today* (July 1983) p. 109 and M. Teich and G. Dodeles. "Mind Control: How to Get It, How to Use It, How to Keep It." *Omni* (October 1987) pp. 53–60.

page 217. Easing off: P. Ekman, R.W. Levenson, and W.V. Friesen. "Autonomic Nervous System Activity Distinguishes Among Emotions." *Science* (September 16, 1983) pp. 1208–1210; J. Greden et al. *Archives of General Psychiatry,* 43 (1987) pp. 269–274; see note 16, Teich and Dodeles; and R.B. Zajonc. "Emotion and Facial Efference: A Theory Reclaimed." *Science,* 228, 4695 (April 5, 1985) pp. 15–21.

page 218. A common: See, for example, S.S. Hendler. *The Oxygen Breakthrough* (New York: Pocket Books, 1989); R. Fried. *The Breath Connection* (New York: Plenum, 1991); R. Cailliet and L. Gross. *The Rejuvenation Strategy* (New York: Doubleday, 1987) p. 52; K. Sedlacek. *The Sedlacek Technique: Finding the Calm Within* (New York: McGraw-Hill, 1989); J.H. Riskind and C.C. Gotay. "Physical Posture: Could It Have Regulatory or Biofeedback Effects on Motivation and Emotion?" *Motivation and Emotion,* 6, 3 (1982) pp. 273–298; and G.E. Weisfeld and J.M. Beresford. "Erectness of Posture as an Indicator of Dominance or Success in Humans." *Motivation and Emotion,* 6, 2 (1982) pp. 113–131.

page 219. In this ICS: See, for example, G. Nadler and S. Hibino. *Breakthrough Thinking* (Rocklin, CA: Prima Publishing, 1990) and G. Nadler and S. Hibino, with Farrell, J. *Creative Solution Finding* (Rocklin, CA: Prima Publishing, 1995).

page 220. Practice this: See M. Csikszentmihalyi. *Flow: The Psychology of Optimal Experience* (New York: HarperCollins, 1991); M. Csikszentmihalyi. *The Evolving Self* (New York: HarperCollins, 1993); and M. Csikszentmihalyi. *Finding Flow* (New York: Basic Books, 1997) p. 21.

page 223. Preserving some: See C. Peterson and L.M. Bossio. *Health and Optimism* (New York: Free Press, 1991) and M.E.P. Seligman. *Learned Optimism* (New York: Knopf, 1991).

page 225. Researchers have: D. Tice. Study results reported in *The New York Times* (December 30, 1992) p. C6.

page 225. Cardiologists have: R.S. Eliot and D.L. Breo. *Is It Worth Dying For?* Rev. ed. (New York: Bantam, 1989).

page 225. For some: K.S. Peterson. "To Fight Stress, Women Talk, Men Walk." *USA Today* (August 7, 2000) p. D1 and S. Taylor et al. *Psychological Review* (autumn, 2000).

page 226. Research indicates: J.W. Pennebaker, J.K. Kiecolt-Glaser, and R. Glaser, "Disclosure of Traumas and Immune Function." *Journal of Consulting and Clinical Psychology,* 56 (1988) pp. 239–245.

Chapter 22

page 229. They also: See, for example, J.L. Locke. *The De-Voicing of Society* (New York: Simon & Schuster, 1998); N. Nicholson. "How Hard-Wired Is Human Behavior?" *Harvard Business Review* (July/August 1998) pp. 134–147; N. Nicholson. *Executive Instinct* (New York: Crown Business Books, 2000); D.M. Ruiz. *The Four Agreements* (San Rafael, CA: Amber-Allen Publishing, 1997); and B. Blanton. *Radical Honesty* (New York: Dell, 1996).

page 229. According to: See, for example, J.P. Kotter. *Matsushita Leadership* (New York: Free Press, 1997); G. Nadler and S. Hibino. *Breakthrough Thinking* (Rocklin, CA: Prima Publishing, 1990); and G. Nadler and S. Hibino. *Creative Solution Finding* (Rocklin, CA: Prima Publishing, 1995).

page 229. Over 90: P. Drucker. *Creative Living* (autumn, 1997).

page 232. There is: See P. Drucker. *Creative Living* (autumn, 1997).

page 232. Unfortunately when: See, for example, R.B. Zajonc. "Styles of Explanation in Social Psychology." *The European Journal of Social Psychology* (September/October 1989).

Chapter 23

page 234. Schweitzer thought: A. Schweitzer. In *What Does It Mean to Be Human?* Ed. F. Franck (New York: St. Martin's Press, 2000) pp. 3–4.

page 235. As Walt: J. Loving. *Walt Whitman: The Song of Himself* (Berkley, CA: University of California Press, 1999).

page 237. But lying: B. Blanton. *Radical Honesty* (New York: Dell, 1996).

page 237. Yet one: J. Kotter. *Leading Change* (Boston: Harvard Business School Press, 1997).

page 238. I remember: J. Porte (Ed.). *Emerson in His Journals* (Boston: Harvard University Press, 1982).

page 239. Constructive conflict: D. Tjosvold. *Learning to Manage Conflict* (New York: Lexington Books, 1993).

page 240. There are: See, for example, R. Schank. *Coloring Outside the Lines: Raising a Smarter Kid by Breaking All the Rules* (New York: HarperCollins, 2000) and R.S. Sternberg. *Successful Intelligence* (New York: Simon & Schuster, 1997).

page 242. When describing: M. Giovagnoli. *Angels in the Workplace* (San Francisco: Jossey-Bass, 1999).

page 242. New research: See J. Collins. "Level 5 Leadership." *Harvard Business Review* (January 2001) pp. 67–76.

page 242. When Dr. Schweitzer: See A. Schweitzer. In *What Does It Mean to Be Human?* Ed. F. Franck (New York: St. Martin's Press, 2000), pp. 3–4.

page 242. Consider the: For an intriguing glimpse into one person's view of the soul of an angel, see K. Goldman. *The Angel Book* (New York: Simon & Schuster, 1992).

Chapter 24

page 247. I recall: Kierkegaard. In C. Handy. *Waiting for the Mountain to Move* (San Francisco: Jossey-Bass, 1999).

page 248. There are: F. Nietzsche. *Twilight of the Idols* (New York: Penguin Books, 1968).

page 248. His writings: J.B. Stockdale. *Courage Under Fire: Testing Epictetus's Doctrines in a Laboratory of Human Behavior* (Stanford, CA: Stanford University, Hoover Institution, 1993, Essay No. 6).

page 249. Abraham Maslow: A. Maslow. *Toward a Psychology of Being* (New York: Harper & Row, 1978).

page 250. All these: R.P. Feynman. *The Pleasure of Finding Things Out* (New York: Perseus Books, 1999).

page 252. "The way . . .": R. Tarquinio. "One Foot in Eternity." Lyric Mood CD; Acoustic Alliance, Vol. 1, #90401.

Chapter 25

page 253. The death: I am not certain if this name is correct. I was a young boy when this story was told and my grandfather once said he wanted to let this man rest in peace. So I am guessing that he used a pseudonym.

page 255. As Abraham: A. Heschel. *What Is Man?* (Stanford: Stanford University Press, 1965).

page 255. According to: C. Barks. *The Essential Rumi* (New York: HarperCollins, 1995).

page 255. Martin Luther: M.L. King, Jr. *Letter from the Birmingham Jail* (New York: HarperCollins, 1963/1994).

page 255. Caring takes: See K.S. Peterson. "Why Is Everyone So Short-Tempered?" *USA Today* (July 18, 2000) pp. A1–2.

page 255. Engage in: W. Wordsworth. "Lines Composed a Few Miles Above Tintern Abbey" (1798).

page 256. Over the: L. Cameron. *The Music of Light: The Extraordinary Story of Hikari and Kenzaburo Oe* (New York: Free Press, 1998).

page 257. The Supreme: G.E. White. *Justice Oliver Wendell Holmes: Law and the Inner Self* (New York: Oxford University Press, 1993).

page 258. "What you . . .": Y. Chadha. *Gandhi: A Life* (New York: Wiley, 1997).

page 258. Consider the: M.W. Edelman. Commencement address, Washington University, St. Louis (May 15, 1992).

page 259. Gandhi said: See Y. Chadha. *Gandhi: A Life* (New York: Wiley, 1997).

page 261. "On the . . .": See A. Heschel. *What Is Man?* (Stanford: Stanford University Press, 1965).

Chapter 26

page 262. Each of: To learn more, see J.W. Gauld. *Character First* (San Francisco: Institute for Contemporary Studies, 1993).

page 268. As Harvard: R. Lewontin. *Human Diversity* (New York: Scientific American Library, 1995) p. 42.

page 269. Walter Benjamin: M.W. Jennings. *Walter Benjamin: Selected Writings: Volume 2, 1927–1934* (Cambridge, MA: Belknap Press/Harvard University Press, 1999).

page 269. Write a: For a memorable exploration of this theme, see B. Greene and D.G. Fulford. *Notes on the Kitchen Table* (New York: Doubleday, 1998).

page 270. When Abraham: H. Holzer (Ed.). *Lincoln as I Knew Him* (Chapel Hill, NC: Algonquin Books, 1999).

INDEX

ABOUT THE AUTHOR

Praised as "a national treasure" by Stanford Business School Professor Michael Ray, Robert K. Cooper is a faculty member in the Lessons in Leadership Distinguished Speaker Series™ sponsored by university business schools from coast to coast.

An acclaimed educator on how exceptional leaders and teams liberate untapped human capacities and excel under pressure, Cooper is also recognized for his pioneering work on the practical application of emotional intelligence and the neuroscience of trust, initiative, leadership, and commitment.

In his life, he has been a newspaper delivery boy, housepainter, farm worker, martial artist, All-American athlete, U.S. Marine, rock climber, carpenter, surveyor, university honor student, independent scholar, health and fitness instructor, newspaper columnist, co-developer of measurement systems on peak performance, chair of the board for a metrics firm specializing in leadership advancement and applied intelligence, consultant to a global technology consortium, advisor to organizational leaders, and a public speaker. He has learned from scientists, inventors, teachers, refugees, star performers in many fields, and people in all walks of life.

In a recent survey of managers and professionals from more than 90 organizations, his work was compared to 20 widely recognized leadership authorities. Cooper rated highest on every scale, including inherent value, usefulness, applicability, delivery, and overall results. His articles have been published in *Strategy & Leadership,* and his books, including *The Performance Edge,* and *Executive EQ,* have sold nearly four million copies.

Cooper serves as managing director of Advanced Excellence Systems, a leadership consulting firm. He is an adjunct professor in the Ph.D. program at the Union Institute Graduate College in Cincinnati. In addition to graduate work at the University of Michigan and University of Iowa, he completed his undergraduate degree with honors at the University of Minnesota and earned his Ph.D. at the Union Institute Graduate College in health and psychology with an emphasis on leadership.

Cooper has designed and presented leadership development and professional education programs for many organizations, including 3M, Arthur Andersen, Ford Motor Company, Sun Microsystems, Marriott, Morgan Stanley Dean Witter, Scientific-Atlanta, SmithKline Beecham, Delta Air Lines, Georgia-Pacific, Children's Healthcare, Fireman's Fund Insurance, Novartis, Qualcomm, Coca-Cola, Allstate Insurance, Methodist Hospitals, and Pinkerton Security.

He holds instructor-level certifications from several leading preventive medicine institutions. He served in the U.S. Marine Corps during the Vietnam War. An All-American athlete, he is a recipient of the University of Michigan's Honor Trophy Award for "outstanding achievement in scholarship, athletics, and leadership." He lives in Ann Arbor, Michigan, with his wife and children.

To learn about Robert Cooper's live seminars, speaking
schedule, books, videos, audio programs, and leadership
articles, please visit his Web site:
www.theother90percent.com
e-mail address:
robertcooper@theother90percent.com